Pivotal

Interpretations

of American History

VOLUME I ★

HARPER TORCHBOOKS

A reference-list of Harper Torchbooks, classified by subjects, is printed at the end of this volume.

Pivotal Interpretations of American History

Vol. I ★ Edited by CARL N. DEGLER

HARPER TORCHBOOKS, The Academy Library

HARPER & ROW, Publishers, New York

PIVOTAL INTERPRETATIONS OF AMERICAN HISTORY: VOLUME I

Printed in the United States of America.

First edition: HARPER TORCHBOOKS, 1966
Harper & Row, Publishers, Incorporated
New York, N.Y. 10016.

Library of Congress Catalog Card Number: 66-10532.

Contents

Volume I

Introduction

BY CARL N. DEGLER

As a consequence of the "paperback revolution," the teaching and learning of American history have deepened considerably in the past decade. High school and college students and general readers of history now have access to books in paper editions which, only a dozen years ago, few could get their hands on because of the limited number of copies available in the college or public libraries. One of the purposes of this collection is to further this direct acquaintance and to encourage the close critical analysis of historical works. Many important contributions to American history appear first, and frequently only, in the scholarly journals, which most students and general readers neither see nor have access to. Often these articles announce significant and new approaches to the past, which any serious student of American history should know and be able to study at first hand. That is the first purpose of this collection.

The second purpose is to bring together scholarly articles of importance. The articles included here are not simply "interesting" or "new" interpretations; in fact, several are twenty-five years old. Rather they have been selected because they are turning points in the study of American history—that is, they persuasively and successfully challenged a widely accepted view.

Certainly one of the most engrossing and stimulating aspects of historical study is that our view of the past is constantly changing. Indeed, if it did not, historians would be guilty of dogmatism and be slavish purveyors of revealed truth from earlier historians. But this mutability of historical interpretation is often exasperating to nonprofessional readers and especially to undergraduate students, who do not understand why or how these changes take place. This sense of exasperation is especially acute when readers are confronted by two different or contrary interpretations, without any sound basis for judgment between them. The result, too often, is that students of history gain the impression that virtually any or all interpretations, especially new ones, are valid, that all interpretations, in a word, are equal in the intellectual market place.

Nothing could be more self-defeating to the critical study of history. The fundamental aim behind the contemporary emphasis on novel interpretations, clashing views, and new viewpoints, is to sharpen the reader's critical faculties, to stimulate him to think about and evaluate what he is reading. But when the conflicting-interpretation approach results, as I'm afraid it often does, in making the "latest" interpretation equivalent to the best, or what is worse, results in the best being merely a "matter of opinion," then the critical aim is surely lost.

For all interpretations are not equal. Of all students of human behavior, historians are the least ready to talk of the "true" knowledge of their subject. For this reluctance there is surely good reason. Human behavior in a civilized community, which is the subject of the historian as distinguished from the anthropologist, is immensely varied and awesomely complex. And when to this difficulty is added the fact that all the participants in the story are dead and beyond interrogation, it is easy to understand why many historians hesitate to place much confidence in the long-range validity of conclusions drawn from historical inquiry. Yet historians would be the last persons to say that "anything goes" in their subject. Otherwise, any answer on an examination would be acceptable, and any fable would be indistinguishable from history. Far more than many will admit, historians recognize truth in their subject and, as all students know, penalize those who deviate too far from it.

Moreover, on a professional level historians acknowledge that certain interpretations and generalizations are no longer acceptable. As an example, take one that is contained in this collection. No historian conversant with the literature of American history talks any longer about the safety valve of the western frontier in the way that Frederick Jackson Turner seemed to do some forty-five years ago in his book of essays, *The Frontier in American History*. Thanks to the investigations of Carter Goodrich and Sol Davidson, that bit of interpretation has been seriously modified. That is not to say that the general question of the effect of the frontier on the economy has been settled by that article, for it has not. Nor does it mean that someone, sometime, may not unearth a body of materials that will show that many urban workers did, in fact, migrate to the western frontier because of lack of employment and economic opportunity in eastern cities. But until that new body of data is before us, the modifications that Goodrich and Davidson made in the Turner safety valve thesis will be the accepted view. In that respect, at least, the study of history is similar in approach to that of natural science, where all discoveries or new factual information are subject to revision, but until they are in fact revised, they serve as accepted knowledge or truth.

It is for that reason that I have called the articles included in this collection "pivotal." Upon the original publication of them, the study of American history took a new "turn," which was so well sustained that it precluded a return to the old view. Put another way, this collection of articles rests on the assumption that there is a body of knowledge about the American past that, given our present state of knowledge and understanding, can be denominated as true.

One further basis for the selection of these articles should be made clear. All of them, to be sure, are reinterpretations. But there are two kinds of reinterpretative studies. The most common kind is that which looks at an accepted or familiar body of factual material in a new way, usually within a new frame of reference or from a novel set of assumptions. An example of this is the way American slavery has been reinterpreted in the work of Kenneth M. Stampp as compared with that of Ulrich B. Phillips. Phillips, who was a Southerner, wrote his principal work on slavery in 1918, when racism and doubts about the equality of the Negro were common elements in the thought of all educated Americans, Northerners as well as Southerners. Not surprisingly, Phillips found slavery a benign institution largely because he believed the Negro to be suited to the institution. Kenneth Stampp, a Northerner, writing almost fifty years later, used many of the same facts and sources as Phillips, while adding much new material as well. But Stampp was convinced of the equality of Negroes, for he wrote in an age when that conviction enjoyed the support of enlightened opinion and scientific investigation alike. His conclusion was that slavery crippled the Negro socially, intellectually, and emotionally.

Another example of seeing old facts from a new viewpoint is Howard K. Beale's seminal article, "On Rewriting Reconstruction History," *American Historical Review*, XLV (July 1940), 807–827. Unlike Stampp, Beale did not bring much new research to his article. What he did do, though, was to ask searching questions about the standard interpretation of Reconstruction from the vantage of the lower class whites and the Negroes, instead of from the viewpoint of the disfranchised and dispossessed white Southerners who had been the principal point of reference of earlier historians.

The second type of reinterpretation is the overturning of past interpretations by digging out new factual information, which leads to a new conclusion about the past. In many cases the new factual information is searched for in order to show that a new approach is possible. Such was undoubtedly the case in Stampp's reappraisal of Phillips's conception of slavery. In such instances the two avenues of reinterpretation actually overlap.

It is this second category of new interpretations that this collection illustrates and makes accessible to readers of American history. To be sure, in several articles a new frame of reference is often included as well as a new body of factual material. But, with one possible exception (No. 20), in no case has any article been included unless it also supports its view with a substantial amount of new factual data. Indeed, it is my view that such interpretative articles are the only kind that the undergraduate or general reader, as distinguished from the professional historian, is capable of judging or analyzing. Highly interpretative articles or new ways of looking at old facts too often bewilder college students who do not and, understandably enough, cannot have the factual knowledge to judge the validity of an interpretation drawn by a trained historian. If they do, they probably wouldn't need to be taking a general course in American history.

Each of the articles in this collection contains new factual information as well as a novel reinterpretation drawn from those facts. Thus the reader learns not only new facts but can observe how those facts are marshaled by a professional historian in support of a broad interpretation. The introductions to the articles are frankly didactic. Each one explicitly points out how the article departed from an older view, why the new interpretation is persuasive (or why it fails to be completely so), what were the principal methods the author used in securing and arranging his new facts, and finally, how subsequent historians have responded to the thesis of the article. Without getting into long lists of books and articles, each introduction, in short, attempts to place the article in the broad context of American history, both as a body of knowledge and as a scholarly discipline.

Professional historians will undoubtedly notice omissions from this highly selective collection of pieces from the vast body of published research in American history. Some of the omissions are attributable to my ignorance. I tried to compensate for that weakness by calling upon a number of friends in the profession for suggestions and criticisms of my original list. For that help, which I know has made this a better collection than I could have compiled alone, I am greatly indebted to Robin Brooks, Stuart Bruchey, Clyde Griffen, Charles C. Griffin, John Higham, and Clarence Ver Steeg. But the ultimate choice of articles was mine; hence defects of commission or omission must be charged against me, not against them. My selections finally rested upon my conclusion as to the state of our craft, and for any defects in this compilation I can plead only what all anthologists must retort to such charges: this is my view of the matter, and I am stuck with it. The responsibility for the introductions, of course, is entirely mine. My indebtedness for assistance extends also to the editors of the journals in which these articles originally appeared and to the authors of them, all of whom graciously granted permission to reprint their respective properties here. Finally, as always, I am much beholden to my wife, Catherine Grady Degler, who is not only a source of encouragement but also a detached and first-rate critic of my prose and logic. My dependence upon her talents grows with the years.

A FURTHER WORD OF INTRODUCTION TO STUDENTS

The introductions to the articles are designed to aid you in your own analysis and judgment of the article. These introductions have two aims. The first is to provide you with some background for appreciating the significance of the article in the writing of American history and to give you some idea of the subject and approach of the article. For that reason there is merit in reading the introduction prior to reading the article. The second purpose is to provide a critical appraisal of the article by explaining why it can be viewed as pivotal in the study of American history and by examining the historical method employed by its author. Obviously that part of the introduction will make more sense to you after you have read the article. Hence it would be worthwhile to reread the introduction after you have gotten some familiarity with the content of the article. In that way you can determine whether you agree with the introduction's analysis of the article. It is important to recognize that these introductions are simply that and no more—they are not final, but only the view of one historian looking at the work of another. You have before you the evidence of the article as well as the judgment of the editor. But if you disagree with the conclusions advanced in the introductions, you should have a better-supported conclusion, not simply "yours" as opposed to "mine."

A FURTHER WORD OF INTRODUCTION TO INSTRUCTORS

A good number of the omissions my fellow historians may discover here can be attributed to the premises on which the compilation was made. Since the primary aim was to reprint only pivotal interpretations, no effort has been made to include "differing" or interesting interpretations merely for the sake of making a balance between opposing views or to "cover" all periods of American history. Indeed, whole periods of history in which much important scholarly work has recently been done, but in which the accepted view has not undergone any substantial revision, are not represented. There is only one article, for example, treating the years beyond the 1920s. In fact, there is not a single article on the New Deal, though that subject certainly is of central importance in the teaching of history in American colleges and universities. The fact of the matter is that our view of the New Deal has not been seriously challenged. Indeed, one might say that our view of it is still in the process of being settled, as research only begins to probe into the voluminous records of the period. The conception of a First and a Second New Deal, which Basil Rauch in his *History of the New Deal* (New York, 1944) first discerned, has been recently discounted, notably in *The Politics of Upheaval* (Boston, 1960) by Arthur M. Schlesinger, Jr., and in William Leuchtenberg's *Franklin D. Roosevelt and the New Deal* (New York, 1963). But no articles of important revisionism have yet appeared.

If such is the situation with the 1930s, even less likely are pivotal articles to be expected for later years, when our "standard" interpretation has not yet hardened. In fact, even the earlier decade of the 1920s reveals a remarkable and unfortunate paucity of revisionist articles that meet the test of factual as well as interpretive contributions. Undoubtedly the best revisionist article is Henry May's piece that has been included here, but it is nonetheless a dubious inclusion, since it is really a survey of new points of view rather than a contribution in its own right.

On the other hand, the colonial period, which is usually not treated with any completeness in surveys of American history, is represented here by as many as three articles. Such an "imbalance," it appears to me, is dictated by the large amount of revisionist writing that is being done in the colonial field; it would have been both misleading and self-defeating to try to force a balance by arbitrarily establishing a "quota" of articles on colonial history.

There is yet another reason for some of the gaps in the coverage in this collection. Many alterations in our conception of the American past occur not in articles but in books. Since the books are usually readily available in paperback and, in any case, cannot easily be cut down to fit into an anthology of this size, they have been resolutely left out, though some of the most trenchant and enduring criticisms of past views are therefore excluded. But there did not seem to be any value in excising books in order to make another one.

Some obviously pivotal articles do not appear because they have since been incorporated in books or are readily available in other collections. Bray Hammond's "Banking in the Early West: Monopoly, Prohibition and Laissez-Faire," *Journal of Economic History*, VIII (May 1948), 1–25, for example, would have qualified for a collection of this design, but it now appears in his book *Banks and Politics in America from the Revolution to the Civil War* (Princeton, 1957). Certainly I would have included at least one of Sidney Mead's provocative essays on the character of American Protestantism and the doctrine of separation of church and state except for the recent publication of most of his articles in a volume entitled *The Lively Experiment* (New York, 1963).

Finally, it will be noticed that no review articles have been included, again for the simple reason that they do not fit the requirements laid down. Certainly Robert Lively's "The American System: a Review Article," *Business History Review*, XXIX (March 1955), 81–96, which assessed the literature on governmental support of internal improvements, and Bernard Weisberger's "Dark and Bloody Ground of Reconstruction Historiography," *Journal of Southern History*, XXV (November 1959), 427–47, are excellent exemplars of their genre, but they do not, and make no pretense of, adding new knowledge.

1

AT LEAST since the appearance, in 1850, of Hawthorne's novel of Puritan Salem, *The Scarlet Letter,* the image of the crabbed, bigoted, grim-faced Puritans has been a commonplace in both popular and scholarly writing. Even the descendants of the Puritans, as Hawthorne himself demonstrated, helped to establish and perpetuate the portrait of the Puritan as distrustful when not simply fearful of sex. Charles Francis Adams, the son of John Quincy and the grandson of John Adams, focused attention upon the matter with a lecture before the Massachusetts Historical Society entitled "Some Phases of Sexual Morality and Church Discipline in Colonial New England," Massachusetts Historical Society *Proceedings,* 2nd Series, VI (1891), 477–516. Although Adams was primarily concerned with the eighteenth-century church records, he rather clearly implied that there was great concern about and therefore control over sexual matters among the seventeenth-century Puritans.

In the 1920s, during the era of Prohibition, for which the seventeenth-century Puritans, as Edmund Morgan makes clear, would have had only disdain, the image of the Puritans as kill-joys reached a high point. All American inhibitions about the elemental fact and force of sex were traced back to them. H. L. Mencken, the irreverent sage of Baltimore, used the Puritan image as a club to beat those who did not exhibit his social values. More important as a purveyor of the image among scholars and students, as well as among general readers, was Vernon L. Parrington's massive and engrossing *Main Currents in American Thought,* the first volume of which appeared in 1927 and received the Pulitzer Prize. Parrington's treatment of the Puritans was unsympathetic, largely because he portrayed them as dogmatic, overly ascetic, and humorless. His view became for the next two decades virtually the standard conception of the Puritan. Also during the twenties, James Truslow Adams published his trilogy on New England history from the founding to the nineteenth century, the first volume of which, *The Founding of New England* (Boston, 1921), had vigorously portrayed the Puritans as bluenoses who imposed their restrictive conception of life on an unwilling and less ascetic majority.

Curiously enough, at the very time that the Parrington-Adams approach to the Puritans was dominating the scholarly and popular field, a quite different attitude was growing among scholars associated with Harvard, the first Puritan college in America. In 1925 Kenneth Murdock published his realistic and essentially favorable biography of Increase Mather, father of the better-known Cotton Mather. But the real thrust behind the new approach came from two other Harvard professors. One was Samuel Eliot Morison, professor of history and eventually the author of several books on his university and the Puritans in general. The other was Perry Miller, a professor of English, whose *The New England Mind: The Seventeenth Century* (New York, 1939) marked a turning point in the treatment of the Puritans. For once they were treated as human beings with concern for ideas and with a credibility that writers like Parrington had long obscured.

But if Miller's book rehabilitated the Puritans in the field of intellectual history, the picture of the Puritans as narrow-minded on the subject of sex remained largely unchanged. That had not been a concern of Miller. It is true that in 1932 Henry Bamford Parkes in "Morals and Law Enforcement in Colonial New England," *New England Quarterly*, V (July 1932), 431–52, rescued the Puritans from the charges of hypocrisy that Charles Francis Adams laid against them forty years earlier, but that was all. Therefore, it can be said that Edmund Morgan's article brought about a significant change in historical judgment regarding Puritan attitudes on sex. After reading Morgan's article it is no longer possible to see whatever asceticism or fear of sexuality there is in America as stemming from the seventeenth-century Puritans. If any group in the past is to be blamed as the "originators," it is the early nineteenth-century Victorians.

Morgan's article is much broader than the title implies. By focusing his attention on the subject of sex, Morgan succeeds in concretely demonstrating the realistic and forthright character of Puritanism. However much one might ascribe this realism to the rough-and-tumble life of the seventeenth century—and it was a dangerous and crude time—the fact remains that the early American Puritans were no shrinkers from life. His presentation of Puritan attitudes is also important because he shows so well that on the subject of sexual matters, as well as in religion, government, and society in general, the Puritans were advocates of the "middle way." They tried to walk the line between the asceticism of the monastery and the license of paganism.

One of the pitfalls in an article like this, which seeks to describe the attitudes of a large group of people, is the establishing of the representativeness of the evidence. Obviously, unless the examples Morgan chooses reflect the attitudes of most of the people of the time, his collection of quotations will not convince the reader. This article is effective and convincing simply because the evidence he uses does not depend upon the number of examples, but upon the kinds.

Actually, he uses two kinds: quotations from books by Puritan divines, which demonstrate what the ideals of the society were; and examples drawn from court records, which describe the practices of the society. What is the special merit of court records? It is simply that they are by nature representative. One does not have to sift a great number of examples to find out which ones are representative, because courts by their very function reflect the standards of society. It is instructive, though, to reflect upon the limitations of court decisions. What would be some obvious ones in writing social history, for example? For Morgan's purposes the writings of the Puritan divines were very appropriate pieces of evidence, since it would be expected that the divines would be the most rigorous in suppressing freedom in sexual matters. But it is also clear that for another purpose the very same sources might be quite inappropriate. Under what circumstances would that be true?

Mr. Morgan is professor of history at Yale University. His most recent works on the Puritans are *The Puritan Dilemma: The Story of John Winthrop* (Boston, 1958), *The Gentle Puritan: A Life of Ezra Stiles, 1727–1795* (New Haven, 1962), and *Visible Saints: The History of a Puritan Idea* (New York, 1963).

The Puritans and Sex

BY EDMUND S. MORGAN

HENRY ADAMS once observed that Americans have "ostentatiously ignored" sex. He could think of only two American writers who touched upon the subject with any degree of boldness—Walt Whitman and Bret Harte. Since the time when Adams made this penetrating observation, American writers have been making up for lost time in a way that would make Bret Harte, if not Whitman, blush. And yet there is still more truth than falsehood in Adams's statement. Americans, by comparison with Europeans or Asiatics, are squeamish when confronted with the facts of life. My purpose is not to account for this squeamishness, but simply to point out that the Puritans, those bogeymen of the modern intellectual, are not responsible for it.

At the outset, consider the Puritans' attitude toward marriage and the role of sex in marriage. The popular assumption might be that the Puritans frowned on marriage and tried to hush up the physical aspect of it as much as possible, but listen to what they themselves had to say. Samuel Willard, minister of the Old South Church in the latter part of the seventeenth century and author of the most complete textbook of Puritan divinity, more than once expressed his horror at "that Popish conceit of the Excellency of Virginity." [1] Another minister, John Cotton, wrote that

> Women are Creatures without which there is no comfortable Living for man: it is true of them what is wont to be said of Governments, *That bad ones are better than none*: They are a sort of Blasphemers then who dispise and decry them, and call them *a necessary Evil,* for they are *a necessary Good.*[2]

These sentiments did not arise from an interpretation of marriage as a spiritual partnership, in which sexual intercourse was a minor or incidental matter. Cotton gave his opinion of "Platonic love" when he recalled the case of

SOURCE: Reprinted by permission from *The New England Quarterly,* XV (December 1942). Copyright 1942 by the New England Quarterly.

[1] Samuel Willard, *A Compleat Body of Divinity* (Boston, 1726), 125 and 608–613.

[2] John Cotton, *A Meet Help* (Boston, 1699), 14–15.

one who immediately upon marriage, without ever approaching the *Nuptial Bed,* indented with the *Bride,* that by mutual consent they might both live such a life, and according did sequestring themselves according to the custom of those times, from the rest of mankind, and afterwards from one another too, in their retired Cells, giving themselves up to a Contemplative life; and this is recorded as an instance of no little or ordinary Vertue; but I must be pardoned in it, if I can account it no other than an effort of blind zeal, for they are the dictates of a blind mind they follow therein, and not of that Holy Spirit, which saith *It is not good that man should be alone.*[3]

Here is as healthy an attitude as one could hope to find anywhere. Cotton certainly cannot be accused of ignoring human nature. Nor was he an isolated example among the Puritans. Another minister stated plainly that "the Use of the Marriage Bed" is "founded in mans Nature," and that consequently any withdrawal from sexual intercourse upon the part of husband or wife "Denies all reliefe in Wedlock vnto Human necessity: and sends it for supply vnto Beastiality when God gives not the gift of Continency."[4] In other words, sexual intercourse was a human necessity and marriage the only proper supply for it. These were the views of the New England clergy, the acknowledged leaders of the community, the most Puritanical of the Puritans. As proof that their congregations concurred with them, one may cite the case in which the members of the First Church of Boston expelled James Mattock because, among other offenses, "he denyed Coniugall fellowship vnto his wife for the space of 2 years together vpon pretense of taking Revenge upon himself for his abusing of her before marryage."[5] So strongly did the Puritans insist upon the sexual character of marriage that one New Englander considered himself slandered when it was reported, "that he Brock his deceased wife's hart with Greife, that he wold be absent from her 3 weeks together when he was at home, and wold never come nere her, and such Like."[6]

There was just one limitation which the Puritans placed upon sexual relations in marriage: sex must not interfere with religion. Man's chief end was to glorify God, and all earthly delights must promote that end, not hinder it. Love for a wife was carried too far when it led a man to neglect his God:

[3] *A Meet Help,* 16.

[4] Edward Taylor, Commonplace Book (manuscript in the library of the Massachusetts Historical Society). 12.

[5] Records of the First Church in Boston (manuscript copy in the library of the Massachusetts Historical Society), 12.

[6] Middlesex County Court Files, folder 42.

> . . . sometimes a man hath a good affection to Religion, but the love of his wife carries him away, a man may bee so transported to his wife, that hee dare not bee forward in Religion, lest hee displease his wife, and so the wife, lest shee displease her husband, and this is an inordinate love, when it exceeds measure.[7]

Sexual pleasures, in this respect, were treated like other kinds of pleasure. On a day of fast, when all comforts were supposed to be foregone in behalf of religious contemplation, not only were tasty food and drink to be abandoned but sexual intercourse, too. On other occasions, when food, drink, and recreation were allowable, sexual intercourse was allowable too, though of course only between persons who were married to each other. The Puritans were not ascetics; they never wished to prevent the enjoyment of earthly delights. They merely demanded that the pleasures of the flesh be subordinated to the greater glory of God: husband and wife must not become "so transported with affection, that they look at no higher end than marriage itself." "Let such as have wives," said the ministers, "look at them not for their own ends, but to be fitted for God's service, and bring them nearer to God." [8]

Toward sexual intercourse outside marriage the Puritans were as frankly hostile as they were favorable to it in marriage. They passed laws to punish adultery with death, and fornication with whipping. Yet they had no misconceptions as to the capacity of human beings to obey such laws. Although the laws were commands of God, it was only natural—since the fall of Adam—for human beings to break them. Breaches must be punished lest the community suffer the wrath of God, but no offense, sexual or otherwise, could be occasion for surprise or for hushed tones of voice. How calmly the inhabitants of seventeenth-century New England could contemplate rape or attempted rape is evident in the following testimony offered before the Middlesex County Court of Massachusetts:

> The examination of Edward Wire taken the 7th of october and alsoe Zachery Johnson. who sayeth that Edward Wires mayd being sent into the towne about busenes meeting with a man that dogd hir from about Joseph Kettles house to goody marches. She came into William Johnsones and desired Zachery Johnson to goe home with her for that the man dogd hir. accordingly he went with her and being then as far as Samuell Phips his house the man over tooke them. which man caled himselfe by the name of peter grant would have led the mayd but she oposed itt three times: and coming to Edward Wires house the said grant would have kist hir but

[7] John Cotton, *A Practical Commentary . . . upon the First Epistle Generall of John* (London, 1656), 126.

[8] *A Practical Commentary*, 126.

she refused itt: wire being at prayer grant dragd the mayd between the said wiers and Nathanill frothinghams house. hee then flung the mayd downe in the streete and got atop hir; Johnson seeing it hee caled vppon the fellow to be sivill and not abuse the mayd then Edward wire came forth and ran to the said grant and took hold of him asking him what he did to his mayd, the said grant asked whether she was his wife for he did nothing to his wife: the said grant swearing he would be the death of the said wire. when he came of the mayd; he swore he would bring ten men to pul down his house and soe ran away and they followed him as far as good[y] phipscs housc where they mett with John Terry and George Chin with clubs in there hands and soe they went away together. Zachy Johnson going to Constable Heamans, and wire going home. there came John Terry to his house to ask for beer and grant was in the streete but afterward departed into the towne, both Johnson and Wire both aferme that when grant was vppon the mayd she cryed out severall times.

Deborah hadlocke being examined sayth that she mett with the man that cals himselfe peeter grant about good prichards that he dogd hir and followed hir to hir masters and there threw hir downe and lay vppon hir but had not the use of hir body but swore several othes that he would ly with hir and gett hir with child before she got home.

Grant being present denys all saying he was drunk and did not know what he did.[9]

The Puritans became inured to sexual offenses, because there were so many. The impression which one gets from reading the records of seventeenth-century New England courts is that illicit sexual intercourse was fairly common. The testimony given in cases of fornication and adultery—by far the most numerous class of criminal cases in the records—suggests that many of the early New Englanders possessed a high degree of virility and very few inhibitions. Besides the case of Peter Grant, take the testimony of Elizabeth Knight about the manner of Richard Nevars's advances toward her:

The last publique day of Thanksgiving (in the year 1674) in the evening as I was milking Richard Nevars came to me, and offered me abuse in putting his hand, under my coates, but I turning aside with much adoe, saved my self, and when I was settled to milking he agen took me by the shoulder and pulled me backward almost, but I clapped one hand on the Ground and held fast the Cows teatt with the other hand, and cryed out, and then came to mee Jonathan Abbot one of my Masters Servants, whome the said Never asked wherefore he came, the said Abbot said to look after you, what you doe unto the Maid, but the said Never bid Abbot goe about his businesse but I bade the lad to stay.[10]

One reason for the abundance of sexual offenses was the number of men in the colonies who were unable to gratify their sexual

[9] Middlesex Files, folder 48.
[10] Middlesex Files, folder 71.

desires in marriage.[11] Many of the first settlers had wives in England. They had come to the new world to make a fortune, expecting either to bring their families after them or to return to England with some of the riches of America. Although these men left their wives behind, they brought their sexual appetites with them; and in spite of laws which required them to return to their families, they continued to stay, and more continued to arrive, as indictments against them throughout the seventeenth century clearly indicate.

Servants formed another group of men, and of women too, who could not ordinarily find supply for human necessity within the bounds of marriage. Most servants lived in the homes of their masters and could not marry without their consent, a consent which was not likely to be given unless the prospective husband or wife also belonged to the master's household. This situation will be better understood if it is recalled that most servants at this time were engaged by contract for a stated period. They were, in the language of the time, "covenant servants," who had agreed to stay with their masters for a number of years in return for a specified recompense, such as transportation to New England or education in some trade (the latter, of course, were known more specifically as apprentices). Even hired servants who worked for wages were usually single, for as soon as a man had enough money to buy or build a house of his own and to get married, he would set up in farming or trade for himself. It must be emphasized, however, that anyone who was not in business for himself was necessarily a servant. The economic organization of seventeenth-century New England had no place for the independent proletarian workman with a family of his own. All production was carried on in the household by the master of the family and his servants, so that most men were either servants or masters of servants; and the former, of course, were more numerous than the latter. Probably most of the inhabitants of Puritan New England could remember a time when they had been servants.

Theoretically no servant had a right to a private life. His time, day or night, belonged to his master, and both religion and law required that he obey his master scrupulously.[12] But neither religion nor law could restrain the sexual impulses of youth, and if

[11] Another reason was suggested by Charles Francis Adams in his scholarly article, "Some Phases of Sexual Morality and Church Discipline in Colonial New England," *Proceedings* of the Massachusetts Historical Society, XXVI, 477–516.

[12] On the position of servants in early New England see *More Books*, XVII (September, 1942), 311–328.

those impulses could not be expressed in marriage, they had to be given vent outside marriage. Servants had little difficulty in finding the occasions. Though they might be kept at work all day, it was easy enough to slip away at night. Once out of the house, there were several ways of meeting with a maid. The simplest way was to go to her bedchamber, if she was so fortunate as to have a private one of her own. Thus Jock, Mr. Solomon Phipps's Negro man, confessed in court

> that on the sixteenth day of May 1682, in the morning, betweene 12 and one of the clock, he did force open the back doores of the House of Laurence Hammond in Charlestowne, and came in to the House, and went up into the garret to Marie the Negro.
>
> He doth likewise acknowledge that one night the last week he forced into the House the same way, and went up to the Negro Woman Marie and that the like he hath done at severall other times before.[13]

Joshua Fletcher took a more romantic way of visiting his lady:

> Joshua Fletcher . . . doth confesse and acknowledge that three severall nights, after bedtime, he went into Mr Fiskes Dwelling house at Chelmsford, at an open window by a ladder that he brought with him. the said windo opening into a chamber, whose was the lodging place of Gresill Juell servant to mr. Fiske. and there he kept company with the said mayd. she sometimes having her cloathes on, and one time he found her in her bed.[14]

Sometimes a maidservant might entertain callers in the parlor while the family were sleeping upstairs. John Knight described what was perhaps a common experience for masters. The crying of his child awakened him in the middle of the night, and he called to his maid, one Sarah Crouch, who was supposed to be sleeping with the child. Receiving no answer, he arose and

> went downe the stayres, and at the stair foot, the latch of doore was pulled in. I called severall times and at the last said if shee would not open the dore, I would breake it open, and when she opened the doore shee was all undressed and Sarah Largin with her undressed, also the said Sarah went out of doores and Dropped some of her clothes as shee went out. I enquired of Sarah Crouch what men they were, which was with them. She made mee no answer for some space of time, but at last shee told me Peeter Brigs was with them, I asked her whether Thomas Jones was not there, but shee would give mee no answer.[15]

In the temperate climate of New England it was not always necessary to seek out a maid at her home. Rachel Smith was seduced in an open field "about nine of the clock at night, being darke, neither

[13] Middlesex Files, folder 99.
[14] Middlesex Files, folder 47.
[15] Middlesex Files, folder 52.

moone nor starrs shineing." She was walking through the field when she met a man who

> asked her where shee lived, and what her name was and shee told him. and then shee asked his name, and he told her Saijing that he was old Good-man Shepards man. Also shee saith he gave her strong liquors, and told her that it was not the first time he had been with maydes after his master was in bed.[16]

Sometimes, of course, it was not necessary for a servant to go outside his master's house in order to satisfy his sexual urges. Many cases of fornication are on record between servants living in the same house. Even where servants had no private bedroom, even where the whole family slept in a single room, it was not impossible to make love. In fact many love affairs must have had their consummation upon a bed in which other people were sleeping. Take for example the case of Sarah Lepingwell. When Sarah was brought into court for having an illegitimate child, she related that one night when her master's brother, Thomas Hawes, was visiting the family, she went to bed early. Later, after Hawes had gone to bed, he called to her to get him a pipe of tobacco. After refusing for some time,

> at the last I arose and did lite his pipe and cam and lay doune one my one bead and smoaked about half the pip and siting vp in my bead to giue him his pip my bead being a trundell bead at the sid of his bead he reached beyond the pip and Cauth me by the wrist and pulled me on the side of his bead but I biding him let me goe he bid me hold my peas the folks wold here me and if it be replyed come why did you not call out I Ansar I was posesed with fear of my master least my master shold think I did it only to bring a scandall on his brothar and thinking thay wold all beare witnes agaynst me but the thing is true that he did then begete me with Child at that tim and the Child is Thomas Hauses and noe mans but his.

In his defense Hawes offered the testimony of another man who was sleeping "on the same side of the bed," but the jury nevertheless accepted Sarah's story.[17]

The fact that Sarah was intimidated by her master's brother suggests that maidservants may have been subject to sexual abuse by their masters. The records show that sometimes masters did take advantage of their position to force unwanted attentions upon their female servants. The case of Elizabeth Dickerman is a good example. She complained to the Middlesex County Court,

[16] Middlesex Files, folder 44.
[17] Middlesex Files, folder 47.

> against her master John Harris senior for profiring abus to her by way of forsing her to be naught with him: . . . he has tould her that if she tould her dame: what cariag he did show to her shee had as good be hanged and shee replyed then shee would run away and he sayd run the way is befor you: . . . she says if she should liwe ther shee shall be in fear of her lif.[18]

The court accepted Elizabeth's complaint and ordered her master to be whipped twenty stripes.

So numerous did cases of fornication and adultery become in seventeenth-century New England that the problem of caring for the children of extra-marital unions was a serious one. The Puritans solved it, but in such a way as to increase rather than decrease the temptation to sin. In 1668 the General Court of Massachusetts ordered:

> that where any man is legally convicted to be the Father of a Bastard childe, he shall be at the care and charge to maintain and bring up the same, by such assistance of the Mother as nature requireth, and as the Court from time to time (according to circumstances) shall see meet to Order: and in case the Father of a Bastard, by confession or other manifest proof, upon trial of the case, do not appear to the Courts satisfaction, then the Man charged by the Woman to be the Father, shee holding constant in it, (especially being put upon the real discovery of the truth of it in time of her Travail) shall be the reputed Father, and accordingly be liable to the charge of maintenance as aforesaid (though not to other punishment) notwithstanding his denial, unless the circumstances of the case and pleas be such, one the behalf of the man charged, as that the Court that have the cognizance thereon shall see reason to acquit him, and otherwise dispose of the Childe and education thereof.[19]

As a result of this law a girl could give way to temptation without the fear of having to care for an illegitimate child by herself. Furthermore, she could, by a little simple lying, spare her lover the expense of supporting the child. When Elizabeth Wells bore a child, less than a year after this statute was passed, she laid it to James Tufts, her master's son. Goodman Tufts affirmed that Andrew Robinson, servant to Goodman Dexter, was the real father, and he brought the following testimony as evidence:

> Wee Elizabeth Jefts aged 15 ears and Mary tufts aged 14 ears doe testyfie that their being one at our hous sumtime the last winter who sayed that thear was a new law made concerning bastards that If aney man wear aqused with a bastard and the woman which had aqused him did stand vnto it in her labor that he should bee the reputed father of it and should mayntaine it Elizabeth Wells hearing of the sayd law she sayed vnto vs that If shee should bee with Child shee would bee sure to lay it vn to won

[18] Middlesex Files, folder 94.
[19] William H. Whitmore, editor, *The Colonial Laws of Massachusetts. Reprinted from the Edition of 1660* (Boston, 1889), 257.

who was rich enough abell to mayntayne it wheather it wear his or no and shee farder sayed Elizabeth Jefts would not you doe so likewise If it weare your case and I sayed no by no means for right must tacke place: and the sayd Elizabeth wells sayed If it wear my Caus I think I should doe so.[20]

A tragic unsigned letter that somehow found its way into the files of the Middlesex County Court gives more direct evidence of the practice which Elizabeth Wells professed:

der loue i remember my loue to you hoping your welfar and i hop to imbras the but now i rit to you to let you nowe that i am a child by you and i wil ether kil it or lay it to an other and you shal have no blame at al for I haue had many children and none have none of them. . . . [*i.e.,* none of their fathers is supporting any of them.] [21]

In face of the wholesale violation of the sexual codes to which all these cases give testimony, the Puritans could not maintain the severe penalties which their laws provided. Although cases of adultery occurred every year, the death penalty is not known to have been applied more than three times. The usual punishment was a whipping or a fine, or both, and perhaps a branding, combined with a symbolical execution in the form of standing on the gallows for an hour with a rope about the neck. Fornication met with a lighter whipping or a lighter fine, while rape was treated in the same way as adultery. Though the Puritans established a code of laws which demanded perfection—which demanded, in other words, strict obedience to the will of God, they nevertheless knew that frail human beings could never live up to the code. When fornication, adultery, rape, or even buggery and sodomy appeared, they were not surprised, nor were they so severe with the offenders as their codes of law would lead one to believe. Sodomy, to be sure, they usually punished with death; but rape, adultery, and fornication they regarded as pardonable human weaknesses, all the more likely to appear in a religious community, where the normal course of sin was stopped by wholesome laws. Governor Bradford, in recounting the details of an epidemic of sexual misdemeanors in Plymouth, wrote resignedly:

it may be in this case as it is with waters when their streames are stopped or damned up, when they gett passage they flow with more violence, and make more noys and disturbance, then when they are suffered to rune quietly in their owne chanels. So wickednes being here more stopped by strict laws, and the same more nerly looked unto, so as it cannot rune in a comone road of liberty as it would, and is inclined, it searches every wher, and at last breaks out wher it getts vente.[22]

[20] Middlesex Files, folder 52.
[21] Middlesex Files, folder 30.
[22] William Bradford, *History of Plymouth Plantation* (Boston, 1912), II, 309.

The estimate of human capacities here expressed led the Puritans not only to deal leniently with sexual offenses but also to take every precaution to prevent such offenses, rather than wait for the necessity of punishment. One precaution was to see that children got married as soon as possible. The wrong way to promote virtue, the Puritans thought, was to "ensnare" children in vows of virginity, as the Catholics did. As a result of such vows, children, "not being able to contain," would be guilty of "unnatural pollutions, and other filthy practices in secret: and too oft of horrid Murthers of the fruit of their bodies," said Thomas Cobbett.[23] The way to avoid fornication and perversion was for parents to provide suitable husbands and wives for their children:

> Lot was to blame that looked not out seasonably for some fit matches for his two daughters, which had formerly minded marriage (witness the contract between them and two men in *Sodom*, called therfore for his Sons in Law, which had married his daughters, Gen. 19. 14.) for they seeing no man like to come into them in a conjugall way . . . then they plotted that incestuous course, whereby their Father was so highly dishonoured. . . .[24]

As marriage was the way to prevent fornication, successful marriage was the way to prevent adultery. The Puritans did not wait for adultery to appear; instead, they took every means possible to make hubsands and wives live together and respect each other. If a husband deserted his wife and remained within the jurisdiction of a Puritan government, he was promptly sent back to her. Where the wife had been left in England, the offense did not always come to light until the wayward husband had committed fornication or bigamy, and of course there must have been many offenses which never came to light. But where both husband and wife lived in New England, neither had much chance of leaving the other without being returned by order of the county court at its next sitting. When John Smith of Medfield left his wife and went to live with Patience Rawlins, he was sent home poorer by ten pounds and richer by thirty stripes. Similarly Mary Drury, who deserted her husband on the pretense that he was impotent, failed to convince the court that he actually was so, and had to return to him as well as to pay a fine of five pounds. The wife of Phillip Pointing received lighter treatment: when the court thought that she had overstayed her leave in Boston, they simply ordered her "to depart the Towne and goe to Tanton to her husband." The courts, moreover, were not satisfied

[23] Thomas Cobbett, *A Fruitfull and Usefull Discourse touching the Honour due from Children to Parents and the Duty of Parents towards their Children* (London, 1656), 174.

[24] Cobbett, 177.

with mere cohabitation; they insisted that it be peaceful cohabitation. Husbands and wives were forbidden by law to strike one another, and the law was enforced on numerous occasions. But the courts did not stop there. Henry Flood was required to give bond for good behavior because he had abused his wife simply by "ill words calling her whore and cursing of her." The wife of Christopher Collins was presented for railing at her husband and calling him "Gurley gutted divill." Apparently in this case the court thought that Mistress Collins was right, for although the fact was proved by two witnesses, she was discharged. On another occasion the court favored the husband: Jacob Pudeator, fined for striking and kicking his wife, had the sentence moderated when the court was informed that she was a woman "of great provocation." [25]

Wherever there was strong suspicion that an illicit relation might arise between two persons, the authorities removed the temptation by forbidding the two to come together. As early as November, 1630, the Court of Assistants of Massachusetts prohibited a Mr. Clark from "cohabitacion and frequent keepeing company with Mrs. Freeman, vnder paine of such punishment as the Court shall thinke meete to inflict." Mr. Clark and Mr. Freeman were both bound "in XX £ apeece that Mr. Clearke shall make his personall appearance att the nexte Court to be holden in March nexte, and in the meane tyme to carry himselfe in good behaviour towards all people and espetially towards Mrs. Freeman, concerneing whome there is stronge suspicion of incontinency." Forty-five years later the Suffolk County Court took the same kind of measure to protect the husbands of Dorchester from the temptations offered by the daughter of Robert Spurr. Spurr was presented by the grand jury

> for entertaining persons at his house at unseasonable times both by day and night to the greife of theire wives and Relations &c The Court having heard what was alleaged and testified against him do Sentence him to bee admonish't and to pay Fees of Court and charge him upon his perill not to entertain any married men tò keepe company with his daughter especially James Minott and Joseph Belcher.

In like manner Walter Hickson was forbidden to keep company with Mary Bedwell, "And if at any time hereafter hee bee taken in company of the saide Mary Bedwell without other company to bee forthwith apprehended by the Constable and to be whip't with ten stripes."

[25] Samuel E. Morison and Zechariah Chafee, editors, *Records of the Suffolk County Court, 1671–1680, Publications* of the Colonial Society of Massachusetts, XXIX and XXX, 121, 410, 524, 837–841, and 1158; George F. Dow, editor, *Records and Files of the Quarterly Courts of Essex County, Massachusetts* (Salem, 1911–1921), I, 274; and V, 377.

Elizabeth Wheeler and Joanna Peirce were admonished "for theire disorderly carriage in the house of Thomas Watts being married women and founde sitting in other mens Laps with theire Armes about theire Necks." How little confidence the Puritans had in human nature is even more clearly displayed by another case, in which Edmond Maddock and his wife were brought to court "to answere to all such matters as shalbe objected against them concerning Haarkwoody and Ezekiell Euerells being at their house at unseasonable tyme of the night and her being up with them after her husband was gone to bed." Haarkwoody and Everell had been found "by the Constable Henry Bridghame about tenn of the Clock at night sitting by the fyre at the house of Edmond Maddocks with his wyfe a suspicious weoman her husband being on sleepe [*sic*] on the bedd." A similar distrust of human ability to resist temptation is evident in the following order of the Connecticut Particular Court:

> James Hallett is to returne from the Correction house to his master Barclyt, who is to keepe him to hard labor, and course dyet during the pleasure of the Court provided that Barclet is first to remove his daughter from his family, before the sayd James enter therein.

These precautions, as we have already seen, did not eliminate fornication, adultery, or other sexual offenses, but they doubtless reduced the number from what it would otherwise have been.[26]

In sum, the Puritan attitude toward sex, though directed by a belief in absolute, God-given moral values, never neglected human nature. The rules of conduct which the Puritans regarded as divinely ordained had been formulated for men, not for angels and not for beasts. God had created mankind in two sexes; He had ordained marriage as desirable for all, and sexual intercourse as essential to marriage. On the other hand, He had forbidden sexual intercourse outside of marriage. These were the moral principles which the Puritans sought to enforce in New England. But in their enforcement they took cognizance of human nature. They knew well enough that human beings since the fall of Adam were incapable of obeying perfectly the laws of God. Consequently, in the endeavor to enforce those laws they treated offenders with patience and understanding, and concentrated their efforts on prevention more than on punishment. The result was not a society in which most of us would care

[26] *Records of the Suffolk County Court,* 442–443 and 676; John Noble, editor, *Records of the Court of Assistants of the Colony of Massachusetts Bay* (Boston, 1901–1928), II, 8; *Records of the Particular Court of Connecticut, Collections* of the Connecticut Historical Society, XXII, 20; and a photostat in the library of the Massachusetts Historical Society, dated March 29, 1653.

to live, for the methods of prevention often caused serious interference with personal liberty. It must nevertheless be admitted that in matters of sex the Puritans showed none of the blind zeal or narrow-minded bigotry which is too often supposed to have been characteristic of them. The more one learns about these people, the less do they appear to have resembled the sad and sour portraits which their modern critics have drawn of them.

2

A CARDINAL belief of most Americans is that in their country everything is always getting better and better. They have found it almost axiomatic, for example, to believe that political democracy in the United States was a development of the last century only, and that the colonial period was the era of a narrowly based franchise and the exclusion of the masses from the political process. Since one of the measures of political democracy is the absence of property qualifications on the franchise, the presence of such restrictions during the colonial period was readily interpreted as evidence that a wide suffrage did not obtain until after the Revolution. Professional historians, too, have fallen into this habit of equating property qualifications automatically with severe limitations on the number of voters. The first few pages of Katherine Brown's article gives ample evidence of the scholarly belief in this view.

This article illustrates two important developments in recent writing about colonial history. One has already been mentioned in the introduction to the previous selection, namely, the changing view of seventeenth-century Puritanism. One aspect of the standard myth of the Puritans has been that they were essentially oligarchs who perpetuated themselves in power by carefully and rigorously excluding from government all those who did not agree with them. Such a conception, for example, runs through Thomas Jefferson Wertenbaker's *The Puritan Oligarchy* (New York, 1947). If only in passing, Brown's article clearly shows that the religious qualifications for the early franchise were neither as rigidly applied nor as restrictive as usually assumed. A similar point from a slightly different angle is made by Edmund S. Morgan in "New England

Puritanism: Another Approach," *William and Mary Quarterly*, 3rd Series, XVIII (April 1961), 236–242. There Morgan shows that the "halfway" covenant, rather than being an answer to the demands of those outside the church for a greater voice in church and state, was actually an attempt on the part of those in power to entice more people into active participation in church affairs. Indeed, many righteous nonmembers simply refused to join the church, though urged to do so, out of a sense of unworthiness. The moral for the historian is that he must always be on guard against reading back into the past the values that he accepts in his own time. Because participation in government today is considered fundamental to a good, democratic society, we are therefore prone to assume that men in other and earlier communities equally desired the opportunity to hold office or to vote. Actually, as Brown points out, such participation often brought new and onerous duties, which caused men to shun or evade the privileges of governmental activity. Both Parrington and J. T. Adams, by reading back into the days of the Puritans the values of the twentieth century, neither enlighten us nor understand the Puritans.

The second development in the writing of colonial history illustrated by Brown's article is broader in significance than the Puritans. Indeed, her article is representative of a number of studies which have recently brought about a sharp alteration in the historiography of colonial history. The alteration is the recognition that government in the American colonies of the seventeenth and eighteenth centuries was much more democratic than usually thought. One of the important works in the elaboration of this viewpoint is the book by Katherine Brown's husband, Robert E. Brown, *Middle Class Democracy and the Revolution in Massachusetts, 1691–1780* (Ithaca, N. Y. 1955), which persuasively argues for the middle of the eighteenth century what Mrs. Brown is here asserting for the early seventeenth century—that is, that the wide distribution of property rendered property qualifications no serious restriction on a wide suffrage. Since the article and book first appeared, other historians have begun to substantiate the Browns' point of view for areas outside of Massachusetts. Much the same point of view, for example, is taken by Chilton Williamson in his *American Suffrage from Property to Democracy, 1760–1860* (Princeton, 1960) and in Charles S. Grant's *Democracy in the Connecticut Frontier Town of Kent* (New York, 1961). A recent investigation of the other Massachusetts colony of the seventeenth century by George Langdon, Jr., "The Franchise and Political

Democracy in Plymouth Colony," *William and Mary Quarterly*, 3rd Series, XX (October 1963), 513–526, draws much the same conclusion about the breadth of the franchise as Katherine Brown. There are several aspects of historical investigation or method that Brown's article illustrates. For one thing, it demonstrates the inconclusiveness that often results when sources are limited and records are laconic. (Notice the specific questions that she raises in the middle of her article but cannot find final answers for.) For another, it illustrates the need for imagination and resourcefulness if the historian is to squeeze the maximum of information from the limited sources available.

The article is also a good example of taking a very large subject, like the degree of democracy in colonial society, and reducing it to manageable proportions by narrowing the definition of terms. In this article Brown defines a democratic franchise, in effect, as one in which more than one half of the adult males may vote. Obviously there are broader and perhaps even more meaningful definitions, but certainly in any discussion of political democracy the simple numerical breadth of the suffrage is important. To have taken too broad a definition of the conception of democracy would have been very unmanageable because so many elements would have to be considered. (For examples of how other historians have handled a similar problem see selections 5 and 8). Once this narrow definition has been established, other historians can go on to explore further the character and the extent of democracy more broadly defined. The Browns have continued their re-evaluation of the extent of the suffrage in colonial America in a recent book, *Virginia, 1705–1786: Democracy or Aristocracy?* (East Lansing, Mich., 1964).

For a critique of the Browns' narrow definition of democracy see John Cary, "Statistical Method and the Brown Thesis on Colonial Democracy," with a rebuttal by Robert E. Brown, in *William and Mary Quarterly*, 3rd Series, XX (April, 1963), 251–276.

Mrs. Brown lives in East Lansing, Michigan, where her husband is professor of history at Michigan State University. Her most recent elaboration of the position taken in the present article is "Puritan Democracy: A Case Study," *Mississippi Valley Historical Review*, L (December 1963), 377–396.

Freemanship in Puritan Massachusetts

BY B. KATHERINE BROWN

ARISTOCRACY, oligarchy, theocracy—these are the terms modern writers generally choose to characterize Puritan government in early Massachusetts. It was undemocratic society, they tell us, from the beginning in 1629 until the arbitrary Governor Andros took over in 1686. The colony was divided into political classes—the minority who could vote ruled the majority who could not. The minority, the freemen, were those who, since they belonged to the established Puritan church, were eligible to take the oath of freedom and were thus permitted to enjoy all political privileges in the Commonwealth. The freemen, they say, comprised only about one fifth of the adult male population and were in general the most substantial citizens. They were hostile to every democratic tendency, so the story goes, and were jealous of their social position in the class-conscious society of the early Bay Colony.[1]

When we examine these secondary accounts more closely, we find many fundamental inconsistencies and contradictions, both between authorities and within individual interpretations. Such inconsistencies and contradictions cast a strong shadow of doubt on the accuracy of the accepted story.

For example, historians disagree on the extent of democracy in

SOURCE: Reprinted by permission of the American Historical Association from the *American Historical Review*, LIX (July 1954).

[1] Vernon Louis Parrington, *Main Currents in American Thought* (New York, 1930), I, 21; John D. Hicks, *The Federal Union* (Boston, 1937), p. 29; Thomas Jefferson Wertenbaker, *The Puritan Oligarchy* (New York, 1947), p. viii; Charles M. Andrews, *The Colonial Period of American History* (New Haven, 1934), I, 443; George H. Haynes, *History of Representation and Suffrage in Massachusetts, 1620–1691* (Baltimore, 1894), p. 16; Perry Miller, *Orthodoxy in Massachusetts, 1630–1650* (Cambridge, 1933), pp. 243–44; Oliver Perry Chitwood, *A History of Colonial America* (New York, 1931), pp. 140, 141. Some of the earlier historians did not picture early Massachusetts as a class-ridden oligarchy. See for example, Mellen Chamberlain, "Remarks . . . ," in *Proceedings of the Massachusetts Historical Society*, 2d series, VII (Boston, 1891–92), 241–42, and Charles F. Adams, "Genesis of the Massachusetts Towns," *ibid.*, VII, 207–10.

one basic part of the political structure—the town meeting. V. L. Parrington declares that Puritan town meetings were not democratic,[2] while J. D. Hicks believes the local government was democratic from the very beginning.[3] C. M. Andrews does not agree with either of these writers. Although a small body of freemen controlled all political affairs until 1648, he says, after that time every man who had taken the oath of fidelity and was twenty-four years old could vote and offer motions or petitions in town meetings.[4] Still another authority is at odds with Andrews' interpretation. Samuel Eliot Morison believes that the percentage of church members and voters in early Massachusetts was quite high but that by 1670 the franchise was limited to about one fourth of the adult males.[5] It is difficult to understand how four major authorities could hold such different views about one vital point in Puritan government.

Not only are there major disagreements between authorities but there are also important inconsistencies within specific accounts. Parrington, for example, succeeds in thoroughly confusing the conflict between the deputies, who were freemen, and the magistrates, who were also freemen, with the supposed struggle of the unenfranchised to gain some political power.[6] It is obvious that the two controversies cannot be mixed: the one concerned a struggle within the "oligarchy" and the other between the oligarchy and an outside force. And as a result of his confusing the two disputes, Parrington sometimes calls the deputies, who were freemen of course and therefore full-fledged members of the oligarchy, "representatives of the people." [7]

J. T. Adams, too, confuses the conflict *within* the oligarchy with a supposed opposition *to* the oligarchy. "It is clear," he wrote, "that real grievances and the democratic influences at work in the town meeting were likely to develop into attacks upon the arbitrary power of the very limited body of freemen. The form that the struggle assumed was that of a contest, lasting twenty years, between the deputies and the magistrates, with the clergy constantly on the side of the latter." Later in the same work, Adams, like Parrington, claims

[2] Parrington, I, 21; see also James T. Adams, *The Founding of New England* (Boston, 1921), p. 152.

[3] Hicks, p. 57; also Samuel Eliot Morison and Henry S. Commager, *The Growth of the American Republic* (New York, 1950), I, 56.

[4] Andrews, I, 459–60.

[5] Samuel Eliot Morison, *Builders of the Bay Colony* (Cambridge, 1930), pp. 340–41.

[6] Parrington, I, 16–50, *passim*.

[7] *Ibid.*, p. 21.

that the deputies represented public opinion rather than the oligarchy.[8]

Furthermore, Adams contradicts himself by stressing first the strong opposition to the oligarchy throughout the period and then calmly concluding that no real opposition existed. In the beginning, he says, one of the two major elements in the political history of Massachusetts under the old charter was "the struggle of a part of the colonists themselves, for toleration and liberty, against the governing class." Owing to the church-membership restriction for voting, "the unenfranchised class was so large, and the disadvantage under which it labored was so palpably unjust, that the demand for reform was growing steadily louder."[9] But Adams then startles the reader by concluding that after all the ordinary man in early Massachusetts probably cared no more about government than the ordinary man elsewhere.

> In fact, at a little later period, the more accurate election returns would seem to indicate that he then cared even less. The small minority that ran the government and the churches was naturally active and vocal. But the fact that four fifths of the people were reasonably content to join no church, and to have no voice in the government, certainly does not argue, in that time and place, any very high degree of political, religious, or intellectual interest as compared with the rest of America.[10]

Such somersaults in logic are a bit alarming when they concern a basic interpretation. Was there a "struggle" or wasn't there?

C. M. Andrews, makes an even more serious error by building his interpretation of the Puritan period on an admitted lack of evidence. In time, Andrews points out, four classes appeared in Puritan Massachusetts society: (1) the freemen, "always a minority in every town and in the colony as a whole"; (2) the church members who never offered to become freemen; (3) the inhabitants who were neither freemen nor church members "but who had taken the oath of fidelity and therefore were in accord with the general purpose and aims of the colony"; and finally (4) those who were neither freemen nor church members and so were "in the colony but not of it." "It is impossible," he continues, "to conjecture, even roughly, what were the relative sizes of these four groups." But he promptly does the impossible: the third group was the largest, the second the smallest, and "the fourth the only one, the loyalty of which to Puritan principles can be seriously questioned."[11] In other words, three of the four

[8] Adams, *Founding of New England*, pp. 154–55, 257.
[9] *Ibid.*, pp. 155–56, 253.
[10] *Ibid.*, p. 443.
[11] Andrews, I, 437–38.

groups, or a majority, were in sympathy with Puritan aims. But a few pages later Andrews characterizes Massachusetts from 1634 on as undemocratic, as a society in which "a privileged class was in command, whose deputies in no way represented the colony as a whole." [12] If it were impossible to estimate "even roughly" the number of freemen in the colony, how could Andrews conclude that Massachusetts was highly undemocratic?

From these conflicting and contradictory reports, it would seem that we need to know more about freemanship in Puritan Massachusetts before we can say with any certainty how democratic or undemocratic the colony really was. Who could be a freeman, who wanted to be a freeman, and how limited was the franchise? The answers to these questions will tell us a great deal about Puritan society.

Freemanship in Massachusetts rested first on a corporation or company charter granted to the company in England in 1629 and later on laws passed in the colony. The charter provided for a general court or meeting of company officials and stockholders to make laws governing company affairs. Among the powers of the general court was that of admitting new members, or freemen, to the privileges of the company. In the colony, the charter was used as a constitution for a civil government rather than merely a business corporation, and freemen who were admitted to the company became citizens with political privileges. Rules governing the admission of new freemen, or citizens, were altered from time to time by the general court. What these new rules were and how they were put into practice will show much about the number of freemen.

The first major change in the rules for admitting freemen, and the basis for the interpretation that early Massachusetts was undemocratic, came in 1631. The general court passed an order that no man should be admitted to freemanship but such as were members of some of the churches in Massachusetts.[13] It has been assumed that only the few were church members, and consequently only the few could be freemen. Perry Miller, for example, stresses that the law was put over on the people by a few aristocratic leaders, leaders who aimed at retaining their position.[14] The extent to which this law

[12] *Ibid.*, I, 443.

[13] *Records of the Governor and Company of Massachusetts Bay, 1628–1686*, ed. N. B. Shurtleff (Boston, 1853–54), I, 87. Hereafter this work will be cited as *Mass. Records*.

[14] Miller, *Orthodoxy in Mass.*, pp. 243–44.

limited the number of freemen and therefore restricted democracy is the heart of our problem.

Although evidence is scanty on the exact number of church members at this period, there is some indication that the first settlers were mostly orthodox in their religious beliefs and therefore might well have approved a law restricting freemanship to church members. An official company letter dated April 17, 1629, outlined how carefully all those in the company's service were screened in religious beliefs. Colony officials were warned that, if in spite of care to purge the unorthodox, some "libertines" were found, they should be punished and corrected or be returned to England.[15]

Another way to determine the contemporary popularity of the 1631 law is to find out who was responsible for putting over the restriction. Records show that in October, 1630, over one hundred men "desired" to be made freemen. At the next court meeting, May 18, 1631, the records list those who were "made" freemen, many of whom were on the 1630 list.[16] The problem then is whether these men were admitted to freemanship before the church restriction law was passed, or whether the law was put over on the people by a few leaders.

Edward Johnson, one of those made free in 1631, stated clearly that the first group of men were made freemen before the law was passed restricting freemanship to church members. "At this Court," he wrote, "many of the first Planters came and were made free, yet afterward none were admitted to this fellowship, or freedome, but such as were first joyned in fellowship with some one of the Churches of Christ. . . ."[17] Since Johnson was present at both the 1630 and 1631 meetings and wrote his history only twenty years later, his story might well be accurate. Thomas Hutchinson, who probably had access to more contemporary documents than any other Massachusetts historian, agreed with Johnson.[18]

Other evidence that the 1631 law was put over *by* and not *on* the people is found in the wording of the early records. Descriptions of the first general court meetings picture a democratic, not a "patriarchial undertaking," as described by Parrington.[19] In the first court of October, 1630, the proposal that the "ffreemen" should have

[15] *Mass. Records*, I, 393.

[16] *Ibid.*, I, 79–80, 366–67.

[17] Edward Johnson, *The Wonder-Working Providence of Sions Saviour in New England (1628–1651)*, ed. William F. Poole (Andover, Mass., 1867), p. 66.

[18] Thomas Hutchinson, *History of the Colony and Province of Massachusetts-Bay*, ed. L. S. Mayo (Cambridge, Mass., 1936), I, 24–25.

[19] *Main Currents*, I, 20.

the power of choosing the assistants was "fully assented unto" by a general vote of "the people." [20] And at the next general court, May 18, 1631, the above law was explained and elaborated and the church restriction order added "with the full consent of all the comons" then present.[21] The "comons" apparently meant the people in general, for John Winthrop tells us that on May 17, 1631, "all the freemen of the commons were sworn to this government." [22] Had there been a struggle about adoption of the order restricting the franchise at this meeting, we might assume Winthrop would have mentioned it in his *Journal.*

If these first Massachusetts settlers were orthodox Puritans in general and if the law was passed after the freemen of the commons were admitted, we can hardly conclude that the law was put over on the people by a few aristocratic leaders to keep the government in their own hands.

By 1635 the colony of Massachusetts had outlined the basic franchise rules that were to be followed until the year 1647, the date of the next major change in voting procedure. The oath required of all freemen for participation in political activities was put into final form in 1634.[23] And on September 3, 1635, the court ordered that none but freemen should have any vote in town affairs, although nonfreemen were allowed to vote for military officers.[24] In this early period, then, only freemen could legally vote and hold office in town and province government.

While the famous *Body of Liberties* of 1641 did not directly alter the franchise, some minor changes favoring nonfreemen can be seen in this first compilation of Massachusetts laws. Where originally the general court had declared that it alone could admit freemen, now this right was given also to the county courts. In addition, every man "whether Inhabitant or fforreiner, free or not free" was allowed to attend any court, council, or public meeting and propose measures if it were done "in convenient time, due order, and respective manner." [25] But the *Body of Liberties* did not specifically allow nonfreemen to vote or hold office.

[20] *Mass. Records*, I, 79.
[21] *Ibid.*, I, 87.
[22] *Winthrop's Journal, 1630–1649*, ed. James Kendall Hosmer (New York, 1908), I, 63.
[23] *Mass. Records*, I, 117.
[24] *Ibid.*, I, 161, 188.
[25] *The Colonial Laws of Massachusetts, Reprinted from the Edition of 1660, with the Supplements to 1672, Containing also, The Body of Liberties of 1641* (Boston, 1889), pp. 24, 35. Hereafter this work will be referred to as *Mass. Laws of 1660.*

If, legally, only freemen could participate in politics, two questions must be answered: (1) how well was the law enforced, since we know that laws do not always represent actual conditions, and (2) approximately what portion of the adult males were freemen before 1647?

Records of the town meetings show that in many Massachusetts towns during this early period "inhabitants" as well as legal freemen came to the meetings and voted. In Dorchester, for instance, the town scribe recorded that by "An agreement made by the whole consent and vote of the Plantation" on October 8, 1633, there would be a "generall meeting of the inhabitants of the Plantation att the meeteing house" every Monday before the general court to elect town selectmen.[26] Furthermore, in 1645 when the town composed "The Directory"—a set of rules to govern town affairs—the terms inhabitant and freemen were used interchangeably, and there is no indication in this town constitution of a cleavage between freemen and nonfreemen.[27]

In Boston too, the language in the town records implies that most men were included in the meetings. For example, the record of May 13, 1639 began: "Att a Generall Meeting upon particular or private Generall notice giveing from house to house." And at this meeting both deputies to the general court and new selectmen were elected.[28] If the number of people participating in these town meetings had been very limited, the notice would probably not have been given from house to house. Furthermore, it was the "townesmen" who made the town rates and divided the town's land—privileges supposedly reserved for freemen only.[29]

The language of the Salem and Woburn town records is also definite about nonfreemen as well as freemen coming to the meetings and voting. Woburn elected its first selectmen in 1644 "with the general consent of all the freemen and other inhabitants then present." [30] And in 1646 Salem agreed "that all the towne's men and freemen" should meet every second day for four weeks together to consider the public good of the town.[31] Language of this type in the con-

[26] *Dorchester Town Records,* in *Report of the Record Commissioners of the City of Boston* (Boston, 1883), IV, 3.

[27] *Dorchester Town Records,* pp. 289–91.

[28] *Report of the Record Commissioners of the City of Boston,* II, 41. Hereafter this work will be cited as *Boston Town Records.*

[29] *Ibid.,* II, 57–58.

[30] Samuel Sewall, *The History of Woburn, Middlesex County, Mass.* (Boston, 1868), p. 24.

[31] Quoted in Joseph B. Felt, *Annals of Salem* (Salem, Mass., 1845), I, 350.

temporary records suggests that the 1631 law was not so restrictive after all.

Another method of determining real practices in town government is to compare the names of town selectmen with the official list of freemen. In spite of the law, town selectmen were not always freemen in the legal sense. A few weeks after the order was passed permitting only freemen to vote in town affairs, Watertown records read: "Agreed by the Consent of the Freemen that these 11 freemen shall order all the Civill Affaires for the Towne for the yeare following, & to divide the Lands." Then the record named the eleven "freemen."[32] Checking these names with the list of freemen shows that four of the eleven were not legal freemen at the time. Two of the four were made freemen about eight months later on May 25, 1636, and the remaining two never did appear on the official list.[33] It would seem, then, that (1) Watertown elected some nonfreemen to office before they were made free, and (2) the term "freeman" probably was used by the people of that day in two meanings—either to indicate a legal freeman, a church member who had taken the freeman's oath, or to indicate a man not in bondage, not a servant or a slave. Apparently the Watertown scribe was using "freeman" in the latter and more popular sense.

Like Watertown, other Massachusetts towns elected nonfreemen to office. In Dorchester, five of the twelve selectmen plus the bailiff chosen on October 2, 1636, were not on the list of freemen.[34] This is also true of three of the ten Dorchester selectmen in 1637, and five of the ten selectmen in 1638.[35] Boston elected one "Wm. Tynge" deputy in 1639 and selectman in 1644, but Tynge cannot be found on the official list.[36] And in 1645, one of the Boston selectmen and one of the constables—Thomas Fowle and William Frankling—were not freemen.[37] Woburn chose freemen for its selectmen in 1644, but two of the three surveyors of highways elected that year were nonfreemen.[38]

Studying the official lists answers some questions for us, but also

[32] *Watertown Records* . . . (Watertown, Mass., 1894), I, 2.

[33] *Boston Town Records*, XXIX, 133, 134, 136, 137.

[34] *Dorchester Town Records*, p. 19. The nonfreemen's names were Mr. Glouer, Henry Withington, John Hollman, Cristofer Gibson, Mr. Joanes, and the bailiff, Joseph Flood. Two of these, Gibson and a Mr. Ralfe Glouer, are listed on the 1630 list of men who desired freemanship but are not on the official list of freemen in 1631. See *Mass. Records*, I, 80, 366–79.

[35] *Dorchester Town Records*, pp. 24, 35; *Mass. Records*, I, 366 ff.

[36] *Boston Town Records*, II, 46, 79; *Mass. Records*, I, 366–79; II, 291–95.

[37] *Boston Town Records*, II, 84, 86; *Mass. Records*, I, 366–79; II, 291–95.

[38] Sewall, *Woburn*, p. 25; *Mass. Records*, I, 366–79; II, 291–95. Ralph Hill, possibly one of the surveyors, was made free, May 26, 1647, three years later.

it brings up a number of problems. Why, for instance, did Mr. Richard Bellingham, John Winthrop, Sr., John Humfry, Thomas Dudley, William Coddington, Increase Nowell, and Symon Bradstreet wait until May 25, 1636, to take the freeman's oath? Certainly these men were active in politics well before that date. According to John Cotton, Mr. Humfry was made an assistant in London before coming to the colony but had not joined a church in the colony yet "by reason of the unsetledness of the congregation" where he lived.[39] This explains Humfry's negligence in becoming a legal freeman, but what about the other six political leaders? Could it be that the line between freeman and nonfreeman was not so rigid as the law implies?

Another question brought up by studying the lists of freemen concerns the completeness of the lists as we know them today. When a Watertown selectman, a nonfreeman, was chosen eight months or more before his name appeared on the list, the man obviously was not a legal freeman at the time of his election. But what of the many other selectmen whose names never do appear on the lists? Were they actually never freemen or could it be that the official lists are not complete?

There is some evidence indicating that not all the names of the freemen were recorded. In 1637 when the colony was torn with dissension over the unorthodox religious opinions of Mrs. Anne Hutchinson, a number of her sympathizers were disfranchised by the general court. Two of those men, Mr. John Wheeleright and Sergeant Boston, were never enfranchised if being listed among the freemen was necessary.[40] And why, for instance, was one Mr. William Jennison listed on the 1630 list of those *desiring* freedom but not listed on the 1631 list of freemen admitted? And yet, in 1635 Watertown named him one of the freemen elected as a selectman.[41] Perhaps future study will clarify this problem.

Still another means of discovering the limitations of freemanship in this period is to find out what social classes were represented by the freemen. Were they from the upper rungs of the social ladder only—the wealthy, the educated, the gentlemen—or could anyone become a freeman?

The records again provide the answer: in the earliest days of the Puritan government, when, in theory, freemanship was limited to the few, the jump from servant to freeman was short and easy. In Bos-

[39] See John Cotton, "Letter of Cotton to Lord Say & Seal" (1636), in Thomas Hutchinson, *The History of the Colony of Massachusetts-Bay . . .* (London, 1760 [i.e., 1765]), Appendix, p. 498.

[40] *Mass. Records,* I, 207, 366–79.

[41] *Boston Town Records,* XXIX, 133; *Watertown Records,* I, 2.

ton, for example, in 1639, one Francis Dowse, "servant to our brother George Burdon," was allowed an inhabitant and became a freeman a year and a half later.[42] Another example was Thomas Joanes. On May 3, 1642, the general court gave Joanes, "servant to Willi: Richrdson," liberty to dispose of himself. Four years later Thomas Joanes was made a freeman.[43] One Thomas Reeves, who was set free by the court in May, 1644, was made a freeman in May, 1645.[44] As a final instance, on October 28, 1639, the town of Boston granted a house plot to John Robinson, "late servant to our brother Mr. Newgate."[45] This former servant became a freeman June 2, 1641.[46]

A detailed check of two servants gives more insight into how rapid the climb from servant to freeman could be in the early Bay Colony. In 1632 the general court ordered two of Israell Stoughton's servants, Alexander Miller and John Wipple, to pay their master for their wasteful use of powder and shot.[47] Since Israell Stoughton was a Dorchester resident, the Dorchester town records furnish us additional material on his two helpers. On September 1, 1634, the town granted "Alexander Miller servant to Mr. Stoughton" three acres of land. In 1635 he was granted three more acres and four years later he was listed among the "inhabitants" in the division of town lands. On May 2, 1638, he was made a freeman. In other words, it took a little more than two years for wayward servant Miller to become a freeholder and four more years to become a freeman.[48] The record of servant John Wipple is similar but he was not made a freeman until 1640.[49]

There is other evidence, too, that freemanship in this early period was not restricted to any one social and economic stratum. John Martin, a Boston shipcarpenter, and John Palmer, a Boston carpenter, became freemen soon after becoming inhabitants in the town.[50] Carpenters would not generally be considered among the exclusive set in Puritan society. On the other hand, Winthrop noted that one Briscoe of Watertown, "a rich man, a tanner," lost £200 worth of goods when his barn burned down. Briscoe was not a church member, not a freeman, and in 1643 wrote a pamphlet objecting to

[42] *Boston Town Records*, II, 45; *Mass. Records*, I, 379.
[43] *Mass. Records*, II, 4, 294.
[44] *Ibid.*, II, 67, 294.
[45] *Boston Town Records*, II, 43.
[46] *Mass. Records*, I, 378.
[47] *Ibid.*, I, 100.
[48] *Dorchester Town Records*, pp. 7, 10, 30, 37; *Mass. Records*, I, 374.
[49] *Dorchester Town Records*, pp. 27, 76, 140; *Mass. Records*, II, 376.
[50] *Boston Town Records*, II, 22, 51; *Mass. Records*, I, 376, 378.

support of the minister by taxation.[51] Obviously when an ordinary carpenter could be a freeman, and a rich man, not a freeman, could live in Massachusetts and even object to the local administration, freemanship was not socially nor economically restrictive.

Perhaps the most conclusive evidence that freemanship was not limited to gentlemen nor to any one social class is to be seen by the following description of a freeman. On May 26, 1647, Mighill Smith was made a freeman according to the official list, and on that same date appeared this statement: "It is ordered, y^{t} ye fine of Mighill Smith, for his puting in of three beanes at once for one mans election, it being done in simplicity, & he being pore & of an harmles disposition, it is orde^{r}ed his fine is suspended till furth^{r} ord^{r} from ye Gen^{r}all Co^{r}te." [52] Freeman Smith surely was not from the top rung of the Puritan social ladder.

As to the actual number of freemen in the colony at this time, contemporary opinion varied, but the scale weighed heaviest on the democratic side. Thomas Lechford, a Church of England man who came to Massachusetts in 1638, offered contradictory evidence. At one point, he complained that many men were excluded from freemanship. Wrote Lechford: "Now the most of the persons at *New-England* are not admitted of their Church, and therefore are not *Freemen*. . . ." [53] At another time, however, he declared that Massachusetts was a good country and yielded many products "if that popular elections destroy us not." [54] On the other hand, Nathaniel Ward, author of the *Body of Liberties*, believed the freemen were too numerous and held too much power. In his oft-quoted letter of 1639 to John Winthrop, he asked:

> That you would please to advise throughly with the counsell, whether it will not be of ill consequence to send the Court business to the common consideration of the freemen. I feare it will too much exauctorate the power of that Court to prostrate matters in that manner. I suspect both Commonwealth & Churches have discended to lowe already; I see the spirits of people runne high & what they gett they hould. They may not be denyed their proper & lawfull liberties, but I question whether it be of God to interest the inferiour sort in that which should be reserved *inter optimates penes quos est sancire leges.*[55]

[51] *Winthrop's Journal*, II, 88, 91.
[52] *Mass. Records*, II, 189.
[53] Thomas Lechford, *Plain Dealing; or, Newes from New-England* (London, 1642), reprinted in *Collections of the Mass. Hist. Soc.*, 3d series, III (Cambridge, Mass., 1833), 81.
[54] Thomas Lechford, *Note-book, 1638–1641*, ed. Edward E. Hales (Cambridge, Mass., 1885), p. 287.
[55] Letter of Nathaniel Ward to John Winthrop, in Thomas F. Waters, *Ipswich In the Massachusetts Bay Colony* (Ipswich, Mass., 1905), Appendix C, p. 505.

It is of significance that Ward was concerned over the great power and low social status of the freemen, not the nonfreemen. The fact that he used "people" synonymously with "freemen" implies broad suffrage. Furthermore, the general court seemed to agree with Ward when it declared in 1641 that better order was needed in elections because the freemen had grown "to so great a multitude as wilbee overburthensome to the country." [56]

According to figures given by Samuel Eliot Morison, the actual percentage of freemanship in this period was quite high. He cites a 1638–1640 list of Roxbury householders containing sixty-nine men of whom fifty-eight were church members and voters.[57] In other words, eighty-four per cent or about five to one of the men in the town of Roxbury were freemen. This is quite the opposite of the figure usually given.

While most authorities follow Lechford and assume that men wanted freemanship but could not attain it and consequently label Puritan society as undemocratic, there is evidence that many men avoided freemanship because of the duties and obligations which freemanship entailed. In 1643 the general court ordered "concerning members that refuse to take their freedom, the churches should bee writ unto, to deale wth them." [58] And a few years later, Edward Winslow, Massachusetts agent in England, declared that in every town there were many freemen but there were also many who were not free by choice. If they were understanding men and able to be helpful, he explained, it was primarily their own fault. They avoided freemanship because of the responsibilities involved.[59] This certainly gives a different connotation to nonfreemanship in the colony. Obviously the freemen wanted to include, not exclude, more men in the suffrage, and many men were nonfreemen by choice, not by necessity.

Freeman, too, were primarily responsible for events which led up to the 1647 law giving nonfreemen equal rights with freemen in town government. In 1644, according to Winthrop, a proposal was made in the general court "for all the English within the united colonies to enter into a civil agreement for the maintenance of religion and our civil liberties, and for yielding some more of the freeman's privileges to such as were no church members that should join in this government." Nothing was concluded on the matter, however, but letters were written to the other colonies to advise with them about it.[60]

[56] *Mass. Records*, I, 333.

[57] Morison, *Builders of the Bay Colony*, Appendix, pp. 340–41.

[58] *Mass. Records*, II, 38.

[59] Edward Winslow, "New-Englands Salamander Discovered," in *Collections Mass. Hist. Soc.*, 3d series, II (Cambridge, 1830), 137, 139.

[60] *Winthrop's Journal*, II, 163–64.

The freemen, it seems, wanted all the help they could muster in the face of threatened trouble with the Dutch and Indians. Two years later, in 1646, the general court drew up a law "allowing non-freemen equal power with the freemen in all town affairs, and to some freemen of such estate, etc., their votes in election of magistrates." But near the end of this court session and before the law was passed, a controversial petition to enlarge the franchise was presented by Dr. Robert Childe and action on the law as well as the petition was referred to the next meeting.[61]

The petition by Dr. Robert Childe and six others, which delayed the court's action on enlarging rights of nonfreemen, demanded more civil and religious rights for Church of England men in the colony and threatened to apply to parliament for help if their demands were not granted. The petition asked that the court give liberty to members of the Church of England to be taken into Massachusetts congregations "to enjoy with you all those liberties and ordinances Christ hath purchased for them," and also that "Civil liberty and freedome be forthwith granted to all truly *English*, equall to the rest of their Country-men." These requests were not unreasonable, but the petition did not stop there. It insinuated that Massachusetts was dangerously independent of England and concluded with a threat that if their demands were not heeded, the petitioners would appeal to parliament, "who we hope will take our sad conditions into their serious considerations."[62]

Given the already increasing sentiment in the colony for enlarging the franchise, Dr. Childe's petition might not have occasioned so much disturbance had it not contained a definite threat to apply over the heads of Massachusetts leaders to parliament if the general court refused Childe's requests. This threat was a direct challenge to the entire position of the Puritan colony and to every freeman there.

In the upheaval following this challenge and in the contemporary writings about it, it becomes clear that the petition was not merely a move by the unenfranchised to gain more political freedom. It was a move originally agitated by one of the patentees, Mr. William Vassal, who came over in 1630 and who was dissatisfied with the Massachusetts government.[63] The seven signers of the Childe petition were

[61] *Ibid.*, II, 271–72.

[62] Major John Childe, *New-Englands Jonas Cast up at London* . . . (London, 1647), reprinted in Peter Force, *Tracts and Other Papers* . . . (Washington, 1836), IV, No. 3, pp. 11–13.

[63] *Winthrop's Journal*, II, 271; William Hubbard, *General History of New England* (*1680*), ed. T. M. Harris, in *Collections Mass. Hist. Soc.*, 2d series, V, VI (Boston, 1848), 499–500.

a mixture of freemen and nonfreemen: Mr. Samuel Maverick of Salem was a freeman,[64] Mr. Thomas Fowle was a Boston leader but not a freeman, and three others according to Winslow were mere strangers and had no property within the government.[65] One of the petitions to parliament later confiscated by the general court was signed by twenty-five nonfreemen, "(pretending to be in the name, and upon the sighs and tears, of many thousands)." But, according to Winthrop, most of these men were Marblehead fishermen, some of whom had come from Newfoundland the previous year, or young men servants who had little religion in them.[66]

The Childe petition failed, but the next general court nevertheless passed a law in 1647 extending the freemen's privileges to nonfreemen in town affairs. Any inhabitant of twenty-four years of age, the law said, who had taken the oath of fidelity (required of all male residents) could be on the jury, could vote in town meetings and could be elected a selectman. The only restriction in town affairs was the requirement that a major part of the town selectmen be freemen.[67] From this time on, then, the law sanctioned a broad-based local franchise and only in province elections did the church restriction clause of 1631 apply.

Although for over a decade after 1647 there was a letdown in the pressure for additional change in the franchise, during this period there appears a sharper division between freemen and nonfreemen. The *Massachusetts Laws of 1648*, unlike the *Body of Liberties* in 1641, sharply divided the freemen from nonfreemen.[68] And some of the town records show more definite distinction between the two groups. In 1653, for example, the Dorchester town records clearly warned all "freemen" to meet for choice of magistrates and all "the planters inhabtance" to meet for other town business.[69] Boston started to separate the meetings of freemen and inhabitants in 1658, but it was 1659 before the town openly made a rule for their separation.[70]

The more definite division between freemen and nonfreemen did

[64] *Winthrop's Journal,* II, 316.
[65] Winslow, "New-Englands Salamander Discovered," p. 123.
[66] *Winthrop's Journal,* II, 307–308.
[67] *Mass. Records,* II, 197.
[68] *The Laws and Liberties of Massachusetts Reprinted from the Copy of the 1648 Edition in the Henry E. Huntington Library, with an Introduction by Max Farrand* (Cambridge, 1929), pp. A2, 23, 50–51. Hereafter this work will be cited *Mass. Laws of 1648.*
[69] *Dorchester Town Records,* p. 315.
[70] *Boston Town Records,* II, 133, 148, 149; for a similar change in Salem see *Town Records of Salem, Massachusetts* (Salem, 1913, 1934), II, 4, 8, 9.

not engender any obvious opposition to the church and government in the colony however. In fact there seemed to be a lack of any real disturbance during this period. There was apparently still a great degree of uniformity in religious beliefs in most of the towns. In 1661, for instance, the Watertown selectmen complied with an order of the general court and took a survey of the town to determine whether all inhabitants were obeying the law which required "the knowledg of God & excerising reading to the advancing of Catachising." They found that only four families were neglecting their duty.[71] Ten years earlier Johnson had given the Watertown population as 160 families.[72] If only four out of 160 Watertown families were neglecting their religious instruction, there could not have been much dissension in the town on the religious score. Furthermore, the very fact that Johnson himself does not mention any political turmoil, any growing threat of a large body of nonfreemen to enlarge their political rights, is good indication that there was none. Johnson, who wrote his historical work during this period, was one of the "aristocracy" and would have been definitely concerned about any major move to upset the status quo.

Not only was there no great demand for increased freemanship at this time but some men were still avoiding the obligations of freedom. A 1647 law is clear on this matter: "*Wheras there are within this Jurisdiction many members of Churches who to exempt themselves from all publick service in the Common-wealth will not come in, to be made Freemen,*" the court ordered that such members should not be exempt from public service. They must serve when elected constables, jurors, selectmen, or surveyors of highways, and if they refused when legally chosen they must pay the same fine freemen were liable to in such cases.[73] If church members were refusing to become freemen, it is logical to assume that non-church members might be equally reluctant—a fact which must be considered in any discussion of the franchise.

The only minor change in franchise requirements between 1647 and 1664 was the addition in 1658 of a property qualification for town voting. According to the law, all English inhabitants of twenty-four years who had taken the oath of fidelity and who were "Rated at *twenty pound* estate in a single Country Rate" could vote and hold office in town affairs.[74] This new property qualification did not

[71] *Watertown Records,* I, 71.
[72] Johnson, *Wonder-Working Providence,* p. 74.
[73] *Mass. Laws of 1648,* p. 23.
[74] *Mass. Laws of 1660,* p. 76 [196].

provide any real restriction on voting, however, as the tax laws illustrate. A horse was rated at £10, a cow at £3, and even single men in Watertown who had no visible estate were to be rated £15.[75] Moreover, according to Johnson, at this time in the colony even the poorest man owned a house and land of his own—certainly enough property to qualify him for the vote.[76]

Actually, there is evidence that during this period the majority of adult men were freemen. According to one Captain Breedon, who was summoned to appear before the Council for Foreign Plantations in London, March 11, 1660, two thirds of the soldiers were freemen.[77] If two thirds of the soldiers, which included all men over sixteen years,[78] were freemen in 1660, then almost all free adult males in 1660 must have been freemen, for approximately thirty-four per cent of all settled males over sixteen years were minors or servants.[79] Breedon's estimate coincides with figures on Roxbury about this time cited by Samuel Eliot Morison. His claim was that of the fifty-seven men in Roxbury fifty-four were voters.[80]

In the 1660's the final major legal change was made in province voting, a change which slightly widened the franchise. The king of England sent a royal commission to investigate the colonies, and at the insistence of the king and the commissioners, the general court repealed the 1631 law restricting freemanship to church members, and adopted a new franchise requirement. The new law, passed in August, 1664, gave the vote to all church members in full communion. But it also enfranchised all Englishmen twenty-four years of age who presented a certificate from the ministers of their town that they were orthodox in religion and another certificate from the selectmen that they were freeholders and "rateable to the country in a single country rate," without poll tax and in the usual manner of valuation, to the value of ten shillings.[81]

In view of the current interpretation that the 1664 property qualification excluded most men from the vote,[82] the contemporary debate over the issue deserves some special attention. Displeased about the new law, the royal commissioners wrote to the general

[75] *Mass. Records,* IV, Pt. I, pp. 288–89; *Watertown Records,* I, 33.
[76] Johnson, p. 210.
[77] *Calendar of State Papers, Colonial Series, America and West Indies, 1677–1680,* ed. W. Noel Sainsbury and J. W. Fortescue (London, 1896), p. 297.
[78] *Mass. Laws of 1660,* p. 57 [177].
[79] *Boston Town Records,* I, 46–48.
[80] Morison, *Builders of the Bay Colony,* pp. 340–41.
[81] *Mass. Records,* IV, Pt. 2, pp. 117–18, 134.
[82] See for example, J. T. Adams, *The Founding of New England,* p. 331; Wertenbaker, *Puritan Oligarchy,* pp. 305–306.

court on May 18, 1665, warning them the king would not be happy to find the law allowed the vote to "him only who pajeth ten shillings to a single rate to be of competent estate." In a town of one hundred inhabitants, the commissioners complained, hardly three men were to be found who paid that much and not one church member in a hundred paid that amount.[83]

The general court defended its law, claiming it did not restrict many from the franchise. The law was not "exclusive," the court maintained, and furthermore some type of religious discipline was required of any Christian society. It "is no other then what is required of his majestjes subjects in England; & as for the manner of the exercise of ecclesiasticall discipline, although the godly orthodox are variously minded therein, yet this is no barr to any in the enjoyment of any civil priviledge heere." And, added the court, the small compensation for officeholding in the colony made those elected not "the objects of envy for any personall benefit they have thereby." In fact many had greatly reduced their estates by having to serve in office.[84]

War between the English and Dutch prevented the royal commissioners from carrying on the debate, however, and the law continued in force until the charter was revoked in 1686.

The actual wording of this law along with a check on the tax customs of the day reveals the retort of the general court to be correct, not the interpretation of the royal commissioners. The law was not exclusive. It said those freeholders were qualified to vote who were *rated* in a single country rate to the value of ten shillings, not those who *paid* ten shillings. This made a great difference. A tax rating was the assessed valuation of a man's taxable property. The commissioners were correct in saying few men in a town *paid* ten shillings tax, but they confused the amount paid with the amount rated.

Tax valuations for that day show it would be rare indeed if a man did not own enough property to be *rated* ten shillings. In 1653 all single persons in Watertown without visible estates were rated at £15 for ministry and town charges.[85] After the early 1650's the amount paid in country (that is, province) tax was one penny for every twenty shillings ratable estate,[86] and a law in 1657 showed clearly how estates were to be valued. Houses and lands

83 *Mass. Records,* IV, Pt. 2, p. 205.
84 *Ibid.,* IV, Pt. 2, p. 221.
85 *Watertown Records,* I, 33.
86 *Boston Town Records,* X, 48.

were to be rated at "an equall and indifferent value" according to their worth in the town where they were located. Animals were to be rated as follows: every three-year-old horse at £10; those between two and three years at £7; those between one and two years at £5; cows at £3; sheep at 25*s.*; swine at 20*s.*; every ass of one year at 40*s.*; and so on.[87] In other words, anyone who owned one half of a swine or one sixth of a cow would be *rated* enough to qualify for the franchise.

Not only is the valuation law itself evidence that few would be excluded from the vote by a ten-shilling property qualification, but a check of the valuation records for Boston in 1676 shows that ninety-five per cent of the men listed on the Boston tax list had ample property to qualify. A very few houses were valued as low as £5, and none lower. Most of them were rated £10 or over and a few as high as £300. But even if a man couldn't qualify with real estate, such items as horses, cows, swine, sheep, mills, and other estates (money at interest, or trades) were also rated.[88] Since all males over sixteen years were listed for poll tax on the tax records, it is very possible that some of the disqualified five per cent would be younger sons and servants under the voting age.

With the repeal of the church restriction clause and the passage of the 1664 law, province voting rules for the remainder of the Puritan period were set. Was the new law exclusive or did the relaxation of the church restriction allow a flood of new voters?

The altered regulation apparently resulted in little change in the complexion of the voting population or voting habits. A comparison of records before and after the change discloses no unusual turnover in officeholders.[89] The Boston town records still show that notices for freemen's meetings were given from "house to house"—an indication that being a freeman was not too rare.[90] And, according to Samuel Sewall, some men continued to be hesitant about joining the church (still an easy means to freemanship) because of their personal unsettled condition and the responsibilities involved.[91] But even in this late period the majority favored the Puritan way. For example, in 1680 one unsympathetic traveler, Jasper Danckaerts, wrote: "They [in New England] are all Independents in matters of religion, if it can be called religion; many of them perhaps more for the purposes of enjoying the benefit of its privileges

[87] *Mass. Records,* IV, Pt. 1, pp. 288–89.
[88] *Boston Town Records,* I, 60–67.
[89] *Mass. Records,* IV, Pt. 2, pp. 1, 116–17, 141–43, 294.
[90] *Boston Town Records,* VII, 24, 38.
[91] *Samuel Sewall's Diary,* ed. Mark Van Doren (New York, 1927), p. 14.

than for any regard to truth and godliness."[92] And William Stoughton and Peter Bulkeley, Massachusetts agents in England, stated that although the non-church-members could be freemen, the number who were not members was "inconsiderable."[93]

In fact, available statistics for this period indicate the majority of men in Boston were freemen. As early as 1665 Boston complained that their town was under-represented, that the number of Boston freemen was "very lardg" and that the town deserved more representation.[94] In 1679 Boston was still complaining, and declared their "great Towne" consisted of "neere twentie times twentie" or about four hundred freemen.[95] Other figures found in Boston tax records for 1674 show that sixty-six to sixty-eight per cent of the total ratable males (that is, over sixteen years) were masters of families.[96] And in 1678 and 1679, a total of 991 males over sixteen years took the required oath of allegiance in Boston.[97] So if sixty-six per cent of the males over sixteen were masters of families, there would be 654 masters of families or adult householders in Boston in 1678–1679. If 400 of the 654 were freemen, at least sixty-one per cent of all adult men in Boston would have been freemen in 1679. Furthermore, it should be remembered that Boston was the only town with any organized churches other than Congregational and therefore would probably have had the lowest percentage of freemen among the adult male residents of any town in the colony.[98] But even sixty-one per cent freemen is a reasonable majority and far different from the percentage usually assumed by most authorities.

During the last few years of the Puritan period, an increase in the property qualification for town voting may have provided some restriction for a few of the nonfreemen in local affairs. By an order of 1670, the property qualification for the town franchise was raised from a £20 to an £80 ratable estate, but the sum was not to exclude any person from the privilege of voting formerly granted to him.[99] No explanation for the change is given in the

[92] *Journal of Jasper Danckaerts, 1679–1680,* ed. Bartlett B. James and J. Franklin Jameson (New York, 1913), p. 274.

[93] *Calendar of State Papers, 1677–1680,* pp. 261, 269; and for a slightly later period see Cotton Mather, *Magnalia Christi Americana,* 2d ed. (Hartford, 1855), I, 86–87.

[94] *Boston Town Records,* VII, 26.

[95] *Ibid.,* VII, 134.

[96] *Ibid.,* I, 38–39, 46–48, 49–53.

[97] *Ibid.,* XXIX, 164, 169.

[98] See Mather, *Magnalia,* I, 86–87.

[99] *Mass. Records,* IV, Pt. 2, p. 464.

laws and there seems to have been no noticeable opposition to the new qualification. At best it would have affected few men, for all freemen still had the franchise as well as all nonfreemen who formerly voted under the twenty-pound restriction. The new order, however, would affect any prospective voters who were nonfreemen in the final years of the Puritan regime.

In spite of this change the majority of adult men apparently could still vote in town affairs. A 1679 list of those in Ipswich "that by law are allowed to have there votes in Town affairs" contained 125 names.[100] Early in 1678 the town also listed all the commoners. Along with absentee owners, widows, and rights of the school, 161 male commoners were named.[101] Some of these 161 men might have been minors who could not have voted anyway, but for safety we will assume that all 161 men were adults. It appears, then, that approximately 125 out of 161 or 77.6 per cent of the men in Ipswich were allowed to vote in town affairs.

What does all this evidence mean?

It can mean that our modern notions about Puritan Massachusetts need some revision. Throughout the seventeenth century, the colony was surprisingly uniform in religion. Voting was limited to freemen at first, but as the number of nonfreemen grew the restrictions were gradually relaxed and much of that relaxation was due to pressure by freemen. Many men were nonfreemen by choice, not by compulsion. And the property qualification which replaced the religious restriction on province voting in 1664 was not large enough to exclude many men from the franchise. In other words, the franchise laws changed as the complexion of the population changed and Puritan Massachusetts practiced more democracy than most current writers indicate. Massachusetts was not as aristocratic, as undemocratic, as we have been led to believe.

[100] Waters, *Ipswich in the Mass. Bay Colony*, I, 91–93. Waters came to quite a different interpretation through what I believe to be a mishandling of evidence. In his total number of adult males which he combined from several lists, he has included all absentee owners, widows, and many obvious duplicate names. See pp. 98–106.

[101] This list is given in *New England Historical and Genealogical Register*, VII (Boston, 1853), 77–79.

3

NOT all nations, any more than all persons, can write about their history critically, for to do so requires maturity of insight and psychological security. One reason interpretations of the coming of the American Revolution have differed is the fact that Americans and historians have differed in their ability to look critically at the American past. For generations after the Revolution the colonists' argument that they had revolted against the tyranny of the mother country provided the central theme for historians who wrote about the coming of the Revolution. The nation was born out of a struggle for liberty, it was said. Undoubtedly the need to create a new nationalism as well as the continuing difficulties with Great Britain in the first half century of the Republic helped to make that view prevalent. But in the twentieth century, as Americans and historians alike became more secure and therefore more critical of their past and their origins as a people, they began to find flaws in the familiar arguments. The contention, for example, that the colonial revolt stemmed essentially from "taxation without representation" seemed to many historians too narrow a base for a revolution. After all, such an argument was in essence constitutional. Was such an argument likely to engage the energy and concern of many ordinary colonists? Could such abstract questions explain the willingness to accept hardship and danger that the drive to revolution certainly entailed?

Because their answers to these questions were generally negative, many historians turned to what they considered a more realistic view of the springs that move men in general and in the American Revolution in particular. They thought economic motives needed to be emphasized if the forces behind the Revolution were to be made credible. Arthur M. Schlesinger in his *Colonial Merchants and the American Revolution, 1763–1776* (New York, 1918) followed the philosophical lead of Charles A. Beard in *An Economic Interpretation of the Constitution,* which had appeared only five years earlier. Schlesinger treated the coming of the Revolution as a conflict between English and American merchants in which the constitutional issue of "no taxation without representation" was merely a public and more acceptable rhetoric for powerful and private interests.

Schlesinger's approach was only one way of suggesting that the usual explanation for the coming of the Revolution was both inadequate and uncritical. Other historians, examining the records and documents of the time, also found that the colonial accusations against the British, even on narrow constitutional issues, did not show the mother country to be as tyrannical or unreasonable as either the revolutionary rhetoric or tradition portrayed it. Among such works were Randolph G. Adams's *Political Ideas of the American Revolution* (Durham, N.C., 1922) and Carl Lotus Becker's two influential works *The Eve of the Revolution* (New Haven, 1918) and *The Declaration of Independence* (New York, 1922). For these historians the real weakness of the American case was revealed by the inconsistencies of the colonists' constitutional argument. Of all arguments, a constitutional one requires logic and consistency; if it can be shown that an argument used in one place is forgotten in another, then suspicion grows that the constitutional objection is simply a cover for a deeper and more self-interested objection. These historians pointed out that the American pamphleteers shifted their constitutional ground as British actions changed in response to colonial objections. Such a procedure certainly belied the colonists' concern for constitutional scruples.

Needless to say, those historians who thought the economic antagonisms between American and British merchants lay at the heart of the dispute found the shifting of American constitutional arguments grist for their mill. It demonstrated what they already believed, namely, that constitutional issues were not the real concerns but only the rhetorical sugar-coating by which more deep-felt issues were made palatable.

By the time Edmund Morgan published his article, the alleged shift in the Americans' constitutional argument had become commonplace in scholarly and textbook treatments of the prerevolutionary decade. Between the passage of the Stamp Act (1765) and the passage of the Townshend Acts (1767), historians believed, the

Americans revised their constitutional arguments to meet the threat of new taxes. Morgan's article, however, now makes it impossible to find any shifting in the colonial constitutional position.

As a consequence, it is not surprising that the constitutional explanation for the coming of the Revolution has once more become the most widely held view among historians. Certainly there are other reasons why the economic interpretation of the coming of the Revolution has been largely abandoned, at least one of which is explored in selection No. 4. But Morgan's article made its contribution by showing that the constitutional argument was not to be impugned simply on the grounds of inconsistency.

Morgan has used three methods in establishing his conclusion in this article. As he writes early in the article, "One cannot rely on newspapers and pamphlets nor on the resolutions adopted by informal gatherings of small groups, for these may represent the view of factions or the idiosyncracies of a single man." Hence he has based the first part of his article on the resolutions of official bodies of Americans, their assemblies. There he has sought out the meanings of the words "external" and "internal" taxation, for these are the words at issue. Later, however, in analyzing Daniel Dulany's pamphlet he goes a step further. There he closely examines the context of Dulany's words, which misled both contemporaries and historians. Finally he concludes by showing how the mistaken view of the colonial argument was arrived at by men at the time and later by historians. His analysis in this final part is perhaps one of the best examples of why the historian, in trying to get at the meaning of the past, must be careful not only to see events as men of the time saw them but to be aware also that different men living at the same time in the past may define words differently, thus confusing each other as well as historians.

One further observation may be made about Morgan's expert analysis. Precisely what the Americans contended for is important to get straight, and Morgan has helped us in doing that. But that the British misunderstood the colonials and thus charged them with inconsistency is also important. For that belief was certainly an important cause for the growing rift between the mother country and the colonies. But only when the historian knows that a misconception has taken place can he then call attention to it as a cause for the dispute. Thus Morgan's work does more than simply set the record straight; it makes a contribution to our understanding of why the Revolution came about.

After the publication of his article, Mr. Morgan and his wife, Helen

M. Morgan, published a full length study, *The Stamp Act Crisis* (Chapel Hill, 1953). His brief, cogent, and eminently lucid summary of the whole revolutionary era, *The Birth of the Republic, 1763–89* (Chicago, 1956), has subsequently appeared in paperback.

Colonial Ideas of Parliamentary Power, 1764-1766[1]

BY EDMUND S. MORGAN

I

THE distinction between internal and external taxes, said Charles Townshend, was "ridiculous in everybody's opinion except the Americans'."[2] The House of Commons was disposed to agree. Members had declared at the time of the Stamp Act that the distinction was meaningless. Some thought that the Americans were fools for espousing such sophistry; others thought that they were knaves, who would seize any pretext to avoid paying for their own protection. And knaves the Americans certainly appeared to be when they objected to the Townshend Duties almost as vehemently as they had to the Stamp Act. The colonists in fact seemed to be a ridiculous group of hypocrites, who capered from one pious notion of their rights to another. Their conduct was shameful and their efforts to justify it even more so. First they quibbled about external taxes and internal taxes. When this distinction failed them, they talked about taxes for regulating trade as against taxes for

SOURCE: Reprinted by permission from the *William and Mary Quarterly*, 3rd Series, V (July 1948). Copyright, 1948, by The Institute of Early American History and Culture.

1 This paper, in a shortened version, was read at a meeting of the American Historical Association at Cleveland on December 28, 1947. I wish to express my thanks to the members of the Association who offered comments at that time and to the members of my graduate seminar at Brown University, who criticized the paper at an earlier reading. I also wish to thank Mr. Bernhard Knollenberg, who read the manuscript and made several valuable suggestions.

2 Quoted in J. C. Miller, *Sam Adams: Pioneer in Propaganda* (Boston, 1936), 115.

revenue. Before long they were denying that Parliament had any authority to tax them, and finally they concluded that they were simply not subject to Parliament at all. The frivolous way in which they skipped from one of these views to the next was sufficient evidence that they had no real devotion to any principle except that of keeping their pockets full.[3]

The modern historian, who has thrown off the mantle of patriotism and Whigism for the more sober garments of impartiality, has tended to accept the Tory analysis of American resistance to taxation. He does not always cast doubt on the sincerity of the successive theories of American constitutional rights, but he agrees with Charles Townshend that it was the Americans who distinguished between internal and external taxes, that they abandoned this distinction for another, which likewise proved untenable, and so on until they reached the Declaration of Independence. Thus in the book which examines the American theories most closely, Doctor Randolph G. Adams' *Political Ideas of the American Revolution*,[4] the American advance toward independence is broken down into three stages:

> In the first, the colonies admitted the right of Parliament to levy customs duties (external taxes), but denied the right of Parliament to levy excise taxes (internal taxes) upon them. In the second, the colonies conceded the right of Parliament to regulate the trade of the Empire, and hence exercise a legislative authority over the unrepresented colonies, but denied the right of Parliament to levy taxes of any kind whatever, internal or external. In the third stage of the controversy, the colonies admitted the right of Parliament to act as a quasi-imperial superintending power over them and over all the dominions, but denied that Parliament had any legislative authority over the colonies as a general proposition, on the ground that the colonies were not represented in Parliament.[5]

The first two stages of American Revolutionary thinking, as

[3] See William Knox, *The Controversy between Great-Britain and her Colonies Reviewed* (London, 1769), 34–35: "When the repeal of the stamp-act was their object, a distinction was set up between internal and external taxes; they pretended not to dispute the right of parliament to impose external taxes, or port duties, upon the Colonies, whatever were the purposes of parliament in laying them on, or however productive of revenue they might be. . . . but when parliament seemed to adopt the distinction, and waiving for the present the exercise of its right to impose internal taxes, imposed certain duties on merchandizes imported into the Colonies, . . . the distinction between internal and external taxes is rejected by the colony advocates, and a new one devised between taxes for *the regulation of trade*, and taxes for the *purpose of revenue*."

[4] New York, 1939 (second edition).

[5] P. 69. For similar views by other historians, see C. P. Nettels, *The Roots of American Civilization* (New York, 1940), 634–635; C. L. Becker, *The Declaration of Independence* (New York, 1942, 1945), 80–134; H. J. Eckenrode, *The Revolution in Virginia* (Boston and New York, 1916), 28.

defined by Doctor Adams, have received less attention and are consequently less well understood than the last stage. My purpose is to examine the colonial ideas of Parliamentary power in the period covered by Doctor Adams' first stage, the period of the Stamp Act crisis.

It will be remembered that the Stamp Act was under discussion in the colonies from the spring of 1764 to the spring of 1766. Although it was in force for less than four months before its repeal in February, 1766, the colonists had begun to consider it as soon as they received news of the resolution passed by Parliament on March 10, 1764, the resolution which declared, "That, towards further defraying the said Expences, it may be proper to charge certain Stamp Duties in the said Colonies and Plantations." [6] The resolution was one of a series which George Grenville had introduced as the basis of his budget for the ensuing year. The others furnished the substance of the Revenue Act of 1764, the so-called Sugar Act, which became a law two months later. But the resolution for a stamp tax was phrased so as to indicate that no action would be taken on it until the next session, though its ultimate passage was almost a certainty.[7] The colonists were thus presented with two measures which threatened their prosperity and which consequently obliged them to think about the relation which they bore to the body which threatened them. They had to consider the Sugar Act, in which Parliament made use of trade regulations to raise money and which in itself would have been sufficient to set discerning minds at work on the question of Parliamentary taxation. At the same time they had to consider the Stamp Act, an act which would directly affect almost every person in the colonies. Of the two, the Stamp Act appeared to most colonists to be the more dangerous, but in formulating their ideas of Parliamentary power they could not afford to neglect either measure; they had to decide in what way their rights were affected both by the internal taxes of the Stamp Act and by the external taxes of the Sugar Act.

Under the pressure of these two acts colonial ideas reached a remarkable maturity during the period under discussion. In some regions and among some persons the theory of complete colonial

[6] *Journals of the House of Commons*, XXIX, 935.

[7] Grenville warned the colonial agents that he would bring in a bill for a stamp tax at the next session of Parliament. See the letter from Jasper Mauduit to Massachusetts, May 26, 1764 (Massachusetts Archives, XXII, 375); the letter from Charles Garth to South Carolina, June 5, 1764 (*English Historical Review*, LIV, 646–648); and the account by William Knox, agent for Georgia, in *The Claim of the Colonies to an Exemption from Internal Taxes Imposed by Authority of Parliament Examined* (London, 1765), 31–35.

autonomy was enunciated. For example a meeting of citizens at New London, Connecticut, on December 10, 1765, adopted resolutions which rehearsed the principles of government by consent, specified that the Stamp Act was a violation of those principles, and finally declared, "That it is the Duty of every Person in the Colonies to oppose by every lawful Means, the Execution of those Acts imposed on them,—and if they can in no other way be relieved to reassume their natural Rights, and the Authority the Laws of Nature and of God have vested them with." [8] If there was any confusion in the minds of the colonists as to how to go about reassuming natural rights, newspaper writers were ready with detailed discussions of the technique of revolution.[9] Short of this, other writers expounded the theory which later found more classic expression in the writings of John Adams and James Wilson, the theory that is assumed in the Declaration of Independence, that the colonies owe allegiance only to the king and are not bound in any way by acts of Parliament.[10]

But in the effort to arrive at what may be called the official colonial position during this period, one cannot rely on newspapers and pamphlets nor on the resolutions adopted by informal gatherings of small groups, for these may represent the views of factions or the idiosyncracies of a single man. Fortunately it is not necessary to depend upon such partial statements, for in every colony except Georgia and North Carolina the formally elected representatives of the people produced some official statement of belief. Five of the colonies which later revolted drew up statements in 1764 while the Stamp Act was pending; nine colonies, including all of the first five, did the same in 1765 after the Act was passed; and in the same year at the Stamp Act Congress, nine colonies combined in a declaration which was formally approved by a tenth. These statements, in the form of resolutions, petitions, memorials, and remonstrances, are the safest index of colonial opinion about Parliamentary power. They were carefully phrased by the regularly elected representatives of the voting population and adopted, in many cases unanimously, after deliberation and debate.

In these formal statements it is scarcely possible to discern a trace

[8] *Boston Post-Boy and Advertiser,* December 16, 1765.

[9] See, for example, *Boston Gazette,* December 2, 1765.

[10] *Maryland Gazette,* May 30, 1765; *Providence Gazette,* May 11, 1765; *Boston Gazette,* February 24, March 3, March 17, 1766. Governor Bernard reported to the Lords of Trade, November 30, 1765, that the Massachusetts politicians were claiming that the colonies "have no Superiors upon Earth but the King, and him only in the Person of the Governor, or according to the terms of the Charter." Bernard Papers, IV, 203, Harvard College Library.

of the ideas which the Americans are supposed to have adopted during the period under discussion. Almost universally the documents deny the authority of Parliament to tax the colonies at all. Nowhere is there a clear admission of the right of Parliament to levy external taxes rather than internal, and only in three cases does such a right seem to be implied. In at least one of these three, the implication which may be suggested by a partial reading is denied by a full consideration of the document and the circumstances under which it was produced.

II

As might be expected, the statements drawn up in 1764 while the Stamp Act was pending were generally not as explicit as those prepared a year later, when the Act had been passed and the colonists had had more time to think over its implications. The clearest of the early statements was that made by the New York Assembly in three petitions, to the King, the Lords, and the Commons, on October 18, 1764. These petitions, in objecting to both the Sugar Act and the proposed Stamp Act, claimed that the colonists should be exempt "from the Burthen of all Taxes not granted by themselves." Far from singling out internal taxes, the New York Assembly stated pointedly:

> . . . since all Impositions, whether they be internal Taxes, or Duties paid, for what we consume, equally diminish the Estates upon which they are charged; what avails it to any People, by which of them they are impoverished? . . . the whole wealth of a country may be as effectually drawn off, by the Exaction of Duties, as by any other Tax upon their Estates.

In accordance with this principle New York admitted the authority of Parliament to regulate the trade of the empire for the good of the mother country, but insisted that

> . . . a Freedom to drive all Kinds of Traffick in a Subordination to, and not inconsistent with, the *British* Trade; and an Exemption from all Duties in such a Course of Commerce, is humbly claimed by the Colonies, as the most essential of all the Rights to which they are intitled, as Colonists from, and connected, in the common Bond of Liberty, with the uninslaved Sons of *Great Britain*.[11]

The statement made by Virginia in 1764 was almost as plain as that of New York. The Virginia Council and House of Burgesses

[11] *Journal of the Votes and Proceedings of the General Assembly of the Colony of New York. Began the 8th Day of November, 1743; and Ended the 23d of December, 1765* (New York, 1766), II, 769–779.

in a petition to the King, a memorial to the House of Lords, and a remonstrance to the Commons, claimed an exemption from all Parliamentary taxation. To the King they asserted their "Right of being governed by such laws, respecting their internal Polity and Taxation,[12] as are derived from their own Consent"; to the Lords they stated their right as British subjects to be exempt from all taxes, "but such as are laid on them by their own Consent, or by those who are legally appointed to represent them"; to the Commons they remonstrated "that laws imposing taxes on the people ought not to be made without the consent of representatives chosen by themselves," and added that they could not discern "by what Distinction they can be deprived of that sacred birthright and most valuable inheritance, by their Fellow Subjects, nor with what Propriety they can be taxed or affected in their estates by the Parliament, wherein they are not, and indeed cannot, constitutionally be represented." [13]

Rhode Island, Connecticut, and Massachusetts took a less precise view of their rights in 1764 than did New York and Virginia, although Massachusetts and Connecticut, at least, cleared up the uncertainty of their position in the following year. In Rhode Island the General Assembly deputed Governor Stephen Hopkins to write a statement of the colony's rights and in addition sent a petition to the King, dated November 29, 1764. Both Governor Hopkins' pamphlet and the petition ignored the constitutional question raised by the Sugar Act, the question of external taxes; they argued against the act simply as a trade regulation which would have ruinous economic consequences. Since none of the colonies at this time denied Parliament's right to regulate colonial trade, Rhode Island, in considering the Sugar Act simply as such a regulation, made no attempt to deny Parliament's right to enact it. Against the proposed Stamp Act Hopkins and the Assembly did raise the question of right. This proposal, if carried into execution, would be "a manifest violation of their just and long enjoyed rights. For it must be confessed by all men, that they who are taxed at pleasure by others, cannot possibly have any property, can have nothing to be called their own; they who have no property can have no freedom, but are indeed reduced to the most abject slavery." The

[12] For the question whether or not the adjective "internal" modifies "taxation" as well as "polity" see the discussion below of the same phrase in the Virginia Resolves of 1765.

[13] *Journals of the House of Burgesses of Virginia 1761–1765* (Richmond, 1907), liv–lvii.

petition to the King recited the same objections and concluded with a request

> that our trade may be restored to its former condition, and no further limited, restrained and burdened, than becomes necessary for the general good of all your Majesty's subjects; that the courts of vice admiralty may not be vested with more extensive powers in the colonies than are given them by law in Great Britain; that the colonists may not be taxed but by the consent of their own representatives, as Your Majesty's other free subjects are.[14]

Thus Rhode Island sidestepped the question of external taxes by ignoring the declared intent of the Sugar Act to raise a revenue. She took a stand upon constitutional grounds only against the proposed Stamp Act, only, in other words, against internal taxes. Yet she did not quite admit Parliament's right to levy external taxes, because she considered the Sugar Act, erroneously to be sure, as a regulation of trade and not as a tax. Her position on external taxes was ambiguous: she didn't say yes and she didn't say no.

Connecticut in 1764 was guilty of the same ambiguity. Connecticut's statement took the form of a pamphlet drawn up by a committee, consisting of Governor Fitch, Ebenezer Silliman, George Wyllys and Jared Ingersoll, deputed by the General Assembly, "to collect and set in the most advantageous light all such arguments and objections as may justly and reasonably [be] advanced against creating and collecting a revenue in America, more particularly in this Colony, and especially against effecting the same by Stamp Duties &c." [15] This committee, of which Governor Fitch was the working member, produced a pamphlet entitled *Reasons why the British Colonies in America should not be charged with Internal Taxes, by Authority of Parliament.*[16] The pamphlet came as close as any American statement to admitting the right of Parliament to levy external taxes. Like the Rhode Island statement, it confined its constitutional objections to internal taxes and failed to consider the problem, raised by the Sugar Act, of whether Parliament could make use of trade regulations as a source of revenue. Instead, it assumed that Parliament would act for the good of the whole in its regulation of trade. "If Restrictions on Navigation, Commerce, or other external Regulations only are established," it said, "the internal Government, Powers of taxing for its Support, an Exemp-

[14] James R. Bartlett, ed., *Records of the Colony of Rhode Island and Providence Plantations* (Providence, 1861), VI, 414–427.

[15] C. J. Hoadly, ed., *Public Records of the Colony of Connecticut* (Hartford, 1881), XII, 256.

[16] New Haven, 1764. Reprinted in Hoadly, XII, 651–671.

tion from being taxed without Consent, and other Immunities, which legally belong to the Subjects of each Colony . . . will be and continue in the Substance of them whole and entire." [17] This was a rather naive view of the situation, but it did not necessarily commit the colony to a constitutional acceptance of external taxes.

The address of Massachusetts to the House of Commons, dated November 3, 1764, like the pamphlets issued by Rhode Island and Connecticut in this year, was not entirely clear on the question of external taxes. Massachusetts affirmed that the American colonists "have always judged by their representatives both of the way and manner, in which internal taxes should be raised within their respective governments, and of the ability of the inhabitants to pay them." The address concluded with the request that "the privileges of the colonies, relative to their internal taxes, which they have so long enjoyed, may still be continued to them." [18] By specifying internal taxes, the address seemed to imply that the inhabitants of Massachusetts did not object to the idea of an external tax imposed by Parliament. This implication was fortified by the rest of the document, which objected to the Sugar Act on economic rather than constitutional grounds as a measure which would ruin the trade of the colony.

Before this address is interpreted as an implied assent to external taxes the circumstances of its origin must be considered. The General Court adopted the address only because the Council refused to concur in a much more inclusive assertion of rights, originally passed by the lower house. In this version the House affirmed that "we look *upon those Duties as a Tax* [i.e. the duties imposed by the Sugar Act], and which we humbly apprehend ought not to be laid without the Representatives of the People affected by them." [19] The abandonment of this earlier version was regarded in Massachusetts as a victory for the Council under the leadership of Lieutenant-Governor Hutchinson, and the House, even though it acquiesced in the new address, did not consider it a proper statement of colonial rights.[20] Accordingly, when they sent it to their agent in London for presentation, they warned him that it did not repre-

[17] *Ibid.*, 661.

[18] Alden Bradford, ed., *Massachusetts State Papers. Speeches of the Governors of Massachusetts from 1765–1775 etc.* (Boston, 1818), 21–23.

[19] Massachusetts Archives, XXII, 414.

[20] See the letters by Governor Bernard, November 17 and 18, 1764, to the Earl of Halifax, to John Pownall, and to Richard Jackson, relating the success of the Council in toning down the petition. Bernard Papers, II, 181–187, 189, 260–264.

sent the views of the House. "The House of Representatives," they said

> were clearly for making an ample and full declaration of the exclusive Right of the People of the Colonies to tax themselves and that they ought not to be deprived of a right they had so long enjoyed and which they held by Birth and by Charter; but they could not prevail with the Councill, tho they made several Tryalls, to be more explicit than they have been in the Petition sent you . . . You will therefore collect the sentiments of the Representative Body of People rather from what they have heretofore sent you than from the present Address.[21]

What the House of Representatives had heretofore sent the agent included a long letter instructing him in the doctrine of natural rights and an explicit statement that any attempt by Parliament to tax colonial trade would be "contrary to a fundamentall Principall of our constitution vizt. That all Taxes ought to originate with the people."[22] The House had also approved and sent to the agent a pamphlet written by one of their members, James Otis, entitled *The Rights of the British Colonies asserted and proved.*[23] In this pamphlet Otis had argued against Parliament's right to tax the colonies and had stated in the most unequivocal manner that "there is no foundation for the distinction some make in England, between an internal and an external tax on the colonies."[24] It would hardly seem proper, then, to draw from the Massachusetts Address the

[21] *Collections of the Massachusetts Historical Society*, LXXIV, 170–171.

[22] *Ibid.*, 39–54, 145–146.

[23] Boston, 1764. See *Journal of the Honourable House of Representatives of His Majesty's Province of the Massachusetts-Bay in New-England, Begun and held at Concord, in the county of Middlesex, on Wednesday the Thirtieth Day of May, Annoque Domini, 1764* (Boston, 1764), 66, 77.

[24] P. 42. Strangely enough these were also the private views of Lieutenant-Governor Hutchinson, who was principally responsible for suppressing the original address of the House. In a piece which he wrote in June or July, 1764, but never published, he argued against the Stamp Act on precisely the same line which was later followed by the House. He pointed out that the Sugar Act had been passed, not for the regulation of trade, but "for the sake of the money arising from the Duties," and that the privileges of the people were no less affected by it than they were by an internal tax. (Massachusetts Archives, XXVI, 90–96.) Moreover, on Nov. 9, 1764, just after he had succeeded in getting the Massachusetts Address toned down, Hutchinson wrote to Ebenezer Silliman in Connecticut, criticizing the Connecticut pamphlet for neglecting to object against external taxes. He told Silliman, who was a member of the Connecticut Committee which drew up the pamphlet, that "the fallacy of the argument lies here it is your supposing duties upon trade to be imposed for the sake of regulating trade, whereas the Professed design of the duties by the late Act is to raise a revenue." (Massachusetts Archives, XXVI, 117–118.) Why Hutchinson should have objected to these views when they came from the Massachusetts House of Representatives is not apparent.

inference that the people of the colonies accepted the right of Parliament to levy external as opposed to internal taxes.

III

At the end of the year 1764, when the five initial colonial statements were all on the books, the colonial position was still a little obscure. New York and Virginia had been plain enough, but Rhode Island, Connecticut, and Massachusetts, while denying Parliament's right to levy a stamp tax, had evaded the question of external taxes. By the close of the following year all signs of hesitation had disappeared. The Stamp Act produced an all-but-unanimous reaction: Parliament had no right to tax the colonies.

The first declaration of rights to be made after passage of the Act was the famous set of resolves which Patrick Henry introduced into the Virginia House of Burgesses on May 30, 1765. As recorded on the Journals of the House of Burgesses there were four of these resolves which passed the House. The first two asserted the right of the inhabitants of Virginia to all the privileges of Englishmen. The third declared "that the Taxation of the People by themselves, or by Persons chosen to represent them" was a "distinguishing Characteristick of *British* Freedom, without which the ancient Constitution cannot exist." The fourth stated that the inhabitants of Virginia had always enjoyed and had never forfeited or yielded up "the inestimable Right of being governed by such Laws, respecting their internal Policy and Taxation, as are derived from their own Consent." [25]

Henry had proposed three more resolutions which either failed of passage or later were expunged from the records. The first of these merely repeated what the others had already implied, namely that the General Assembly of Virginia, in its representative capacity, had "the only exclusive right and power to lay taxes and imposts upon the inhabitants of this colony." The second, more radical, stated "That his Majesty's liege people, the inhabitants of this colony, are not bound to yield obedience to any law or ordinance whatever, designed to impose any taxation whatsoever upon them, other than the laws or ordinances of the General Assembly aforesaid." The last provided that anyone who denied the Assembly's exclusive power of taxation should be considered an enemy of the colony.[26]

[25] *Journals of the House of Burgesses of Virginia 1761–1765*, 360.

[26] *Ibid.*, lxvii. When the Resolves were printed in the newspapers, the three unsuccessful resolves were included along with the others as though they had been passed. The Resolves, so far as the incomplete newspaper records enable

The Virginia Resolves even without the inclusion of Henry's three additional clauses, constituted a clear denial of Parliament's right to tax. The only phrase which could be interpreted as distinguishing between internal and external taxes was the phrase in the third resolution "internal polity and taxation." Here it was possible to read the adjective "internal" to modify "taxation" as well as "polity." That such a reading would have been incorrect is suggested by the fact that in the version of the Resolves which was printed in the newspapers this phrase was changed to read "taxation and internal police."[27] Furthermore this was also the wording in a copy of the Resolves endorsed on the back in Patrick Henry's handwriting.[28]

The Virginia Resolves served as a model for similar declarations in most of the other colonies. Rhode Island, where the Virginia Resolves were first published, was the first to copy them. In September, 1765, the Rhode Island General Assembly passed six resolutions, three of which were adapted from those passed by the Virginia House of Burgesses, two from Henry's unsuccessful resolutions (which had been printed in the newspapers without any indication that they had failed to pass), and one original resolution which, in effect, called upon officers of government to pay no attention to the Stamp Act.[29] On the question of Parliamentary authority the Rhode Island statements, being copied from those of Virginia, were no less definite: the General Assembly of the colony had always enjoyed control over "taxation and internal police" and possessed "the only exclusive right to lay taxes and imposts upon the inhabitants of this colony."[30] Rhode Island in fact went farther than the Virginia Burgesses had been willing to go and farther than any other colony went in the next eight or nine

---

us to tell, were first printed in the *Newport Mercury* on June 24, 1765, and copied in the Boston papers from the version given there. The text printed in the papers, besides including the three unsuccessful resolves, omitted one of those actually passed (the third) and considerably abridged the others. The abridgment did not seriously alter the meaning of the resolves, but the wording was sufficiently changed to suggest that the newspaper text was obtained from an unofficial source, probably from some member of the assembly who had been present when the Resolves were passed. Possibly the source was Henry himself, for the newspaper version, except in its omission of resolution number 3, closely approximates a copy of the resolves which is endorsed on the back in Henry's handwriting. See *Journals of the House of Burgesses*, frontispiece and lxv.

[27] *Newport Mercury*, June 24, 1765; *Boston Post-Boy and Advertiser*, July 1, 1765; *Boston Gazette*, July 1, 1765; *Georgia Gazette*, September 5, 1765.

[28] *Journals of the House of Burgesses of Virginia, 1761–1765*, frontispiece and lxv.

[29] Bartlett, *Records of the Colony of Rhode Island*, VI, 451–452.

[30] *Ibid.*, 452.

years, by calling for direct disobedience to Parliament. She passed the measure which Virginia had rejected and declared that her inhabitants need not submit to a Parliamentary tax. Yet in so doing Rhode Island added a qualification which makes her position on the question of external taxes open to suspicion. In the fifth Rhode Island resolution it was stated that the inhabitants of the colony were "not bound to yield obedience to any law or ordinance designed to impose any internal taxation whatsoever upon them, other than the laws or ordinances of the General Assembly, aforesaid." [31] In Henry's version the word "internal" had not occurred. Rhode Island by inserting it implied that her citizens could disobey an act of Parliament imposing internal taxes but not one imposing external taxes. It should be noted that this distinction did not appear in the assertions of right contained in the preceding resolutions, where the authority of Parliament to tax the colony was denied without qualification. It was only in the summons to rebellion that the Rhode Island Assembly felt obliged to draw back a little. Though their caution on this score was boldness when compared to the stand of the other colonies, which confined themselves to declarations of right, nevertheless the appearance of the word "internal" makes one wonder whether there may not have been a moderate faction in the assembly which would have allowed Parliament a right over external taxes. If there was such a faction, it was not able to insert its views into the resolutions which defined the rights of the colony but only into the one which proposed open rebellion. Moreover, a few weeks later, on November 6, 1765, Rhode Island's popularly-elected governor, Samuel Ward, wrote to General Conway that the colonists were oppressed, because "duties and taxes" were laid upon them without their knowledge or consent.[32]

If the Rhode Island Resolves of 1765 still left some room for doubt on the question of external taxes, the same was not true of the other colonial statements of that year. The Maryland Assembly, on September 28, passed unanimously resolutions denying Parliament's right to tax, in which the only use of the word "internal" was in the familiar phrase "Taxes, and internal Polity." [33] Meanwhile Pennsylvania, on September 21, had drawn up its own set of Resolves, to much the same effect. The first draught of these resolves, written by John Dickinson, included one clause objecting

[31] *Ibid.*
[32] *Ibid.*, 473.
[33] *Maryland Gazette*, October 3, 1765.

specifically to internal taxes,[34] but in the version finally adopted by the assembly there was no mention of the word "internal." The crucial item read: "Resolved therefore, N.C.D. That the taxation of the people of this province, by any other persons whatsoever than such their representatives in assembly, is UNCONSTITUTIONAL, and subversive of their most valuable rights." [35]

Massachusetts, because of the recess of her assembly, did not take action until October, though the newspapers began to agitate for a more spirited statement of rights as soon as they received news of the Virginia Resolves.[36] Accordingly when the assembly was called together in October, it produced a set of resolutions which defined the rights of British subjects and concluded, "that all acts, made by any power whatever, other than the General Assembly of this province, imposing taxes on the inhabitants, are infringements of our inherent and unalienable rights, as men and British subjects; and render void the most valuable declarations of our charter." [37] The Connecticut Assembly likewise cleared up the ambiguity of its earlier statement by a set of resolves modeled partly on those of Virginia and affirming that an act for raising money in the colonies "by duties or taxes" was beyond the authority of Parliament. Connecticut, like Maryland and Rhode Island, included an item copied after the fourth of the Virginia Resolves, in which once again the questionable phrase was rendered as "taxing and internal police." [38]

South Carolina, on November 29, 1765, denied Parliament's right to tax, in a set of eighteen resolves copied from the declarations of the Stamp Act Congress [39] (see below). New York could scarcely state the colonial position more explicitly than she had done the year before, but nevertheless on December 11, 1765, she adopted three more petitions to King, Lords, and Commons, restat-

[34] Charles J. Stillé, *The Life and Times of John Dickinson, 1732–1808* (Philadelphia, 1891), 339–340.

[35] J. Almon, ed., *A collection of interesting, authentic papers, relative to the dispute between Great Britain and America* (London, 1777), 20–21.

[36] See, for example, the *Boston Gazette* of July 8, 1765: "The People of Virginia have spoke very sensibly, and the frozen Politicians of a more northern Government say they have spoke Treason: Their spirited Resolves do indeed serve as a perfect Contrast for a certain, tame, pusillanimous, daub'd, insipid Thing, delicately touch'd up and call'd an Address; which was lately sent from this Side the Water, to please the Taste of the Tools of Corruption on the other." The reference, of course, was to the Massachusetts Address of 1764.

[37] Bradford, *Massachusetts State Papers*, 50–51.

[38] Hoadly, *Public Records of the Colony of Connecticut*, 421–425.

[39] John Drayton, *Memoirs of the American Revolution* (Charleston, S. C., 1821), I, 39–41.

ing the case with the same clarity.[40] New Jersey in the meantime had adopted eleven resolutions copied principally from those of the Stamp Act Congress, with nothing said about internal taxes;[41] and New Hampshire, which did not participate in the Congress, had given formal approval to all the resolutions and petitions of that body.[42]

The Stamp Act Congress had met in New York during October, attended by delegates from Massachusetts, Rhode Island, Connecticut, New York, New Jersey, Pennsylvania, Delaware, Maryland, and South Carolina. These delegates had produced a set of resolutions and three petitions, to the King, the Lords, and the Commons, all denying the authority of Parliament to tax the colonies.[43] Here as in the other formal colonial statements of this year there is no distinction made between internal and external taxes. The Stamp Act Congress has frequently been treated by historians as a rather conservative body of men, possibly because it acknowledged "all due subordination" to Parliament. But as conservatives at the time recognized, this phrase was an empty one unless you stated what subordination was due. It is true that the conservatives, in Massachusetts at least, had hoped to gain control of the Stamp Act Congress.[44] They actually succeeded in securing Timothy Ruggles as one of the Massachusetts delegates, and Governor Bernard wrote at least one letter to Ruggles before the convention urging him to secure submission to the Stamp Act pending its probable repeal.[45] Ruggles remained faithfully conservative, but the true character of the Congress is sufficiently indicated by the fact that, as a conservative, he refused to sign the Resolutions it adopted and was later reprimanded for his refusal by the not-so-

[40] *Journals of the Votes and Proceedings of the General Assembly of the Colony of New York 1743–1765*, II, 795–802.

[41] *New Jersey Archives*, First Series (Paterson, 1902), XXIV, 683–684.

[42] Nathaniel Bouton, ed., *Documents and Records Relating to the Province of New Hampshire* (Nashua, 1873), VII, 92.

[43] Hezekiah Niles, *Principles and Acts of the Revolution* (Baltimore, 1822), 457–460.

[44] Governor Bernard wrote to the Lords of Trade on July 8, 1765, that in Massachusetts, where the proposal for the congress initiated, "It was impossible to oppose this measure to any good purpose and therefore the friends of government took the lead in it and have kept it in their hands in pursuance of which of the Committee appointed by this House to meet the other Committees at New York on 1st of October next. Two of the three are fast friends to government prudent and discreet men such as I am assured will never consent to any undutiful or improper application to the Government of Great Britain." (Sparks Manuscripts 43: British Manuscripts, IV, Harvard College Library).

[45] Bernard Papers, IV, 72. The letter is dated September 28, 1765.

conservative Massachusetts House of Representatives.[46] The Stamp Act Congress, in other words, was no less "radical" than the colonial assemblies which sent delegates to it. Though it acknowledged due subordination to Parliament, it denied without qualification the right of Parliament to tax the colonies.

In sum, during the period of the Stamp Act crisis, fifteen formal statements of colonial rights had been issued. Of these only the three early statements by Rhode Island, Connecticut, and Massachusetts could be interpreted as implying an assent to the constitutionality of external taxes. The statement by Massachusetts was clearly not representative of official opinion, and both the Massachusetts and the Connecticut statements were clarified the following year by resolutions which unequivocally rejected the authority of Parliament to tax the colonies at all.

IV

The question suggested by all these declarations of right is: what did the Americans mean when they admitted due subordination to Parliament and at the same time denied Parliament's right to tax them? What subordination was due? If they did not distinguish between internal and external taxes, but denied all authority to tax, what authority did they leave to Parliament?

The answer is given clearly enough in the documents: the colonists allowed the right of Parliament to legislate for the whole empire in any way that concerned the common interests of all the members of the empire (as yet they made no claim that the colonial assemblies were entirely coordinate with Parliament in legislative authority), but they denied that Parliament's legislative authority extended either to the internal polity of the colonies or to taxation. Not all the colonies insisted on exclusive control of internal polity, for Parliament at this time was not attempting to interfere in this department. The issue of the day was taxation, and what the colonies insisted on most vigorously was that Parliament's supreme legislative authority did not include the right to tax. Taxation and legislation, they said, were separate functions and historically had always been treated as such. Legislation was a function of sovereignty; and as the sovereign body of the empire, Parliament had absolute legislative authority. Under

46 *Boston Gazette*, Feb. 17, 1766. The membership of the Stamp Act Congress has been analysed in an unpublished paper by Mr. David S. Lovejoy, in which it is indicated that of the twenty-seven members only two are known to have become Tories at the time of the Revolution.

this authority Parliament was entirely justified in regulating the trade and commerce of the empire. There was, in other words, nothing unconstitutional about the Acts of Trade and Navigation. But taxes were something else. Taxes were the "free gift" of the people who paid them, and as such could be levied only by a body which represented the people. As far as Great Britain was concerned the House of Commons was a representative body and could therefore tax the people of Great Britain; but since the colonists were not, and from their local circumstances could not be, represented in Parliament, they could not be taxed by Parliament. The only body with a constitutional right to tax them was a colonial assembly, in which the people upon whom the tax would fall would be represented. Thus the Connecticut Assembly in October, 1765, resolved,

> That, in the opinion of this House, an act for raising money by duties or taxes differs from other acts of legislation, in that it is always considered as a free gift of the people made by their legal and elected representatives; and that we cannot conceive that the people of Great Britain, or their representatives, have right to dispose of our property.[47]

According to this distinction the power to levy taxes even in Great Britain was limited to the House of Commons, the representative part of Parliament. The petition from the General Assembly of New York to the House of Commons, December 11, 1765, while expressing "all due submission to the supreme Authority of the *British* Legislature," affirmed

> That all parliamentary Aids in *Great-Britain*, are the free Gifts of the People by their Representatives, consented to by the Lords, and accepted by the Crown, and therefore every Act imposing them, essentially differs from every other Statute, having the Force of a Law in no other Respect than the Manner thereby prescribed for levying the Gift.
>
> That agreeable to this Distinction, the House of Commons has always contended for and enjoyed the constitutional Right of originating all Money Bills, as well in Aid of the Crown, as for other Purposes.
>
> That all Supplies to the Crown being in their Nature free Gifts, it would, as we humbly conceive, be unconstitutional for the People of *Great-Britain*, by their Representatives in Parliament, to dispose of the Property of Millions of his Majesty's Subjects, who are not, and cannot be there represented.[48]

It was this distinction which the members of the Stamp Act Congress had in mind when they acknowledged "due subordina-

[47] *Public Records of the Colony of Connecticut*, XII, 423.
[48] *Journal of the Votes and Proceedings of the General Assembly of the Colony of New York 1743–1765*, II, 800.

tion" to Parliament, for they asked in their petition to the House of Commons,

> Whether there be not a material Distinction in Reason and sound Policy, at least, between the necessary Exercise of Parliamentary Jurisdiction in general Acts, for the Amendment of the Common Law, and the Regulation of Trade and Commerce through the whole Empire, and the Exercise of that Jurisdiction by imposing Taxes on the Colonies.[49]

V

Most members of Parliament would have answered this query with a flat denial that the power of taxation could be distinguished from that of legislation. Taxation, they would have said, was inseparable from sovereignty. But there were some members willing to speak in favor of the colonial view. In the debate on the Declaratory Act in the House of Commons the question arose over a motion made by Colonel Barré to omit from the act the phrase "in all cases whatsoever." This motion was intended to exclude Parliament's authority to tax the colonies, and in the debate which followed, Barré and William Pitt the elder argued for the motion in much the same terms as were used in the colonial statements. Visitors were not admitted to Parliament during this session, so that few accounts of the debate have been preserved, but according to Charles Garth, member for Devizes borough, Wiltshire, and agent for several of the southern colonies, the speakers for Barré's motion contended: "That the Principles of Taxation as distinguished from Legislation were as distinct Principles and Powers as any two Propositions under the Sun." The speakers cited the precedents of the counties palatine of Chester and Durham which had been subject to Parliament's legislative authority but had not been taxed until they were represented. The clergy, it was pointed out, taxed themselves separately but did not have separate legislative power. Another indication that the two functions were separate was that taxes were the free gift of the Commons, and tax bills could not be considered by the Lords or the King until the Commons had made a grant. Other bills remained in the Upper House for the King's signature, but tax bills were sent back to the Commons, whose speaker presented them to the King as the free gift of the Commons. All this, it was said, showed that Parliament

[49] *Proceedings of the Congress at New York* (Annapolis, 1766), 23. The reprint of the proceedings in Niles, *Principles and Acts of the Revolution* is inaccurate at this point.

might legislate as the supreme authority of the realm but that it taxed only in its representative capacity. Since the colonies were not represented in Parliament, they could not constitutionally be taxed by Parliament.[50] In the House of Lords, Lord Camden argued the case to the same effect.[51]

In spite of these arguments Parliament decided by an overwhelming majority [52] to include the words "in all cases whatsoever," and thereby, as far as Parliament was concerned, it was concluded that taxation and legislation were not separate functions and that Parliament's authority over the colonies included the right to tax. But strangely enough the Declaratory Act did not include any explicit statement of the right to tax, so that the colonists could not have recognized that Parliament was denying their position. What the act said was that the King in Parliament had "full power and authority to make laws and statutes of sufficient force and validity to bind the colonies and people of *America*, subjects of the crown of *Great Britain*, in all cases whatsoever." [53] Though the members of Parliament knew that the words "in all cases whatsoever" meant in cases of taxation, there is nothing in the act itself to give the words that meaning. Nor was the ambiguity entirely accidental. When the act was being drawn up, Charles Yorke, the attorney general, suggested that the crucial phrase should read "as well in cases as Taxation, as in all other cases whatsoever." But when he submitted this suggestion to Rockingham, who was then prime minister, Rockingham thought it impolitic to make any mention of the word "taxation." "I think I may say," he wrote to Yorke, "that it is our firm Resolution in the House of Lords—I mean among ourselves—that that word must be resisted." [54] Thus the omission of any mention of taxation was deliberate. By supporting the act as it stood, with the resounding but ambiguous phrase "in all cases whatsoever," the Rockingham government could gain support in Parliament by en-

[50] Garth's account is in *Maryland Historical Magazine*, VI, 287–305. Another account is in *American Historical Review*, XVII, 565–574.

[51] *Archives of Maryland* (Baltimore, 1895), XIV, 267–268.

[52] *Maryland Historical Magazine*, VI, 300; *Archives of Maryland*, XIV, 280; Sir John Fortescue, ed., *The Correspondence of King George the Third* (London, 1927), I, 254.

[53] Danby Pickering, ed., *The Statutes at Large* (Cambridge, England, 1767), XXVII, 20.

[54] British Museum Additional Manuscripts 35430, ff. 37–38 (Rockingham's letter). The exchange of correspondence between Yorke and Rockingham is printed, in part in George Thomas, Earl of Albemarle, *Memoirs of the Marquis of Rockingham* (London, 1852), I, 285–288. The date of Yorke's letter is not given. Rockingham's letter is dated January 25, 1766.

couraging the members to beat the drum of Parliamentary power —behind closed doors—without giving offense to the colonies.

The colonies can hardly be blamed then for not getting the point of the Declaratory Act. They had not generally been informed of the debate which had taken place over the words "in all cases whatsoever," [55] and since the act was accompanied by the repeal of Parliament's most conspicuous attempt to tax them, they might very well interpret it as a simple assertion of legislative authority with no necessary implication of a right to tax. They knew that the Declaratory Act was a copy of the earlier statute of 6 George I regarding Ireland. And they knew also that in spite of this statute Ireland had not been taxed by Parliament. The Massachusetts Assembly even before passage of the Stamp Act had argued from the example of Ireland that the colonies might be dependent on England without allowing England a right to tax them.[56] After passage of the Declaratory Act the Massachusetts agent in London, Richard Jackson, encouraged Massachusetts to believe that the same reasoning was still valid, for he wrote to Governor Bernard that the act would probably affect the colonies as little "as the Power we claim in Ireland, the manner of exercising which you are acquainted with." [57] The same view was expressed by Daniel Dulany of Maryland in a letter to General Conway. According to Dulany the Declaratory Act could not imply a power to tax, because if it did, then the act of 6 George I must give authority to tax Ireland, and such authority had never been claimed or exercised.[58] Thus the fact, so often remarked by historians, that the colonists took little notice of the Declaratory Act does not mean that the colonists were indifferent to the question of principle. They simply did not recognize the Act as a challenge to their views. They could acquiesce in it with a clear conscience and without inconsistency, unaware that their interpretation differed radically from that held in Parliament.[59]

[55] So far as I have been able to discover Garth's account was the only one sent to the colonies, and it was not published at the time.

[56] Massachusetts Archives, XXII, 415. The argument is made in the petition to the King passed by the House of Representatives on October 22, 1764, and non-concurred by the Council.

[57] *Ibid.*, f. 458. The letter is dated March 3, 1766.

[58] Sparks Manuscripts 44, bundle 7, ff. 10–11. The letter is not dated.

[59] George Grenville wrote that the Americans were justified in rejoicing at the repeal of the Stamp Act "especially if they understand by it, as they justly may, notwithstanding the Declaratory Bill passed at the same time, that they are thereby exempted for ever from being taxed by Great Britain for the public support even of themselves." William J. Smith, ed., *The Grenville Papers* (London, 1853), III, 250.

VI

Unfortunately this misunderstanding on the part of the Americans was matched by a similar misunderstanding on the part of many people in England with regard to the colonial position. We have seen that the American protests against the Stamp Act did not distinguish between internal and external taxes but denied that Parliament had any right to tax the colonies. Yet some Englishmen, at least, thought that the American protests were directed only against internal taxes. The American misunderstanding of the Declaratory Act is explicable by the vagueness of the act itself, the absence of any official interpretation of it, and the fact that the Parliamentary debate on it had been closed to the public. But the colonial statements had all been communicated to the British government by the beginning of the year 1766, before Parliament began to consider repeal of the Stamp Act. Why then did Englishmen suppose that the Americans distinguished between internal and external taxes?

Of course not all Englishmen did suppose so; those who took the trouble to read the colonial statements knew better. But apparently many Englishmen, including members of Parliament, did not take that trouble. It should be remembered that the colonial petitions were never formally considered by Parliament. Those sent before passage of the Stamp Act were thrown out because of the procedural rule against receiving petitions on money bills. Those sent for repeal of the Act were excluded for other procedural reasons and because they called the authority of Parliament into question. Thus although the contents of the statements could doubtless have been learned by anyone who wished to discover them, they were never given a regular hearing in Parliament.[60]

In the absence of any direct acquaintance with the colonial statements the average member of Parliament must have gained his impressions from one of two sources: either from the multitude of pamphlets dealing with the Stamp Act or from speeches in Parliament. It is possible but not probable that the authors of pamphlets against the Stamp Act were responsible for creating the impression that the Americans did not object to external taxes. We have already observed an ambiguity in the two pamphlets by Stephen Hopkins and John Fitch which received the approval of Rhode Island and Connecticut respectively in 1764. Both these pamphlets used the phrase "internal taxes" in such a way as to suggest that external

[60] *Collections of the Connecticut Historical Society*, XVIII, 332–335; *Maryland Historical Magazine*, VI, 282–288.

taxes might be constitutionally acceptable, though neither Hopkins nor Fitch explicitly said as much. Two other pamphlets, which enjoyed a wide circulation though not a formal legislative approval, also used the words "internal taxes" in a way which may have helped to bring about a misunderstanding of the American position. Richard Bland in *An Inquiry into the Rights of the British Colonies*[61] demonstrated that the colonists could not constitutionally be subjected to an internal tax by act of Parliament. Anyone reading Bland's conclusions without reading the argument leading to them might get the impression that Bland would have agreed to Parliament's collection of a revenue from customs duties levied in the colonies; but Bland's demonstration of his conclusion showed that Parliament could not constitutionally charge duties in the colony upon either imports or exports. In fact, he even argued that the Navigation Acts were unconstitutional. Bland evidently included in the phrase "internal taxes" the very duties which other people called "external taxes."

Another pamphlet which objected specifically to internal taxes was Daniel Dulany's *Considerations on the Propriety of imposing Taxes in the British Colonies.*[62] This probably had a wider circulation than any other pamphlet against the Stamp Act, and it has frequently been cited as the source of the distinction between internal and external taxes. Although the greater part of Dulany's pamphlet was devoted to general arguments against the constitutionality of Parliamentary taxation, there were a few paragraphs in which he implied that internal taxes alone were unconstitutional. Thus he argued, on page 33, that before the Stamp Act, Parliament had never "imposed an internal Tax upon the Colonies *for the single Purpose of Revenue.*" He went on to deny the contention, which he attributed to the proponents of the Stamp Act, "That no Distinction can be supported between one Kind of Tax and another, an Authority to impose the one extending to the other." Contrary to this erroneous view, he said, "It appears to me, that there is a clear and necessary Distinction between an Act imposing a Tax *for the single Purpose of Revenue*, and those Acts which have been made for the Regulation of Trade, and have produced some Revenue in *Consequence of their Effect* and Operation as *Regulations of Trade.*" According to this distinction Parliament had the right to regulate trade by the imposition of duties, even though those duties should

[61] Williamsburg, 1766.

[62] Annapolis, 1765 (second edition). The succeeding quotations are taken from pp. 30–35.

incidentally produce some revenue. Dulany closed the discussion of this point by affirming: "a Right to impose an internal Tax on the Colonies without their consent, *for the single Purpose of Revenue*, is denied; a Right to regulate their Trade without their Consent is admitted."

It will be observed that in the course of this discussion, which occupied two pages of the pamphlet, Dulany had not made entirely clear what he regarded as constitutional and what he considered unconstitutional. He said that internal taxes for the purpose of revenue were unconstitutional, and he said that duties on trade for the purpose of regulation were constitutional, even though an incidental revenue might attend them, but he failed to say explicitly how he regarded duties on trade for the single purpose of revenue. He failed, in other words, to say how he stood on external taxes; in fact he did not even use the words "external tax" at any point in the pamphlet. His readers would perhaps have been justified in thinking that Dulany admitted external taxes as constitutional, since he explicitly objected only to internal taxes. Yet, unless Dulany was simply confused about the matter, it would appear that in his use of the phrase "internal tax" he included all duties levied in the colonies for the single purpose of revenue. In no other way does Dulany's argument make sense, for he contrasted what he called an internal tax for the single purpose of revenue with duties for the purpose of regulation from which an incidental revenue might arise. The context indicates clearly that the point of the contrast was not the difference between internal taxes as opposed to duties on trade but the difference between an imposition for the purpose of regulation and one for the purpose of revenue. Dulany emphasized the contrast by italicising the phrases: *single purpose of revenue, incidental Revenue*, and *Regulations of Trade*. The whole force of the contrast is lost unless the phrase "internal tax" is taken to include duties on trade collected in the colonies for the purpose of revenue. That this was Dulany's understanding of the term is further indicated in the two paragraphs which follow those summarized above. Here Dulany demonstrated that the duties on trade which had hitherto been collected in the colony had been levied not for the purpose of revenue but for the purpose of regulating trade. The argument which he used to carry this point was drawn from the fact that the customs duties collected in North America brought only £ 1,900 a year into the treasury while they cost £ 7,600 a year to collect. Dulany had taken these figures from a pamphlet by Grenville himself. He concluded with some justice that

> It would be ridiculous indeed to suppose, that the Parliament would raise a Revenue by Taxes in the Colonies to defray Part of the national Expence, the Collection of which Taxes would increase that Expence to a Sum more than three Times the Amount of the Revenue; but, the Impositions being considered in their true Light, as Regulations of Trade, the Expence arising from an Establishment necessary to carry them into Execution, is so far from being ridiculous, that it may be wisely incurred.

Thus Dulany demonstrated that Parliament could not levy what he called an internal tax for the purpose of revenue by showing that Parliament had never levied an external tax for the purpose of revenue. The conclusion seems inescapable that he used the phrase "internal tax" in a loose sense, to cover all taxes collected in the colonies, whether excise taxes or customs duties levied for the single purpose of revenue. That this was his meaning is also suggested by the remainder of the pamphlet, in which he argued against Parliamentary taxation in general terms, as when he stated that "the Inhabitants of the Colonies claim an Exemption from *all* Taxes not imposed by their own Consent." (The italics are Dulany's.)

Dulany's pamphlet, though it was widely acclaimed as a defense of colonial rights, certainly employed a confusing terminology, and it would not be surprising if Englishmen at the time had gained the impression that there was some sort of distinction in it between the constitutionality of internal taxes as opposed to that of customs duties. Though Dulany never used the phrase "external tax" and though most of the pamphlet will make sense only if his use of the phrase "internal tax" is taken to include all taxes collected in the colonies, yet if American historians have derived the impression that he distinguished between internal and external taxes, it is not unreasonable to suppose that contemporary Englishmen received the same impression.

What does seem unlikely, however, is that British statesmen would have assumed, as American historians frequently seem to do, that Daniel Dulany was the proper spokesman for all the colonies. His pamphlet was only one of many, and the others ranged in attitude from complete submission to the authority of Parliament (as in Martin Howrad's *Letter from a Gentleman at Halifax, to His Friend in Rhode Island* [63]) to complete defiance of Parliament (as in the *Considerations upon the Rights of the Colonists to the Privileges of British Subjects* [64]). Most of the pamphlets against the Stamp Act refrained from discussing the question of constitutional right and

[63] Newport, 1765.
[64] New York, 1766.

argued on the grounds of inexpediency or equity.[65] Those which concerned themselves with the constitutional aspects of the question devoted a major part of their attention to the doctrine of virtual representation.[66] This was an easy target, and in centering the constitutional controversy upon it the American protagonists gained a tactical victory; for when their opponents argued that the Americans might be taxed because they were virtually represented, this was tantamount to admitting that the power to tax depended upon representation. Daniel Dulany put his finger on the weakness of the ministerial position when he wrote to General Conway,

> If the right to tax and the right to regulate had been imagined by Mr. Grenville to be inseparable why did he tax his ingenuity to find out a virtual Representation, why did not some able friend intimate to him his Hazard on the slippery ground, he chose, when the all powerful Sovereignty of Parliament might have afforded so safe a footing?[67]

In other words Grenville himself, by arguing for virtual representation (as he did in *The Regulations Lately Made concerning the Colonies, and the Taxes Imposed upon Them, considered*[68]), had admitted that taxation was not a function of sovereignty but rather, as the colonies were contending, the prerogative of a representative body.

There was no reason why the pamphleteers on the American side should have made a distinction between internal and external taxes when arguing the case against virtual representation; and it is not surprising that with the possible exception of those discussed above,

[65] See for example: John Dickinson's *The Late Regulations Respecting the British Colonies on the Continent of America Considered* (London, 1765); *A Letter to a Member of Parliament, Wherein the Power of the British Legislature, and the Case of the Colonists, Are briefly and impartially considered* (London, 1765); *The True Interest of Great Britain, with respect to her American Colonies, Stated and Impartially Considered* (London, 1766); *The Importance of the Colonies of North America, and the Interest of Great Britain with regard to them, considered* (London, 1766); *The Necessity of Repealing the American Stamp Act Demonstrated* (London, 1766); *The Late Occurrences in North America, and Policy of Great Britain, Considered* (London, 1766); and Benjamin Franklin's *The General Opposition of the Colonies to the Payment of the Stamp Duty; and the Consequence of Enforcing Obedience by Military Measures; Impartially Considered* (London, 1766).

[66] See for example: Samuel Cooper, *The Crisis. Or, a Full Defense of the Colonies* (London, 1766), 3–30; Maurice Moore, *The Justice and Policy of Taxing the American Colonies, in Great Britain, Considered* (Wilmington, N. C., 1765), 7–14; Richard Bland, *An Inquiry into the Rights of the British Colonies* (Williamsburg, 1766), 5–12. Daniel Dulany, *Considerations on the Propriety of imposing Taxes in the British Colonies* (Annapolis, 1765), 5–14.

[67] Sparks Manuscripts 44, bundle, 7, f.10.

[68] London, 1765.

none of them seems to have employed the distinction for purposes of argument. The distinction did appear in some of the literature in support of the Stamp Act, where it served as a whipping boy. It was attributed to the Americans and then demolished under the heavy gunfire of constitutional history.[69] It hardly seems likely that the defenders of the Stamp Act would have attributed the distinction to the Americans simply in order to discredit the colonial position. It is much more likely that they and the members of Parliament really believed that the colonists did distinguish between internal and external taxes. The question remains as to how they gained this impression.

The source from which, in all probability, it was derived was the speeches made in Parliament by friends of the colonies during the debates on repeal of the Stamp Act and afterwards, not excepting the brilliant interview given at the bar of the House of Commons by Benjamin Franklin. The member of Parliament who heard that carefully rehearsed performance (or who read it afterwards in print) might very justly have concluded that the Americans had no objection to external taxes, for Franklin, the arch-American, at several points had stated that the Americans objected only to internal taxes.[70] When a member had pointed out that the objection to internal taxes could with equal justice be applied to external taxes, Franklin had replied that the Americans did not reason in that way at present but that they might learn to do so from the English. The wit of Franklin's tongue obscured the fact that he was wrong, but the average member could scarcely have known that. Laughing at Franklin's clever answers, he would probably have forgotten the rather pertinent question put by a member of the opposition: "Do not the resolutions of the Pennsylvania Assembly say, all taxes?" This question was evidently asked by a member who knew something about Pennsylvania's attitude. Franklin's answer to it was not as sprightly as his replies to some of the other questions. The best he could say was that if the Pennsylvania resolutions said all taxes, they meant only internal taxes. Actually it would have been impossible to tell from Franklin's testimony exactly what he thought the constitutional position of the Americans to be. At times he seemed to be saying that the Americans assented to external

69 See *The Rights of Parliament Vindicated, On Occasion of the late Stamp-Act. In which is exposed the conduct of the American Colonists* (London, 1766); *An Examination of the Rights of the Colonies upon Principles of Law* (London, 1766).

70 William Cobbett, ed., *Parliamentary History of England, from the Earliest Period to the Year 1803* (London, 1813), XVI, 137–160.

taxes; at other times he implied that they consented only to the regulation of trade. The performance was a good piece of lobbying for repeal of the Stamp Act, but it gave no clear indication of the American position and certainly could have contributed to the idea that the Americans were willing to accept external taxes.

The speeches of Franklin's friend Richard Jackson, member of Parliament for Weymouth, and agent at various times for Pennsylvania, Connecticut, and Massachusetts, may also have contributed to a false impression of the colonial position. Jackson believed that Parliament had a clear right to tax the colonies by duties on trade. Since Parliament by its admitted right to regulate trade could prohibit any branch of colonial trade, he reasoned, Parliament could also tax any branch of colonial trade.[71] Jackson, moreover, had searched the precedents thoroughly and found that Parliament in the past had imposed external taxes on the trade of Chester and Durham and Wales before those areas were represented in Parliament. At the same time Parliament had refrained from taxing them internally until they were granted representation. When Jackson rehearsed these views before Parliament,[72] he must have been listened to as a man of some authority; for he had the reputation of being extraordinarily learned,[73] and he was, besides, the official agent for several colonies. The average member of Parliament could not have known that he had been elected agent for Massachusetts by the political maneuvers of the royal governor,[74] nor that the Connecticut Assembly had written him a letter deploring his insufficient insistence upon colonial rights,[75] nor that he owed his appointment in Pennsylvania to his friend Benjamin Franklin, who had also misrepresented the colonial position.[76]

What must also have impressed the uninformed member was the famous speech by William Pitt, when the Great Commoner had come out of his retirement to urge the repeal of the Stamp act. On this occasion, Pitt had risen to a statement by George Grenville in which the latter had complained that he could not understand the distinction between internal and external taxes. "If the gentleman

[71] Carl Van Doren, ed., *Letters and Papers of Benjamin Franklin and Richard Jackson 1753–1785* (Philadelphia, 1947), 123–124, 138–139.

[72] *Ibid.*, 194–196; *Collections of the Connecticut Historical Society*, XVIII, 316; Bradford, *Massachusetts State Papers*, 72–73.

[73] Van Doren, *Letters and Papers of Benjamin Franklin and Richard Jackson*, 1–2.

[74] Bernard Papers, III, 277–283.

[75] *Collections of the Connecticut Historical Society*, XVIII, 366–367.

[76] Van Doren, *Letters and Papers of Benjamin Franklin and Richard Jackson*, 87, 100.

does not understand the difference between internal and external taxes," said Pitt, "I cannot help it."[77] Pitt's reply, if left there, might have been somewhat misleading. Anyone who listened to the whole of what he had to say would have known that Pitt, like the colonists, was distinguishing, not between internal and external taxes but between taxation and legislation. In an earlier speech he had stated that "Taxation is no part of the governing or legislative power,"[78] and now he went on to argue that "there is a plain distinction between taxes levied for the purposes of raising a revenue, and duties imposed for the regulation of trade, for the accomodation of the subject; although, in the consequences, some revenue might incidentally arise from the latter."[79] Pitt was following the argument of Dulany, whom he had read and admired;[80] and if historians have misunderstood Dulany's argument, it is not unlikely that the members of Parliament may have misunderstood Pitt's. Though there was a manifest difference between Pitt's and Dulany's acceptance of trade regulations which might incidentally produce a revenue and Jackson's and Franklin's acceptance of external taxes as such, nevertheless all four men were arguing in behalf of the colonies. The average member may have lumped them all together and come out with the simple conclusion that Americans accepted external taxes.

This conclusion would have been strengthened a little later by a speech of Thomas Pownall. Pownall, speaking with some authority as the former governor of Massachusetts, said explicitly that the colonists "*never objected to external taxes*—to imposts, subsidies and duties. They know that the express conditions of their settlements and establishments were, that they should pay these—and therefore they never have had any disputes with government on this head—but have always found reason to be satisfied *in the moderation with which government hath exercised this power.*"[81] Pownall had apparently never read any of the colonial statements. Perhaps he derived some of his ideas from his friend Benjamin Franklin.[82]

[77] *Parliamentary History*, XVI, 105.

[78] *Ibid.*, 99.

[79] *Ibid.*, 105.

[80] W. S. Taylor and J. H. Pringle, eds., *The Chatham Correspondence* (London, 1838–40), III, 192; Moses C. Tyler, *The Literary History of the American Revolution 1763–1783* (New York, 1941), III and n.

[81] *The Speech of Th-m- P-n-ll, Esq . . . in the H—se of C—m-ns, in favor of America* (Boston, 1769), 12.

[82] Pownall cooperated with Franklin on a scheme for raising money in the colonies by interest-bearing paper currency. This scheme was proposed by Franklin as a substitute for the Stamp Tax. For details see V. W. Crane,

Certainly his authority to represent the views of the colonists was long since out of date. But how was the average member to know that? All the friends of America in Parliament seemed to be of opinion that the Americans were resigned to external taxes.

Why the colonial advocates in Parliament should have joined in conveying so false an impression of the colonial position is not entirely clear. A number of reasons might be offered why Pownall or Jackson or Pitt argued as they did: Pownall may have been misinformed; [83] Jackson may have been speaking for himself rather than for the colonies; and Pitt was misunderstood. But Franklin's testimony is more difficult to explain, for Franklin must have been better acquainted with the colonial declarations than he appeared to be. Why should he have contributed to the general misunderstanding? Furthermore why should all the proponents of colonial rights have misrepresented the colonies in the same way?

In the absence of direct information one can only suggest that political circumstances in 1766 required that every friend of the colonies in England refrain from urging the extreme claims put forward by the colonial assemblies and join in representing the colonies as more moderate than they actually were. The immediate object in 1766 was the repeal of the Stamp Act, and repeal was not to be attained by blunt denials of Parliament's authority. Though the colonists seemed to be unaware of this fact and continued on their intransigent course, their friends in England had to seek support where they could find it. They found it in the Rockingham administration, and consequently when they argued for repeal of the Stamp Act, they argued in Rockingham's terms. Now Rockingham's terms, to judge from at least one account, were a recognition of the distinction between internal and external taxes. According to Charles Garth the administration refused to hear the petition of the Stamp Act Congress, because "it tended to question not only the Right of Parliament to impose internal Taxes, but external Duties." [84] Rockingham, it would appear, was prepared to settle the colonial issue by leaving internal taxes to the colonial assemblies.

"Benjamin Franklin and the Stamp Act" *Publications of the Colonial Society of Massachusetts*, XXXII, 56–78. On Pownall's participation, see Pownall's letter to Hutchinson, Dec. 3, 1765, in Massachusetts Archives, XXV, 113.

[83] That Pownall was an unreliable source of information is suggested by the fact that he himself had suggested a stamp tax in his book *The Administration of the Colonies*. Dennys De Berdt later wrote that he was "as irresolute as the Wind, in one days debate a friend to America the next quite with the Ministry." (*Publications of the Colonial Society of Massachusetts*, XIII, 377–378.

[84] *Maryland Historical Magazine*, VI, 285.

Though this was not as much as the colonies demanded, it was more than the rest of Parliament was willing to give, for most members were as ready to assert Parliament's right to levy all taxes as the colonists were to deny it.[85] Rockingham in fact was unable to repeal the Stamp Act on the basis of the distinction between internal and external taxes. Instead he was obliged to agree to the Declaratory Act, though worded in the ambiguous terms already noticed.[86] Rockingham, it is plain, needed all the support he could get, for he could not carry the rest of Parliament even as far as he and his own group were willing to go. In these circumstances it would have been undiplomatic, not to say reckless, for the friends of the colonies to embarrass him by insisting on the politically impossible claims of the colonial declarations. It seems unlikely that there was any formal agreement between the Rockingham group and the other colonial protagonists, whereby the latter agreed to soft-pedal the colonial claims to exclusive powers of taxation, but the pressure of politics undoubtedly dissuaded the friends of the colonies from giving publicity to the colonial declarations, and probably led them to cooperate with Rockingham in adopting a distinction which the colonists would never have allowed.

One conclusion in any case is clear: it was not the Americans who drew the line between internal and external taxes. It was recognized in America at the time by such diverse political personalities as James Otis and Thomas Hutchinson that the distinction was an English one. Otis, as already noticed, in the pamphlet approved by the Massachusetts assembly in 1764, scouted the distinction as one that "some make in England." [87] Hutchinson, in the third volume of his history of Massachusetts, gave credit for it to Pitt. Though it is clear that Pitt did not originate it, Hutchinson evidently thought that he did and was equally certain that the Americans did not accept it; for he averred that in levying the Townshend duties, "government in England too easily presumed, that Mr. Pit's distinction between internal and external taxes would be favourably received in

[85] This fact was reported to the colonists in several letters. See, for example, that of Jared Ingersoll in *Collections of the Connecticut Historical Society*, XVIII, 317–326, and that of Richard Jackson in *ibid.*, 349–351.

[86] Dennys De Berdt wrote to Samuel White at the time of repeal that there were three parties in Parliament so far as the Stamp Act was concerned, one for enforcing, one for repeal with a declaration of right, and one for repeal with a declaration. According to DeBerdt the administration favored the last view but was obliged to take the middle position in order to gain a majority. (*Publications of the Colonial Society of Massachusetts*, XIII, 311–312.)

[87] *The Rights of the British Colonies asserted and proved* (Boston, 1764), 42.

America."[88] There were members of Parliament in England, too, who realized that the distinction was not an American one, for in the debates on the Declaratory Act, Hans Stanley, the member for Southampton, embarrassed the Rockingham administration by pointing out that "The Americans have not made the futile Distinction between internal and external taxes,"[89] and Lord Lyttelton did the same thing in the House of Lords in the debate on the repeal of the Stamp Act, when he stated that "The Americans themselves make no distinction between external and internal taxes."[90] The colonial agents also realized that the colonists were talking bigger at home than their friends in England would admit, and the agents repeatedly requested their constituents to be less noisy about their rights. The colonists in return instructed the agents to be more noisy about them.[91]

The colonists were bumptious, blunt, and lacking in diplomacy, but they were not guilty of the constitutional frivolity with which they have been charged. When they objected to the Townshend Duties in 1767, they had in no way changed the conception of Parliamentary power which they avowed at the time of the Stamp Act: they still admitted the authority of Parliament to regulate trade and to legislate in other ways for the whole empire; they still denied that Parliament had a right to tax them. These views they continued to affirm until the 1770's when they advanced to the more radical position of denying the authority of Parliament to legislate as well as to tax. Though this denial was generally accompanied by an allowance of Parliamentary legislation as a matter of convenience, there can be no question that the later position was constitutionally different from the earlier one. But that the colonists were guilty of skipping from one constitutional theory to another, like so many grasshoppers, is a Tory libel that has too readily been accepted by modern historians. American Revolutionary thought went through two stages, not three; the supposed first stage never existed. If anyone took a more advanced position because of the passage of the Townshend Duties, it was not the colonists. They were already there.

[88] L. S. Mayo, ed., *History of the Province of Massachusetts Bay* (Cambridge, Mass., 1936), III, 130.

[89] *American Historical Review*, XVII, 566.

[90] *Parliamentary History*, XVI, 167.

[91] *Collections of the Connecticut Historical Society*, XVIII, 349–351, 366–367; *Collections of the Massachusetts Historical Society*, LXXIV, 39–54, 145–146; Massachusetts Archives, XXII, 361–363; *Publications of the Colonial Society of Massachusetts*, XIII, 332–333, 335, 337, 354.

4

As suggested in the introduction to the previous selection, by the second decade of the twentieth century the American Revolution was increasingly being explained by reference to economic grievances. Essentially the argument was that the revolutionary crisis came about because the policies of the British government in 1764 and afterwards conflicted with the interests of the growing American merchant class. Restrictions on trade under the Navigation Laws, the limitations on certain kinds of colonial manufacturing, and prohibitions on westward movement were all cited as sources of a growing and uncompromising colonial hostility toward the mother country. References to the allegedly constrictive character of the British mercantilist system were nothing new among American historians. In the nineteenth century, for example, George Bancroft in his massive study of American colonial history had also called attention to the exploitative nature of the British regulations. But whereas Bancroft had seen the constrictive effects of mercantilism as one of several manifestations of English tyranny, twentieth-century historians have seen them as the principal force behind the American drive toward independence. These more modern historians tended to ignore or minimize the constitutional and political complaints which Bancroft had also included in his explanation of the coming of the Revolution.

Viewed from the perspective of both the nineteenth and twentieth centuries, when freedom from government controls over economic affairs had become the accepted way of doing things, the policies of mercantilism seemed an obvious source of colonial discontent. They also seemed to be an important source to those who accepted an economic interpretation of history, in which men's principal reasons for action were held to be the pursuit of economic gain.

Not all historians, of course, as Harper points out in his article, condemned British mercantilism as inimical to colonial interests. But the work of Louis Beer proved unconvincing to historians less Anglophile in persuasion than he. His approach depended too much upon seeing Englishmen of the eighteenth century as more altruistic than they themselves claimed to be. After all, many of them quite frankly admitted that the purpose of their mercantile system was the benefit of the mother country.

But there was more to the question than general theories of human behavior or stated intentions. It was also a matter of historical fact. To test empirically the effect of the mercantile system upon colonial readiness to revolt, two questions had to be answered: (1) Was the mercantile system in fact restrictive of colonial economic activities? Because to nineteenth- and twentieth-century historians it seemed to be so, was not enough. (2) If the system was restrictive, did the American colonists consider these restrictions illegitimate and inequitable? (Earlier, in his monumental study, *The English Navigation Laws* [New York, 1939], Harper had already answered in the affirmative the preliminary question of whether the navigation laws were effective.) The first of these two questions Mr. Harper answers in this article, drawing upon his more thoroughly documented study contained in *The Era of the American Revolution*, edited by Richard B. Morris (New York, 1939). The second one he answers in part here by showing that Americans raised few objections to the navigation system, as the resolves of the Continental Congress in 1774 clearly show.

Since Harper's article appeared, a fuller answer to the second question has been provided in Oliver M. Dickerson, *The Navigation Acts and the American Revolution* (Philadelphia, 1951). Expanding upon Harper's study and adding his own thorough researches, Dickerson demonstrated the absence of any significant colonial opposition to the economic restrictions of the British government.

Harper's article, unlike Beer's volumes on the old colonial system, does not rest for its persuasiveness upon a belief in the benignity of British mercantilism. As he makes clear, Harper is convinced that the navigation system undoubtedly cost the colonists a pretty penny, perhaps as much as seven million dollars per year. Harper, in short, is no apologist for the British mercantile system.

He goes further, however, than simply making concrete what Bancroft and other historians assumed. He asks the additional and necessary question: were the restrictions important to the colonial economy? All policies hurt someone, somewhere, and some time. But what the historian seeking for causes for great events must ask is whether those who are hurt are sufficiently important or numerous to bring to the point of vocal and active opposition those who are not hurt by the policy. One of the ways in which Harper attempts to measure the impact of the costs of the mercantile system is to compare those costs with others that were clearly acceptable to Americans, such as the taxes enacted later by the United States after 1787. This comparative approach should be carefully noted. It provides a means of separating out the social responses to a policy that cannot be ascertained in any other manner. If the historian "listens" only to the complaints of his sources, he is easily beguiled into thinking that the burden of a policy is indeed heavy. But by noting the response of the same people to a similar burden under different circumstances he can test the validity of those complaints. It is important to notice that Harper is measuring the economic effect only of the taxes of the British and of the United States governments in two different periods. He is not drawing any conclusions about the psychological or political sources of discontent. It is altogether possible, of course, that an economic burden placed by an alien authority may be quite intolerable, while an equal burden imposed by a home government may be quite acceptable. The merit of Harper's comparison is that it demonstrates that the economic burden alone—that is, the financial cost—is not the cause of the discontent. Rather it would seem that the political origins of the burden are the active agent of discontent.

Harper's article also illustrates the necessity of taking a quantitative approach to historical problems. Many questions in history ask "how much" or "how many." Such questions obviously can be definitively answered only by counting heads or things. By "counting" the value of English and colonial trade, Harper answered the long-argued question of the cost and impact of the navigation system. Only by collecting such figures could he make the kind of comparison with other periods that he did.

When taken in conjunction with the subsequent book by Dickerson, Harper's work marked a significant turning point in the historiography of the American Revolution. No longer was it possible to argue that the navigation system—as an economic matter—was the principal cause for colonial discontent. It is not surprising, therefore, that since the 1940's the economic interpretation of the American Revolution has been rapidly disappearing from the writings of historians. Harper's article undermined one of the principal economic props of that argument; Morgan's article (No. 3), by showing the unchanging logic of the constitutional arguments of the colonists, reinforced the political explanation. Between them they made most persuasive the political and constitutional interpretation of the causes of the Revolution that now commands the assent of most historians of the period.

Mr. Harper has spent almost all his academic life teaching at the University of California at Berkeley, where he is professor of history, specializing in colonial economic history.

Mercantilism and the American Revolution

BY LAWRENCE A. HARPER

THE cynic who declared that history is the process whereby a complex truth becomes a simplified falsehood may have had in mind interpretations of the American Revolution. Even before the Revolution occurred, Vergennes prophesied that France's loss of Canada would eventually bring it about.[1] The very document which made the severance final attributed the blame to George III, a fashion which has been generally followed, and some years ago was ardently expounded by a former mayor of this city, Big Bill Thompson. These points, however, are called to attention merely to remind us of what Professor Root will expound more fully—that there are many interpretations. Our immediate task is to concentrate upon one—the relation of English mercantilism to the American Revolution.

The term "mercantilism" is one of those words which have dif-

SOURCE: Reprinted by permission of the author and the University of Toronto Press from the *Canadian Historical Review*, XXIII (March 1942).

[1] George Bancroft, *History of the United States of America from the Discovery of the Continent to the Establishment of the Constitution in 1789* (1885 ed., 6 vols.), II, 564.

ferent meanings for different people. On the one hand, George Louis Beer claimed that English mercantilism was a well-balanced system designed for the benefit of the colonies as well as the mother country, and on the other, Sir William Ashley declared that the regulations of English mercantilism were either pious formulas nullified in the actual world of commerce by fraud and evasion, or merely a codification of commercial habits which would have been followed in any case. For reasons which have been explained more fully elsewhere [2] we shall reject Beer's claim that there was no exploitation and accept the statements of the mercantilists themselves that they planned to exploit the colonies for the benefit of the mother country. We shall deny the Ashley view that there was no actual regulation and conclude from more recent studies of the evidence that the English laws did regulate trade and commerce.

These two conclusions provide us with a working definition of English mercantilism in its colonial aspects. It had as its purpose, exploitation, and as its means, regulation. Both phases of the problem, exploitation *and* regulation, are important. To understand the relationship of mercantilism and the Revolution we must not only analyse the extent to which the colonists were exploited but also consider the skill with which they were regulated.

An analysis of how the colonists were exploited is no easy task, as any one knows who has struggled with the many statutory ambiguities involved. The calculations involved in estimating the burdens placed upon the colonial economy are complicated. They call for arithmetical computations involving duties, preferences, or drawbacks of such odd amounts as 1s. 10d. and 15 16/75 of a twentieth of a penny per pound of tobacco. They run afoul of complicated analyses of costs and close decisions about the incidence of taxation. The answer required some thousands of hours of WPA and NYA labour in tabulating the necessary data and hundreds more in analysing and correlating them, the details of which have been compressed in thirty-eight rather dull pages.[3] All that can be attempted here is to state the conclusions and indicate the grounds upon which they are based. We can, however, simplify our analysis of the mercantilist code which exploited the colonies by dividing it into four parts: first, the basic provisions concerning the trans-Atlantic trade; second, the supplementary measures restricting

[2] L. A. Harper, *The English Navigation Laws* (New York, 1939), chap. XIX.

[3] L. A. Harper, "The Effect of the Navigation Acts on the Thirteen Colonies" (in *The Era of the American Revolution*, ed. by Richard B. Morris, New York, 1939).

manufactures; third, the subsidiary rules with reference to the American trade; and fourth, the much discussed measures enacted after the French and Indian War.

In examining the first part, we find that the basic provisions concerning the trans-Atlantic trade placed a heavy burden upon the colonies. By means of the Navigation Acts England attempted both to keep foreign vessels out of the colonies and to enable English merchants to share in the more profitable parts of the trans-Atlantic trade. The enumeration of key colonial exports in various Acts from 1660 to 1766 and the Staple Act of 1663 hit at colonial trade both coming and going. The Acts required the colonies to allow English middlemen to distribute such crops as tobacco and rice and stipulated that if the colonies would not buy English manufactures, at least they should purchase their European goods in England. The greatest element in the burden laid upon the colonies was not the taxes assessed. It consisted in the increased costs of shipment, transshipment, and middleman's profits arising out of the requirement that England be used as an *entrepôt.*

The burdens were somewhat lightened by legislation favouring the colonies, but not as much as usually alleged. The suppression of tobacco production in England, for example, was comparatively unimportant to the colonies since the great quantities of colonial tobacco re-exported caused its price to be determined by a world rather than an English market. Moreover, the motive was not goodwill for the colonists but fiscal, since the heavy revenues derived from tobacco could be collected more easily at the waterfront than upon the farm. Likewise, although colonial shipbuilders and shipowners approved the clauses of the Navigation Acts which eliminated Dutch rivals, they did not need such protection. They had managed to carry cargoes and to build ships which could be sold in the world market before the laws were enacted and they continued to do so after the Revolution. The fact is that colonial shipowners suffered, directly, and colonial shipbuilders, indirectly, under the Navigation Acts since other clauses enabled English shipowners (as contrasted with American) to carry eighty per cent of the trade between the British Isles and the Thirteen Colonies whereas they carried only twenty per cent after the Revolution.[4]

[4] *Ibid.*, 8–10, 37. Richard Champion, *Considerations on the Present Situation of Great Britain and the United States* (London, 1784) declares at pages 27–8 that the ships in the trade between Europe and the Thirteen Colonies totalling 195,000 tons "were generally the property of British merchants, navigated by British seamen" and that they formed "no less than a sixth of our whole

Similarly the drawbacks, bounties, and tariff preferences, of which we are so often reminded, did not materially offset the burdens placed upon the trans-Atlantic trade. The drawbacks paid by English customs authorities on foreign products re-exported to the colonies should not be listed as a benefit to the colonies. There would have been no duties to be drawn back except for the re-

---

shipping," which had previously (p. 13) been stated to be about 1,300,000 tons. Obviously the trans-Atlantic trade of Boston, New York, and Philadelphia included a substantial percentage of colonial-owned ships, but the *trans-Atlantic* trade of those ports was less than that of Virginia, Maryland, and South Carolina, which was overwhelmingly in the hands of British vessels. Thus it seemed wisest to modify Champion's statement somewhat and the estimate of eighty per cent was taken as being a fairly reasonable approximation. Subsequent analyses of the Naval Office lists show that the percentages differed radically from port to port and even within the same port during different years:

OWNERSHIP OF TONNAGE IN TRADE WITH BRITISH ISLES

Ports and years examined		By British	By British and colonial jointly	By colonial	By others	Total
Ports	Exports for					
New York.	1754	340	550	2,585	20	3,495
" ".	1764	1,362	740	2,010	100	4,212
Port York.	1768	2,376		350		2,726
Port Hampton . . .	1758	2,627		465	80	3,172
" " . . .	1766	3,436		1,385	35	4,856
South Carolina. . .	1758	8,649		1,825	670	11,144
" " . . .	1766	13,982	1,691	1,205	605	17,483

An attempt was made to calculate the average for all the colonies on the assumption that the average of the New York percentages would be typical of that of the colonies north of the Mason and Dixon line, while an average of the Virginia and Charleston figures would represent that of the Southern colonies. The averages thus derived were then weighted in accordance with the ratio of Northern (30) and Southern (70) tonnages engaged in the Anglo-American trade in 1769 (Public Record Office, London, Customs 16, vol. 1), with the result that the percentage of British-owned ships was found to be 74.5 per cent and that of colonial-owned ships 16.9 per cent. The procedure, however, involved other complications. Vessels listed as colonial-owned in Virginia and Charleston were listed as colonial but they were probably owned in most cases by Scottish factors who might well be classed as British. Vessels carrying rice to southern Europe were considered to be engaged in trade with the British Isles because they virtually all engaged in a triangular voyage which started and ended there. Owners listed as residing in Madeira, Rotterdam, and elsewhere (3.4 per cent) probably should have been listed as British since only ships of British subjects were allowed to trade in the colonies. Finally, there is the question of how great was the British and how great was the colonial interest in the vessels owned jointly (5.2 per cent). Thus the best estimate now possible would seem to be that the British controlled about 80 per cent of the tonnage in the Anglo-American trade under mercantilism.

quirement that the colonists purchase their European goods in England. The portion of the duties which England retained, while less than it might have been, was obviously greater than nothing at all.[5] Likewise, *bounties paid upon English manufactures* exported to the colonies, were of advantage to the English producer, who received them whether his goods were exported to the colonies or anywhere else, rather than of benefit to the colonial consumer who otherwise would, and often did, buy competitive European goods.[6]

On the other hand, however, the bounties paid upon colonial products were of real advantage to the colonies. They sustained the growth of indigo in South Carolina, did much to foster the development of naval stores in North Carolina, encouraged the lumber industry in New England, and at the end of the colonial period averaged more than £ 65,000 a year for the Thirteen Colonies alone. Similarly the preferences granted colonial products were beneficial in so far as they operated. Although they had no effect upon such commodities as tobacco and rice and their effect upon other commodities is somewhat uncertain, colonial raw silk, naval stores, and lumber definitely benefited. Yet the total sum represented by such preferences was never great and it is doubtful whether the benefit the Thirteen Colonies thus derived amounted to even one-twentieth

[5] It is, of course, true that, if one wishes to consider the fairness of the burdens laid upon the colonists, it is relevant to remember that the allowance of drawbacks enabled them to pay lower taxes upon the same goods than the English were assessed. An analysis of the economic burdens upon the colonies, however, is concerned primarily with ascertaining how much the colonists had to pay, not with determining how fair the assessment was. If one lists the drawbacks as a colonial advantage in such an analysis, the entire tax should be calculated as a colonial burden, in which case one will attain exactly the same result reached in the calculations which follow, since the drawback has already been deducted from the gross tax and the only burden considered has been the net tax retained in Britain.

[6] The grant of the bounty did not depend upon exportation *to the colonies* in the case, of any of the bounty-paid products (cordage, corn, certain fish, beef, pork, gunpowder, linen, sailcloth, silk manufactures, and refined sugar), nor in the case of the candles, glass, hides, lace, thread and fringes, leather manufactures, paper calicoes, silks, salt, soap, and starch, the "exciseable goods" which received specified drawbacks or bounties upon exportation (Samuel Baldwin, *A Survey of the British Customs*, London, 1770, Part II, 19–22). In the case of linens the bounty was paid only for exportations to Africa, America, Spain, Portugal, Gibraltar, Minorca, and the East Indies, but those were the only regions in which British linen had an opportunity to compete successfully. It is also important to note that in the year 1773 the exports to the American colonies of bounty-paid linen totalled £348,464 (of which £168,314 went to the continental colonies), while less than £68,000 worth of bounty-paid linen was exported to the rest of the world. During the same year the continental colonies imported almost the same amount of duty-burdened linens, valued at £137,248, and similar exports to the British Carribbean amounted to £102,754 (Customs 3, vol. 73).

of that obtained by the British West Indian planters who in the year 1773 alone, pocketed £446,000, thanks to a preferential rate which enabled their sugar to hold the English market despite a five-shilling-per-hundred-weight differential in price.[7]

The uncertainties underlying many of our calculations do not permit an exact statement, but judging from calculations for the year 1773, it would seem that after all proper allowances have been made for bounties and other preferences, the net burden imposed upon the Thirteen Colonies by the restraints upon the trans-Atlantic trade was between two million and seven million dollars a year. In these days of astronomical budgets such figures do not seem especially impressive, but the annual per capita burden represented by the lower estimate would come close to meeting all the expenses of operating the national government during Washington's administration, and an annual per capita tax based upon the higher estimate would, in addition to paying the current expenses of government, have raised in twelve years (from 1790–1801) a sum sufficient to pay both the domestic and foreign debt incurred by the United States government during the Revolutionary War.[8]

When we turn to the second part of our discussion, the supplementary measures restricting manufacture, we find a difference of opinion concerning the effect of English restrictions upon manufacturing wool, hats, and iron. The earlier tendency was to dismiss the regulations as immaterial, but recently some have swung the pendulum to the other extreme and argue that the restraints were very important.[9] Neither extreme appears to accord with the facts.

[7] Harper, "Effect of the Navigation Acts," *passim*. As Professor Gipson points out, the British West Indies had their own burdens, such as the 4½ per cent tax in Barbados, but their increasing inability to meet world competition as shown by the decrease in re-exports of sugar from England (Frank W. Pitman, *The Development of the British West Indies*, New Haven, 1915, 156ff.) indicates that retention of England's market was very important to them. Also one must remember that the British fleet, as well as economic interests, helped to prevent their joining the Thirteen Colonies in revolt, just as the Canadians were kept loyal to the mother country partly by their distrust of the Thirteen Colonies and partly by the profits to be derived in the fur trade from an uninterrupted supply of British manufactures.

[8] The estimate of the net burden given here has been modified slightly from that given in Harper, "The Effect of the Navigation Laws," in order to make greater allowances for the possibly beneficial effects of preferential rates on colonial products and for possible errors in estimating the ratio between the pound and the dollar.

[9] Cf. Victor S. Clark, *History of Manufactures in the United States, 1607–1860* (2 vols., Washington, 1916–28) with Miriam Beard, *A History of the Business Man* (New York, 1938); L. M. Hacker, *The Triumph of American Capitalism* (New York, 1940) and "The First American Revolution" (*Columbia University Quarterly*, XXVII, Sept., 1935).

In the case of hats, proximity to the source of supply of furs and the comparatively simple process of manufacturing had led to the development of an industry which appears to have been injured by the legislation,[10] but the hat industry played only a minor part in the total economy. Woollen manufactures were, of course, much more important, but there is much evidence to indicate that the English prohibitions had little material effect. The colonies found that they were handicapped by an inadequate supply of good wool when they tried to develop homespun goods at the time of the Revolution—and even as late as 1791 Hamilton found that an adequate supply of labour was one of the chief stumbling blocks to his programme for encouraging industry. It required an embargo, a war, and a protective tariff before large-scale woollen manufacturing began to develop, and it did not pass beyond the household stage until many years after being freed of English mercantilism—which, incidentally, had never forbidden the manufacture of homespun for domestic use or local distribution.[11]

In the case of iron manufactures the British legislation encouraged the development of pig and bar iron and tried to discourage the manufacture of more advanced forms, but in both respects the influence of the legislation is doubtful. Because of the proximity of iron ore to forests America had a great advantage in producing crude iron, before coke replaced charcoal, and probably did not need legislative encouragement. With such an advantage in producing crude iron it was only natural that some more advanced iron articles would be produced in the colonies, whatever thoroughgoing mercantilists might dream about having the crude iron sent over to England and having it returned in the form of pots, pans, and other manufactures.[12]

The various disallowances of colonial laws which were intended to foster colonial manufacturing further illustrate the English intention of discouraging it but, despite that intent, English mercantilism as a whole probably had a greater tendency to promote than to hinder colonial industry. The colonies' most dangerous industrial competitors were in many respects, not the English, but the Dutch, the Germans, and other Europeans—to say nothing of the natives of India—against whose competition the provisoes of the Staple Act

[10] Harper, "The Effect of the Navigation Acts," 6–7.

[11] *Report on Manufactures,* Dec. 5, 1791, in American State Papers, Finance, I, 123–44; Arthur H. Cole, *The American Wool Manufacture* (2 vols., Cambridge, Mass., 1926), *passim.*

[12] A. C. Bining, *British Regulation of the Colonial Iron Industry* (Philadelphia, 1933); *Pennsylvania Iron Manufacture in the Eighteenth Century* (Harrisburg, 1938).

of 1663 provided a very useful tariff barrier. Moreover, the large sums which mercantilism withheld from the colonies reduced their available cash, and probably forced many colonists to use homespun or other American products instead of buying British.[13]

The third point of our inquiry into colonial exploitation by England should not detain us long. Until the Molasses Act of 1733 the inter-American trade had been left virtually alone except for the requirement that the English colonies trade in English or colonial ships. Even after 1733, the prohibitive duties on foreign sugar, molasses, and rum were usually evaded. Such evasion required bribery, fraud, or concealment which probably served as a mildly protective tariff in favour of the British sugar islands, but the prices quoted in the Thirteen Colonies for sugar, molasses, and rum do not indicate that the legislation had any radical effect upon the trade.[14]

The fourth part of our inquiry—that relating to the period after 1763—is a different matter. The researches of Schlesinger and others have demonstrated how the British measures of that period aroused the resentment of the merchants who unleashed an avalanche of agitation which soon went beyond their control. The agitation was not directed toward revolution at first, but agitation by its very nature promotes conditions favourable for revolution—and revolution followed as a natural sequence. Yet, conceding all the irritation thus aroused, we must still face the questions: Were the measures unduly exploitive? Did they fundamentally upset the economic equilibrium? Were they fatal ills which would inevitably lead to the death of the Empire, or merely minor upsets from which the Empire might have recovered—granted otherwise favourable conditions and good luck?

In reviewing the period it does not seem fair to blame British mercantilism for prescribing regulations which were demanded by the circumstances of the time. The British currency and land policies seem to fall under this category. The restrictions upon paper money undoubtedly distressed those who lacked funds, but they merely affirmed a truth which Americans had to learn from sad experience —that in the eighteenth century at least, no political alchemy could transmute paper into gold. Similarly the Proclamation of 1763 and the Quebec Act of 1774 essentially concerned imperial problems and

13 Cf. Calendar of State Papers, Colonial XXVIII, 225, July 7, 1715; XXXII, 413–14, Sept. 8, 1721; XXXVIII, 326–7, Nov. 5, 1731.

14 See Anne Bezanson, Robert D. Gray, and Miriam Hussey, *Prices in Colonial Pennsylvania* (Philadelphia, 1935); Arthur H. Cole, *Wholesale Commodity Prices in the United States, 1700–1861*, and *Statistical Supplement* (Cambridge, Mass., 1939).

American imitation of the policy after independence was not mere flattery but a tribute to its inherent soundness. The measures disappointed those who had hoped to acquire fortunes from land speculation, but what else could the British have done? Neither they nor the United States government after them could allow private individuals to stir up trouble by moving into Indian territory before the way had been prepared for settlement by negotiations which extinguished the Indians' claim to the area. In view of the British debt it was merely good fiscal policy to charge for the land, and the prices and terms of sale proposed by the British mercantilists seem very reasonable when compared with the prices and terms adopted by the federal government after 1787.[15] And what solution did the Thirteen States themselves find for the conflicting claims to the territory west of the Alleghanies except to create a new governmental unit?

To one who frankly does not profess to be an expert on the point, it is difficult to understand how British mercantilism discriminated materially against the colonists. It is true that in the manœuvering for land grants, British interests sometimes clashed with colonial interests, but we hear fully as much about clashes between different colonial groups. Both the small frontiersmen and the big speculators were charged more for land than they were accustomed to pay, but it was not as much as they were to be charged by the United States government thereafter. In the readjustments which accompanied the establishment of the new policies the fur traders of the Thirteen Colonies suffered somewhat because of the machinations of British opponents but their loss was not great, and in any event by the Revolutionary period trade in furs formed only a negligible fraction of the colonial economy.[16]

[15] The conditions of sale established by the British in 1774, stipulated sale by public auction and a minimum price of 6d. per acre (which however bore an annual quit-rent of ½d. per acre) and terms, cash (New York Colonial Documents, VIII, 410–13). The Ordinance of 1785 stipulated a 640 acre unit of purchase and a minimum price of one dollar an acre, terms, cash. The Land Act of 1796 retained the 640 acre unit of purchase but raised the minimum price to two dollars an acre and stipulated a down payment of one-half, half of the remainder within thirty days, and the balance within one year. The Harrison Land Act of 1800 reduced the unit of purchase to 320 acres but retained the minimum price of two dollars an acre and stipulated a down payment of one quarter, and the balance in four equal yearly payments. The Land Act of 1820 reduced the unit of purchase to 80 acres and the minimum price to $1.25 an acre but abolished the credit system and re-instituted cash terms (Benjamin H. Hibbard, *A History of the Public Land Policies*, New York, 1924).

[16] According to tables compiled by Murray G. Lawson from the Inspector General's accounts (Customs 3), the imports of colonial furs decreased from 1.0 per cent of the total exports from the Thirteen Colonies to England in 1750 to 0.87 per cent in 1755, to 0.51 per cent in 1760, 0.94 per cent in 1765,

The pre-Revolutionary taxation measures, however, are a different matter, and one for which British mercantilism must bear full responsibility.[17] Yet in analysing the figures we find that the average annual revenue raised by the Sugar Acts, the Townshend Acts, and all the other taxes collected in the Thirteen Colonies by the British government amounted to only £31,000. This sum barely exceeded the indirect taxes which were collected on colonial merchandise passing through England. Moreover, both the taxes collected indirectly in England and directly in the colonies failed to equal the bounties which the British government was paying to the colonies —to say nothing of the advantages which they were deriving from preferential duties on their shipments to England. More interesting still, calculated on an annual per capita basis, the taxes collected during the Revolutionary period directly in the colonies and indirectly in England, totalled less than one-seventh of the taxes assessed at the beginning of the century.[18]

Yet even though the amount of taxation was not great, we must consider the possibility that the form of its assessment detrimentally affected colonial interests. The Tea Act, for one, definitely injured the illicit trade in tea by so reducing the price of the legal article that it lessened, if it did not eliminate, the profit from smuggling.[19]

0.6 per cent in 1770, and 0.45 per cent in 1775. These percentages, however, should be further reduced because exports of the Thirteen Colonies to Scotland amounted to about one-half of the exports to England in 1769 (Customs 14, vol. 1B) and the value of exports elsewhere than Great Britain almost equalled the value of exports to Great Britain (T. Pitkin, *A Statistical View of the Commerce of the United States of America: Its Connection with Agriculture and Manufactures . . .*, Hartford, Conn., 1816, 21–3). Thus at the outbreak of the Revolution the fur trade constituted less than one-fifth of one per cent of the total exports of the Thirteen Colonies and probably had never greatly exceeded one-third of one per cent in the second half of the century. An examination of the figures in Pitkin (*ibid.*) discloses (when the £91,486 there given for the value of furs is reduced to almost one-seventh to allow for the inclusion of furs from Canada, Hudson Bay, and similar regions) that the fur trade was less important in 1770 to the Thirteen Colonies than that in spermaceti candles or in horses, to say nothing of the more important staple commodities like indigo, rice, tobacco, or provisions. The decline in importance of the fur trade dates back far before 1763. In New York, the colony most interested in the trade, furs had constituted 32 per cent of the exports to England in 1720 and had declined to 30 per cent in 1730, 23 per cent in 1740, 16 per cent in 1750, 13.8 per cent in 1755, 4.8 per cent in 1760, 10.1 per cent in 1765, 3.3 per cent in 1770, and 2.1 per cent in 1775.

[17] These taxes, of course, differed in many ways from earlier measures but they had very definite economic effects, however political some of their aims may have been. Consequently, it seemed necessary to include them if our discussion of mercantilism was to be complete.

[18] Harper, "Effect of the Navigation Acts," 27–9.

[19] D. Harrington, *The New York Merchant on the Eve of the Revolution* (New York, 1935), 249, 344; A. M. Schlesinger, *The Colonial Merchants and the American Revolution, 1763–1776* (New York, 1918), 262–7.

However unfair smugglers may have thought such tactics, they can hardly be said to have injured the economy of the country—especially since tea was not a pivotal commodity.

Molasses, the rum which was made from it, and the provision trade which accompanied it, however, were vital factors in colonial economy, and historians have often called attention to their importance in such books as *Rum, Romance, and Rebellion.*[20] The Sugar Act of 1764 served notice that the British government intended to make its regulations effective when it lowered the duty on foreign sugar and molasses and prohibited the importation of foreign rum entirely. The provisions concerning sugar and rum were comparatively immaterial since no great quantities were imported, but the duty of 3d. per gallon on molasses was another matter, since literally millions of gallons came from the foreign West Indies.[21] Many feared that the trade could not bear a tax of 3d. per gallon, and in response to their pleas the duty was reduced in 1766 to 1d. per gallon and the tax was assessed on both British and foreign molasses. The excitement aroused by these taxes leads one to look for evidence of the havoc which they wrought in trade, but an examination of the wholesale prices of molasses does not disclose any noticeable change attributable to the legislation.[22] And if we carry our investigations further we find that the tax which the federal government placed and kept upon imports of molasses after 1790 almost equaled the 3d. per gallon placed upon foreign molasses in 1764 and materially exceeded the 1d. duty retained after 1766.[23] In brief, whatever the connection between rum and romance,

[20] By Charles W. Taussig, New York, 1928.

[21] Customs 16, vol. 1 gives the following figures concerning the imports of molasses:

	From Foreign West Indies *Gallons*	From British West Indies *Gallons*
1768	2,803,275	328,675
1769	3,413,367	299,678
1770	3,408,784	226,876

Figures for the importation of rum are not so satisfactory as we could desire, but according to Pitman (*British West Indies*, 208, n. 36) importations of foreign molasses exceeded those of foreign rum 27 to 1 in 1714, 39 to 1 in 1715, 34 to 1 in 1716, and 64 to 1 in 1717. According to the Naval Office Lists for 1764, approximately 38,000 gallons of rum were imported to Boston from the British West Indies as compared with 200 gallons from the foreign West Indies (Public Record Office, London, C.O. 58, vol. 850); at Salem and Marblehead the corresponding figures (for a half year only) were 22,000 and 1,000 (C.O. 5, vol. 850); at New Hampshire 63,000 and none (C.O. 5, vol. 969); at New York 87,000 and 5,000 (C.O. 5, vol. 1228).

[22] *Supra,* note 14.

[23] Adam Seybert, *Statistical Annals . . . of the United States* (Philadelphia, 1818), 398–9, 455–6, 469–70.

the statistics of colonial trade disclose no correlation between rum and rebellion.

In so far as the statistics can be followed, the correlation between wine and rebellion is much closer. The Sugar Act of 1764 had also placed a duty upon wines which gave those imported by way of Britain a preferential rate of £3 per ton. The preference was not sufficient to enable the English to capture the trade in Madeira wine, but it enabled them to gain a flourishing trade in port which previously had been negligible.[24] Yet such an infringement of colonial taste hardly seems to justify a revolt—especially when we note that the quantity involved was not large, and that by the post-Revolutionary period Americans preferred port and other wines to Madeira.[25]

Thus, an analysis of the economic effects of British mercantilism fails to establish its exploitative aspects as the proximate cause of the Revolution. The only measures which afforded a sufficient economic grievance where the *entrepôt* provisions of the Navigation Acts, which governed the trans-Atlantic trade. They helped to create a fundamental economic unbalance, but cannot be connected directly with the Revolution. The colonists had lived under them for more than a century without desiring independence and even in the Revolutionary period with few exceptions the *entrepôt* provisions were accepted as the mother country's due for the protection which she afforded.[26] In fact, the official representatives of the colonies were willing to guarantee the British commercial

[24] In 1750 (before the new tax was placed on Madeira wine) England exported to the Thirteen Colonies 15 tons, 1 hogshead and 13 gallons of Madeira; in 1765 and 1773 (after the imposition of the new tax), the exports were only 22 tons, 1 hogshead, 62 gallons, and 23 tons, 1 hogshead, 48 gallons, respectively. In the case of port, however, England's exportations rose from only 15 tons, 2 hogsheads, and 3 gallons in 1750 to 385 tons, 53 gallons in 1765, and 860 tons, 2 hogsheads, 60 gallons in 1773 (Customs 3, vols. 50, 65, 73).

[25] Seybert, *Statistical Annals,* 164–9, 260.

[26] The necessity of taking considerable space to calculate the burdens laid upon the colonies by mercantilism should not be regarded as a denial that Britain had real contributions to make. The benefits of military and naval protection were very important. British merchants also probably helped the colonists to find markets for their products but it is easy to overemphasize such assistance. During the greater part of the time the *entrepôt* requirements were operative the Dutch were much better qualified to serve efficiently as middlemen in colonial products than the English. Similarly the flattening of the curve of the American tobacco exports after the Revolution is not as significant as it seems at first glance. The destruction wrought by the Revolution, and the interruption to the trade, first by the Revolution, and then by the wars in Europe, would appear to have done much more to discourage tobacco production than the elimination of the laws making Britain an *entrepôt.*

system provided that the measures of political taxation were withdrawn.[27] If there were any inexorable economic forces which were inevitably drawing the colonies toward revolution, they are hard to detect and the colonists were unaware of them.

Anyone who maintains that the Revolution resulted from the inevitable clash of competing capitalisms must reckon with several points: That burdens upon the trans-Atlantic trade were proportionately greater at the beginning of the eighteenth century than in 1776; that the restraints of the land and currency policies were basically the same as those prescribed by the federal government; and that after 1766 the taxes laid on molasses by Britain were less than those imposed by the United States after 1790. He should also explain why the surplus colonial capital alleged to be bursting its confines did not venture into the manufacturing enterprises which the law did not prohibit; why the colonists did not finance their own middlemen in England; and, finally, why they did not pay their debts. If by a clash of expanding capitalism is meant that colonists with money were irritated because their freedom of action was restrained by outside regulation, one must immediately concede that the charge is justified; but such colonial resentment seems more properly classified as a political rather than an economic factor. It is merely an old point dressed in new garb and was better expressed by John Adams when he declared that the American Revolution began when the first plantation was settled.[28]

When we turn, however, from the economic effects of mercantilism to its regulatory aspects, we are faced with a different story. We can establish a direct correlation between mercantilism and the Revolution. Although earlier English regulations had been reasonably satisfactory the regulatory technique of the British government under George III was pitifully defective. As a mother country, Britain had much to learn. Any modern parents' magazine could have told George III's ministers that the one mistake not to

[27] Resolve no. 4 of the "Declaration and Resolves of the First Continental Congress, October 14, 1774" (as quoted in *Documents Illustrative of the Formation of the Union of the American States,* selected, arranged, and indexed by Charles C. Tansill, Washington, 1927, 3) contains the following statement: "But, from the necessity of the case, and a regard to the mutual interest of both countries, we cheerfully consent to the operation of such acts of the British parliament as are bona fide, restrained to the regulation of our external commerce, for the purpose of securing the commercial advantages of the whole empire to the mother country, and the commercial benefits of its respective members, excluding every idea of taxation internal or external, for raising a revenue on the subjects in America without their consent."

[28] *Works of John Adams,* ed. by Charles F. Adams (10 vols., Boston, 1856), X, 313.

make is to take a stand and then to yield to howls of anguish. It was a mistake which the British government made repeatedly. It placed a duty of 3d. per gallon on molasses, and when it encountered opposition, reduced it to 1d. It provided for a Stamp Act and withdrew it in the face of temper tantrums. It provided for external taxes to meet the colonial objections and then yielded again by removing all except one. When finally it attempted to enforce discipline it was too late. Under the circumstances, no self-respecting child—or colonist—would be willing to yield.

Moreover, British reforming zeal came at a very bad time. The colonists were in a particularly sensitive state due to the post-war deflation and the economic distress which accompanied it. The British also attempted to exert unusual control at a time when the removal of the French from Canada had minimized the colonists' dependence upon Britain. Most important of all, the reforms followed one another too rapidly.

In social reform, irritation often is to be measured not so much by what a regulation attempts to achieve as by the extent to which it changes established habits. The early history of English mercantilism itself offers a good illustration of the point. Bitter complaints came from Virginia and Barbados when tobacco and sugar were first enumerated because those colonies had become accustomed to conditions of comparatively free trade, whereas few or no complaints were heard from Jamaica which had developed under the restrictive system.[29] The mercantilist system was geared for leisurely operation and before George III's reign succeeded by virtue of that fact. Its early restraints led to Bacon's rebellion in Virginia but fortunately for the mother country the pressure against New England was deferred until the next decade when it, too, led to an explosion in the form of revolt against Andros.[30] These uprisings were separated both geographically and chronologically so that neither attained dangerous proportions, and both were followed by a reasonably satisfactory settlement of at least some of the colonial grievances.

During the Revolutionary era, however, the tempo of reform was not leisurely. Doubtless all the colonists were not irritated by any one British reform, but each individual had his own feeling of

[29] George L. Beer, *The Old Colonial System, 1660–1754* (2 vols., New York, 1912), I, 162–3 (Virginia); I, 164–5 (Barbados); II, 83 (Jamaica); Harper, *The English Navigation Laws*, 246, n. 37.

[30] Beer, *Old Colonial System*, II, 148ff.; Thomas J. Wertenbaker, *Torchbearer of the Revolution: The Story of Bacon's Rebellion and its Leader* (Princeton, 1940).

grievance which enabled him to agree fervently with the complaints of others against British policy and thus add to the heated tempers of the time. The politician who objected to the political implications in taxation reforms found an audience in the land speculators and frontiersmen who complained that the colonists were being deprived of the reward of their blood and suffering by the Proclamation of 1763 and the Quebec Act of 1774. Debtors and inflationists chimed in to tell of the iniquities of the Currency Act; lawyers and printers could not forget the threat to their interests in the Stamp Act. On Sundays the preachers thundered against the dangers of popery in Quebec and voiced their fear that Britain planned to establish an Anglican Church in the colonies. The merchant was always ready to explain not merely how harmful British taxes were to colonial economy, but how irksome were the new administrative rules and regulations. Such chronological and geographical barriers as existed were overcome and a community of antagonisms was maintained by the Committees of Correspondence and other agitators, but such revolutionary forces could not have succeeded if the different elements of the colonies had not recently experienced a mutual sense of grievance.

In short, many of the misunderstandings which have arisen in connection with mercantilism and the American Revolution have grown out of the failure to distinguish between the two phases of mercantilism: exploitation and regulation. The fact that the colonists were exploited by English mercantilism does not necessarily mean that mercantilism caused the American Revolution. Economic forces are not magnets which inexorably move men in predetermined patterns. For better or for worse, men try to regulate their economic as well as their political destiny. A large part of governmental activity consists in attempting to mould economic conduct and to minimize the friction which results from clashes or constraints. English mercantilism was such an attempt. It succeeded rather well in minimizing friction until 1764. For the next decade it bungled badly, and the penalty was the loss of the Thirteen Colonies.

5

EVER since 1945, upon the publication of *The Age of Jackson* by Arthur M. Schlesinger, Jr., the scholarly study of the Jacksonian era has been a fertile field for re-evaluation and interpretation, as McCormick's opening paragraphs make clear. Although most of this re-evaluation has appeared in books and is therefore outside the scope of this collection, no real consensus has, in any case, emerged from the discussion. The controversy about the nature of the Jacksonians and the direction in which Old Hickory and his supporters were pointing the nation remain subjects of lively but rather inconclusive debate. In all the writing and disputing, though, one aspect of the Jacksonian era has gone unchallenged and is accepted or assumed as true by Arthur Schlesinger and his critics alike. This aspect is the great increase in the electorate during the years of Jackson's prominence. The phrase "mighty democratic uprising," which has become a cliché of writers on the period and which McCormick mentions several times, actually derives from a book written in 1919.

One of the few scholarly articles to call into question this hoary belief in the upsurge in voters in the Age of Jackson was J. R. Pole's "Suffrage and Representation in Massachusetts: A Statistical Note," *William and Mary Quarterly*, 3rd Series, XIV (October 1957), 560–592. By compiling figures for elections in Massachusetts and New Hampshire in the early years of the Republic, Pole showed that in the 1830s the numbers who voted were not extraordinarily large. But his figures were for only two states. McCormick's study, coming a few years later, was therefore of much wider import.

As with so many pivotal interpretations, McCormick's was quite obvious once it was done. Like Pole, he simply counted the number of white males who actually voted in the elections prior to 1828, then compared the results with those for 1828, the year in which the upsurge in voters was traditionally said to have taken place.

A reading of McCormick's article makes it easy to understand how the traditional view got started. If one simply looks at the votes cast for presidents immediately prior to Jackson, the proportion of the population actually voting is obviously quite small. Indeed, as McCormick points out, the total vote doubled between 1824 and 1828. But as his Table II makes evident, had historians pushed back their comparisons further, say to 1808 or 1812, they would have found that the proportions of voters among the white males were not so different then from what they were in 1828. Notice that at this point McCormick introduced an obvious but necessary device of analysis: the *proportion* of the white males voting, in place of simply the *number* of voters. For as he observes, to simply count voters is to fail to take into account the increase in population from one election to another, especially if a large number of years intervene. The proportion of white males voting, of course, can be compared from year to year.

But perhaps the most telling device introduced by McCormick is statistics for elections other than those for president. In this way he is able to show that it was not property qualifications or *general* apathy that kept the electorate small during presidential elections, but the particular apathy toward the presidential races.

The basic question that McCormick set himself to answer is a quantitative one: was there an unprecedented upsurge in voting in 1828 and 1832 that swept Jackson into office? On the basis of his figures for the two Jackson elections and before, the answer must be no. Moreover, by carrying his investigation and compilation of election statistics into subsequent elections he has been able to show that the real upsurge in voter participation came in 1840, not in 1828 or in any of the Jackson years. These are important conclusions. They compel historians to abandon the idea that Jackson's election marked a significant increase in the size of the electorate, and they document the assertion that universal white manhood suffrage virtually prevailed before 1824.

Having established these facts, though, McCormick attempts to draw further interpretive conclusions that do not stand up with equal strength. He lists three reasons usually given for the doubling of the presidential vote in 1828 over 1824: (1) the removal of property qualifications, (2) the influence of the West, and (3) the personal magnetism of Jackson. All of these reasons he finds invalid as a result of his voting statistics.

None of these three reasons, however, is refuted by the statistics provided by him. The first one, to be sure, is conclusively disproved by him—but by reference to the laws on property qualifications, not by his figures. The second one he unconvincingly attempts to refute by arbitrarily singling out those states that showed 70 per cent or more of the white males voting and noting that very few were western states. Such a procedure smacks of a packed deck, for what about the rest of the states? Why look only at those with 70 per cent? What is so sacred about that particular percentage? A less arbitrary figure would have been the average for all the states, which is given in his Table I as 56.3. Obviously any state that exceeded that figure was recording a voting percentage better than the average for the nation. Ten states, according to his figures in Table I, did better than the average; of those, four were western states. Four out of ten does not prove his conclusions wrong, but neither does it warrant his strong negative. A much more direct way of answering the question might have been to calculate the increase in the individual state's votes between 1824 and 1828 to see whether the western states did or did not throw a larger proportion into the election than hitherto. Such an investigation might well support his argument—but that is not the point. It is his method that is weak; it simply doesn't test what he wants to test.

His objection to the third reason is similarly flawed by a rather arbitrary method. Here he uses six states with the highest proportion of white males voting to determine whether Jackson was a catalyst in bringing out the vote. Again the arbitrariness of just six states smacks of rigging the analysis. If instead he had used the states whose proportions of the vote exceeded the average for the nation, then the charge of arbitrariness would not hold—but neither would his conclusion. Of the ten states that showed proportions greater than the average, six supported Jackson, two supported Adams, and two split their votes. Again, this analysis is at best suggestive; much more sophisticated analyses would have to be made to answer conclusively the question he posed. The point is the weakness of his method, not the final accuracy or inaccuracy of his conclusion as such.

Furthermore, the three explanations he offers for the upsurge in voting in 1828 hardly exhaust the possibilities. Is it not possible, for example, that prior to 1828 presidential elections were simply not considered as important as gubernatorial elections, which he uses to show how high the voting proportions went before 1828? After all, today we take it for granted that national elections are the most popular and exciting, but such an attitude was by no means prevalent in the early days of the Republic, when the federal government was small, distant, and new.

If McCormick tries to extract too much from his figures for elections prior to 1840, he reads too much into those for 1840 and after. Like all good researchers, who sense a problem and a clue when they see an anomaly or discontinuity in their data, McCormick seeks to explain the disparity between the proportion of voters in 1832 and 1836 on the one hand and in 1840 and afterwards on the other. The explanation, he says, is that prior to 1840 the voting was so one-sided in some states that the voters did not bother to come out to vote, while in 1840 and later the contests were so close that public interest brought out more voters than ever. He seeks to demonstrate the validity of this interpretation by Table III. Instead he merely shows the dangers that too heavy reliance upon figures can create.

The disparity between the votes for Adams and Jackson in 1828, for example, is certainly great, but that is only after the fact. The people at the time could not have known it; therefore it could not have influenced their behavior. In days of party organization, of course, a region or state would know which party predominated from election to election, and the closeness of a race or lack thereof could influence the voters' decision to go to the polls or not. But by his own statement the 1830s antedated party organizations. In short, he has obviously used his figures without reflecting that the statistics are tools of the historian, used after the event, and often not available to contemporaries. He has, in effect, assumed that people at the time knew what he knows now.

What his figures do seem to establish is that once party organizations got going in 1840 and after, the voters were mobilized and energized, and often without reference to the closeness of the election. In 1840, for example, according to the figures in Table III, eight states showed a spread between the parties that exceeded the national average. According to McCormick's interpretation this disparity should have resulted in a rather small proportion of voters; yet four of these eight (Maine, Tennessee, New Hampshire, and Arkansas) had a proportion of their white males voting that exceeded the national average. Once again the point is not to present an alternative view as correct but simply to show that if another interpretation can be plausibly drawn from the same figures, then McCormick's interpretation ceases to persuade.

Aside from the unwarranted extrapolations McCormick makes from his otherwise valuable statistics, his article undoubtedly documents the achievement of white manhood suffrage at an earlier period than most historians had thought. The validity of this conclusion has since been reached by the avenue of ideas and laws in Chilton Williamson's *American Suffrage from Property to Democracy, 1760–1860* (Princeton, 1960), now the standard study on the suffrage for the period. A recent and important study by David Hackett Fischer, *The Revolution of American Conservatism* (New York, 1965), further supports McCormick's conclusions by showing that in the years between 1800 and 1812 the Federalists, by emulating the popular electioneering techniques of the Jeffersonians, helped to stimulate large voter turnouts long before the Age of Jackson.

Richard P. McCormick is professor of history at Rutgers University. His article "Suffrage Classes and Party Alignments: A Study in Voter Behavior," *Mississippi Valley Historical Review*, XLVI (December 1959), 397–410, which also treats the suffrage in the early Republic, is a brilliant case study of the effects of property qualifications on the size of the electorate and of the lack of class content in voting patterns in the 1830s. It has not been included in this collection simply because it is a case study of only two states and hence not sufficiently wide in its base.

New Perspectives on Jacksonian Politics

BY RICHARD P. MCCORMICK

THE historical phenomenon that we have come to call Jacksonian democracy has long engaged the attention of American political historians, and never more insistently than in the past decade. From the time of Parton and Bancroft to the present day scholars have recognized that a profoundly significant change took place in the climate of politics simultaneously with the appearance of

SOURCE: Reprinted by permission of the American Historical Association from the *American Historical Review*, LXV (January 1960).

Andrew Jackson on the presidential scene. They have sensed that a full understanding of the nature of that change might enable them to dissolve some of the mysteries that envelop the operation of the American democratic process. With such a challenging goal before them, they have pursued their investigations with uncommon intensity and with a keen awareness of the contemporary relevance of their findings.

A cursory view of the vast body of historical writing on this subject suggests that scholars in the field have been largely preoccupied with attempts to define the content of Jacksonian democracy and identify the influences that shaped it.[1] What did Jacksonian democracy represent, and what groups, classes, or sections gave it its distinctive character? The answers that have been given to these central questions have been—to put it succinctly—bewildering in their variety. The discriminating student, seeking the essential core of Jacksonianism, may make a choice among urban workingmen, southern planters, venturous conservatives, farm-bred *nouveaux riches,* western frontiersmen, frustrated entrepreneurs, or yeoman farmers. Various as are these interpretations of the motivating elements that constituted the true Jacksonians, the characterizations of the programmatic features of Jacksonian democracy are correspondingly diverse. Probably the reasonable observer will content himself with the conclusion that many influences were at work and that latitudinarianism prevailed among the Jacksonian faithful.

In contrast with the controversy that persists over these aspects of Jacksonian democracy, there has been little dissent from the judgment that "the 1830's saw the triumph in American politics of that democracy which has remained pre-eminently the distinguishing feature of our society."[2] The consensus would seem to be that with the emergence of Jackson, the political pulse of the nation quickened. The electorate, long dormant or excluded from the polls by suffrage barriers, now became fired with unprecedented political excitement. The result was a bursting forth of democratic energies, evidenced by a marked upward surge in voting.[3] Beard

[1] For a concise survey of the literature on the topic, see Charles G. Sellers, Jr., *Jacksonian Democracy* (Washington, D. C., 1958) or his "Andrew Jackson versus the Historians," *Mississippi Valley Historical Review,* XLIV (Mar. 1958), 615–34. For the most recent treatment of the period, see Glyndon G. Van Deusen, *The Jacksonian Era, 1828–1848,* The New American Nation Series, ed. Henry Steele Commager and Richard B. Morris (New York, 1959).

[2] Sellers, *Jacksonian Democracy,* I.

[3] For representative examples of this viewpoint, see Charles A. and Mary R. Beard, *The Rise of American Civilization* (new ed., 2 vols. in 1, New York,

in his colorful fashion gave expression to the common viewpoint when he asserted that "the roaring flood of the new democracy was . . . [by 1842] foaming perilously near the crest. . . ."[4] Schlesinger, with his allusion to the "immense popular vote"[5] received by Jackson in 1824, creates a similar image. The Old Hero's victory in 1828 has been hailed as the consequence of a "mighty democratic uprising."[6]

That a "new democracy, ignorant, impulsive, irrational"[7] entered the arena of politics in the Jackson era has become one of the few unchallenged "facts" in an otherwise controversial field. Differences of opinion occur only when attempts are made to account for the remarkable increase in the size of the active electorate. The commonest explanations have emphasized the assertion by the common man of his newly won political privileges, the democratic influences that arose out of the western frontier, or the magnetic attractiveness of Jackson as a candidate capable of appealing with singular effectiveness to the backwoods hunter, the plain farmer, the urban workingman, and the southern planter.

Probably because the image of a "mighty democratic uprising" has been so universally agreed upon, there has been virtually no effort made to describe precisely the dimensions of the "uprising." Inquiry into this aspect of Jacksonian democracy has been discouraged by a common misconception regarding voter behavior before 1824. As the authors of one of our most recent and best textbooks put it: "In the years from the beginning of the government to 1824, a period for which we have no reliable election statistics, only small numbers of citizens seemed to have bothered to go to the polls."[8] Actually, abundant data on pre-1824 elections

1933), 540, 546, 550; Wilfred E. Binkley, *American Political Parties: Their Natural History* (New York, 1943), 101, 108, 111, 115, 121; John D. Hicks, *The Federal Union* (2d ed., Cambridge, Mass., 1952), 351, 363–64; William MacDonald, *Jacksonian Democracy, 1829–1837* (New York, 1906), 3, 42, 311; Richard Hofstadter, *The American Political Tradition* (Vintage ed., New York, 1954), 50–52; John Bach McMasters, *A History of the People of the United States* (8 vols., New York, 1883–1913), V, 518; Marvin Meyers, *The Jacksonian Persuasion: Politics and Belief* (Stanford, Calif., 1957), 4, 11; E. E. Robinson, *The Evolution of American Political Parties* (New York, 1924), 101; E. H. Roseboom, *A History of Presidential Elections* (New York, 1957), 91; Arthur M. Schlesinger, Jr., *The Age of Jackson* (Boston, 1947), 12–15, 36.

[4] Beard, *American Civilization*, 550.

[5] Schlesinger, *Age of Jackson*, 36.

[6] Frederick A. Ogg, *The Reign of Andrew Jackson* (New Haven, Conn., 1919), 114.

[7] Roseboom, *Presidential Elections*, 91.

[8] Richard Hofstadter, William Miller, and Daniel Aaron, *The American Republic* (2 vols., New York, 1959), I, 391.

is available, and it indicates a far higher rate of voting than has been realized. Only by taking this data into consideration can voting behavior after 1824 be placed in proper perspective.

The question of whether there was indeed a "mighty democratic uprising" during the Jackson era is certainly crucial in any analysis of the political character of Jacksonian democracy. More broadly, however, we need to know the degree to which potential voters participated in elections before, during, and after the period of Jackson's presidency as well as the conditions that apparently influenced the rate of voting. Only when such factors have been analyzed can we arrive at firm conclusions with respect to the dimensions of the political changes that we associate with Jacksonian democracy. Obviously in studying voter participation we are dealing with but one aspect of a large problem, and the limitations imposed by such a restrictive focus should be apparent.

In measuring the magnitude of the vote in the Jackson elections it is hardly significant to use the total popular vote cast throughout the nation. A comparison of the total vote cast in 1812, for example, when in eight of the seventeen states electors were chosen by the legislature, with the vote in 1832, when every state except South Carolina chose its electors by popular vote, has limited meaning. Neither is it revealing to compare the total vote in 1824 with that in 1832 without taking into consideration the population increase during the interval. The shift from the legislative choice of electors to their election by popular vote, together with the steady popluation growth, obviously swelled the presidential vote. But the problem to be investigated is whether the Jackson elections brought voters to the polls in such enlarged or unprecedented proportions as to indicate that a "new democracy" had burst upon the political scene.

The most practicable method for measuring the degree to which voters participated in elections over a period of time is to relate the number of votes cast to the number of potential voters. Although there is no way of calculating precisely how many eligible voters there were in any state at a given time, the evidence at hand demonstrates that with the exception of Rhode Island, Virginia, and Louisiana the potential electorate after 1824 was roughly equivalent to the adult white male population.[9] A meaningful way of expres-

[9] The only states in which property qualifications were a factor in restricting voting in presidential elections after 1824 were Virginia and Rhode Island. New York did not completely abolish property qualifications until 1826, but the reform of 1821 had resulted in virtually free suffrage. In Louisiana, where voters were required to be taxpayers, the nature of the system of taxation operated to confine the suffrage to perhaps half of the adult white males. See

sing the rate of voter participation, then, is to state it in terms of the percentage of the adult white males actually voting. This index can be employed to measure the variations that occurred in voter participation over a period of time and in both national and state elections. Consequently a basis is provided for comparing the rate of voting in the Jackson elections with other presidential elections before and after his regime as well as with state elections.[10]

Using this approach it is possible, first of all, to ascertain whether or not voter participation rose markedly in the three presidential elections in which Jackson was a candidate. Did voter participation in these elections so far exceed the peak participation in the pre-1824 elections as to suggest that a mighty democratic uprising was taking place? The accompanying data (Table I) provides an answer to this basic question.[11]

Joseph G. Tregle, "Louisiana in the Age of Jackson: A Study in Ego Politics," doctoral dissertation, University of Pennsylvania, 1954, 105–108. To be perfectly accurate, estimates of the size of the potential electorate would have to take into account such factors as citizenship and residence requirements and, in certain states, the eligibility of Negro voters.

[10] After 1840 when the proportion of aliens in the population increased markedly and citizenship became an important requirement for voting, the adult-white-male index becomes less reliable. In order to calculate accurately the number of qualified voters in 1850, the alien adult white males would have to be deducted in those states where citizenship was a qualification for voting. Unfortunately, federal census data on aliens is not obtainable prior to 1890, except for the censuses of 1820 and 1830. In the latter year there were only 107,832 aliens out of a total population of nearly thirteen millions, a fraction so small as to be insignificant. But by 1850, according to one calculation, adult male aliens may have amounted to one-twelfth of the total voting population. J. D. B. De Bow, *Statistical View of the United States* (Washington, D. C., 1854), 50. In certain eastern states the proportion of aliens was higher than the national average. In New York, for example, 18.5 per cent of the total population in 1855 were aliens; the proportion in 1835 had been only 3.79 per cent. Franklin B. Hough, *Census of the State of New York for 1855* (Albany, 1857), xiv, xliii.

[11] The figures on voter participation have been computed from a compilation I have made of returns of state-wide elections covering twenty-five states over the period from 1800 to 1860. For the post-1836 years the returns may be consulted in the *Whig Almanacs* and *Tribune Almanacs* issued by Horace Greeley and, for presidential elections, in W. Dean Burnham's *Presidential Ballots, 1836–1892* (Baltimore, Md., 1955). For the period prior to 1836 the best general sources are the official manuals of certain states, the legislative journals, and the contemporary newspapers. For several states, among them Massachusetts, Connecticut, New Jersey, Maryland, Virginia, North Carolina, and Georgia, it is necessary to use the manuscript sources. The estimate of the adult white male population was computed for each decennial year from the federal census, and the figure for the particular election year was obtained by interpolation. I have computed for each gubernatorial and presidential election in the twenty-five states admitted to the Union by 1836 (exclusive of South Carolina) the percentage of adult white males voting.

In the 1824 election not a single one of the eighteen states in which the electors were chosen by popular vote attained the percentage of voter participation that had been reached before 1824.

TABLE I

Percentages of Adult White Males Voting in Elections

	Highest Known % AWM Voting before 1824		Presidential Elections					
State	Year	% AWM	1824	1828	1832	1836	1840	1844
Maine	1812g	62.0	18.9	42.7	66.2*	37.4	82.2	67.5
New Hampshire	1814g	80.8	16.8	76.5	74.2	38.2	86.4*	65.6
Vermont	1812g	79.9	—	55.8	50.0	52.5	74.0	65.7
Massachusetts	1812g	67.4	29.1	25.7	39.3	45.1	66.4	59.3
Rhode Island	1812g	49.4	12.4	18.0	22.4	24.1	33.2	39.8
Connecticut	1819l	54.4	14.9	27.1	45.9	52.3	75.7*	76.1
New York	1810g	41.5	—	70.4*	72.1	60.2	77.7	73.6
New Jersey	1808p	71.8	31.1	70.9	69.0	69.3	80.4*	81.6
Pennsylvania	1808g	71.5	19.6	56.6	52.7	53.1	77.4*	75.5
Delaware	1804g	81.9	—	—	67.0	69.4	82.8*	85.0
Maryland	1820l	69.0	53.7	76.2*	55.6	67.5	84.6	80.3
Virginia	1800p	25.9	11.5	27.6*	30.8	35.1	54.6	54.5
North Carolina	1823c	70.0#	42.2	56.8	31.7	52.9	83.1*	79.1
Georgia	1812c	62.3	—	35.9	33.0	64.9*	88.9	94.0
Kentucky	1820g	74.4	25.3	70.7	73.9	61.1	74.3	80.3*
Tennessee	1817g	80.0	26.8	49.8	28.8	55.2	89.6*	89.6
Louisiana	1812g	34.2	—	36.3*	24.4	19.2	39.4	44.7
Alabama	1819g	96.7	52.1	53.6	33.3	65.0	89.8	82.7
Mississippi	1823g	79.8	41.6	56.6	32.8	62.8	88.2*	89.7
Ohio	1822g	46.5	34.8	75.8*	73.8	75.5	84.5	83.6
Indiana	1822g	52.4	37.5	68.3*	61.8	70.1	86.0	84.9
Illinois	1822g	55.8	24.2	51.9	45.9	43.7	85.9*	76.3
Missouri	1820g	71.9	20.1	54.3	40.8	35.6	74.0*	74.7
Arkansas		—	—	—	—	35.0	86.4	68.8
Michigan		—	—	—	—	35.7	84.9	79.3
National Average			26.5	56.3	54.9	55.2	78.0	74.9

* Exceeded pre-1824 high
g Gubernatorial election
p Presidential election
\# Estimate based on incomplete returns
c Congressional election
l Election of legislature

Prior to that critical election, fifteen of those eighteen states had recorded votes in excess of 50 per cent of their adult white male population, but in 1824 only two states—Maryland and Alabama—exceeded this modest mark. The average rate of voter participation in the election was 26.5 per cent. This hardly fits the image of the "roaring flood of the new democracy . . . foaming perilously near the crest. . . ."

There would seem to be persuasive evidence that in 1828 the common man flocked to the polls in unprecedented numbers, for the proportion of adult white males voting soared to 56.3 per cent, more than double the 1824 figure. But this outpouring shrinks in magnitude when we observe that in only six of the twenty-two states involved were new highs in voter participation established. In three of these—Maryland, Virginia, and Louisiana—the recorded gain was inconsiderable, and in a fourth—New York—the bulk of the increase might be attributed to changes that had been made in suffrage qualifications as recently as 1821 and 1826. Six states went over the 70 per cent mark, whereas ten had bettered that performance before 1824. Instead of a "mighty democratic uprising" there was in 1828 a voter turnout that approached—but in only a few instances matched or exceeded—the maximum levels that had been attained before the Jackson era.

The advance that was registered in 1828 did not carry forward to 1832. Despite the fact that Jackson was probably at the peak of his personal popularity, that he was engaged in a campaign that was presumably to decide issues of great magnitude, and that in the opinion of some authorities a "well-developed two party system on a national scale" had been established,[12] there was a slight decline in voter participation. The average for the twenty-three states participating in the presidential contest was 54.9 per cent. In fifteen states a smaller percentage of the adult white males went to the polls in 1832 than in 1828. Only five states bettered their pre-1824 highs. Again the conclusion would be that it was essentially the pre-1824 electorate—diminished in most states and augmented in a few—that voted in 1832. Thus, after three Jackson elections, sixteen states had not achieved the proportions of voter participation that they had reached before 1824. The "new democracy" had not yet made its appearance.[13]

[12] Charles G. Sellers, Jr., *James K. Polk: Jacksonian, 1795–1843* (Princeton, N. J., 1957), 166. See also Meyers, *Jacksonian Persuasion*, 11.

[13] It may be suggested that it is invalid to compare voter participation in each state in the presidential contests of 1824, 1828, and 1832 with the highs, rather than the average participation in each state prior to 1824. The object of the comparison is to ascertain whether the Jackson elections brought voters to the polls in unprecedented numbers, as has so often been asserted. Moreover, it is hardly feasible to compare average participation in elections before and after 1824 in many states because of the changes that were made in the methods of electing governors and presidential electors or in certain instances

A comparison of the Jackson elections with earlier presidential contests is of some interest. Such comparisons have little validity before 1808 because few states choose electors by popular vote, and for certain of those states the complete returns are not available. In 1816 and 1820 there was so little opposition to Monroe that the voter interest was negligible. The most relevant elections, therefore, are those of 1808 and 1812. The accompanying table (Table II) gives the percentages of adult white males voting in 1808 and 1812 in those states for which full returns could be found, together with the comparable percentages for the elections of 1824 and 1828. In 1824 only one state—Ohio—surpassed the highs established in either 1808 or 1812. Four more joined this list in 1828—Virginia, Maryland, Pennsylvania, and New Hampshire—although the margin in the last case was so small as to be inconsequential. The most significant conclusion to be drawn from this admittedly limited and unrepresentative data is that in those states where there was a vigorous two-party contest in 1808 and 1812 the vote was relatively high. Consequently, where there was little or no contest in 1824 or 1828, the vote was low.

TABLE II

Percentages of Adult White Males Voting in Presidential Elections

State	1808	1812	1824	1828
Maine	Legis.	50.0	18.9	42.7
New Hampshire	62.1	75.4	16.8	76.5
Massachusetts	Legis.	51.4	29.1	25.7
Rhode Island	37.4	37.7	12.4	18.0
New Jersey	71.8	Legis.	31.1	70.9
Pennsylvania	34.7	45.5	19.6	56.6
Maryland	48.4	56.5	53.7	76.2
Virginia	17.7	17.8	11.5	27.6
Ohio	12.8	20.0	34.8	75.8

NOTE: No complete returns of the popular vote cast for electors in Kentucky or Tennessee in 1808 and 1812 and in North Carolina in 1808 could be located.

—because the state had only recently entered the Union. However, among those states in which average voter participation was obviously higher before 1824 than it was in the three Jackson elections were Alabama, Connecticut, Georgia, Massachusetts, Mississippi, New Hampshire (1809–1817), Pennsylvania, Rhode Island, Tennessee, and Vermont (1807–1815).

When an examination is made of voting in other than presidential elections prior to 1824, the inaccuracy of the impression that "only small numbers of citizens" went to the polls becomes apparent. Because of the almost automatic succession of the members of the "Virginia dynasty" and the early deterioration of the national two-party system that had seemed to be developing around 1800, presidential elections did not arouse voter interest as much as did those for governor, state legislators, or even members of Congress. In such elections at the state level the "common man" was stimulated by local factors to cast his vote, and he frequently responded in higher proportions than he did to the later stimulus provided by Jackson.

The average voter participation for all the states in 1828 was 56.3 per cent. Before 1824 fifteen of the twenty-two states had surpassed that percentage. Among other things, this means that the 1828 election failed to bring to the polls the proportion of the electorate that had voted on occasion in previous elections. There was, in other words, a high potential vote that was frequently realized in state elections but which did not materialize in presidential elections. The unsupported assumption that the common man was either apathetic or debarred from voting by suffrage barriers before 1824 is untenable in the light of this evidence.

In state after state (see Table I) gubernatorial elections attracted 70 per cent or more of the adult white males to the polls. Among the notable highs recorded were Delaware with 81.9 per cent in 1804, New Hampshire with 80.8 per cent in 1814, Tennessee with 80.0 per cent in 1817, Vermont with 79.9 per cent in 1812, Mississippi with 79.8 per cent in 1823, and Alabama with a highly improbable 96.7 per cent in its first gubernatorial contest in 1819. There is reason to believe that in some states, at least, the voter participation in the election of state legislators was even higher than in gubernatorial elections. Because of the virtual impossibility of securing county-by-county or district-by-district returns for such elections, this hypothesis is difficult to verify.

Down to this point the voter turnout in the Jackson elections has been compared with that in elections held prior to 1824. Now it becomes appropriate to inquire whether during the period 1824 through 1832 voters turned out in greater proportions for the three presidential contests than they did for the contemporary state elections. If, indeed, this "new democracy" bore some special relationship to Andrew Jackson or to his policies, it might be anticipated that interest in the elections in which he was the central figure would stimulate greater voter participation than gubernatorial contests, in which he was at most a remote factor.

Actually, the election returns show fairly conclusively that throughout the eight-year period the electorate continued to participate more extensively in state elections than in those involving the presidency. Between 1824 and 1832 there were fifty regular gubernatorial elections in the states that chose their electors by popular vote. In only sixteen of these fifty instances did the vote for President surpass the corresponding vote for governor. In Rhode Island, Delaware, Tennessee, Kentucky, Illinois, Mississippi, Missouri, and Georgia the vote for governor consistently exceeded that for President. Only in Connecticut was the reverse true.[14] Viewed from this perspective, too, the remarkable feature of the vote in the Jackson elections is not its immensity but rather its smallness.

Finally, the Jackson elections may be compared with subsequent presidential elections. Once Jackson had retired to the Hermitage, and figures of less dramatic proportions took up the contest for the presidency, did voter participation rise or fall? This question can be answered by observing the percentage of adult white males who voted in each state in the presidential elections of 1836 through 1844 (Table I). Voter participation in the 1836 election remained near the level that had been established in 1828 and 1832, with 55.2 per cent of the adult white males voting. Only five states registered percentages in excess of their pre-1824 highs. But in 1840 the "new democracy" made its appearance with explosive suddenness.

In a surge to the polls that has rarely, if ever been exceeded in any presidential election, four out of five (78.0 per cent) of the adult white males cast their votes for Harrison or Van Buren.[15] This new electorate was greater than that of the Jackson period by more than 40 per cent. In all but five states—Vermont, Massachusetts, Rhode Island, Kentucky, and Alabama—the peaks of voter participation reached before 1824 were passed. Fourteen of the twenty-five states involved set record highs for voting that were not to be broken throughout the remainder of the ante bellum

[14] These summary statements are based upon an analysis of the compilation referred to in footnote eleven.

[15] It can be calculated that the total of adult white males in the twenty-five states was 3,090,708. The total popular vote was 2,409,682. In the presidential election of 1896 the total vote approximated 80 per cent of the potential electorate. In 1940 and 1952 the comparable figures would be 63 per cent and 65 per cent respectively. These percentages have been calculated on the assumption that the potential electorate in 1896 included all adult male citizens and in 1940 and 1952 all adult citizens.

period. Now, at last, the common man—or at least the man who previously had not been sufficiently aroused to vote in presidential elections—cast his weight into the political balance. This "Tippecanoe democracy," if such a label is permissible, was of a different order of magnitude from the Jacksonian democracy. The elections in which Jackson figured brought to the polls only those men who were accustomed to voting in state or national elections, except in a very few states. The Tippecanoe canvass witnessed an extraordinary expansion of the size of the presidential electorate far beyond previous dimensions. It was in 1840, then, that the "roaring flood of the new democracy" reached its crest. And it engulfed the Jacksonians.

The flood receded only slightly in 1844, when 74.9 per cent of the estimated potential electorate went to the polls. Indeed, nine states attained their record highs for the period. In 1848 and 1852 there was a general downward trend in voter participation, followed by a modest upswing in 1856 and 1860. But the level of voter activity remained well above that of the Jackson elections. The conclusion to be drawn is that the "mighty democratic uprising" came after the period of Jackson's presidency.

Now that the quantitative dimensions of Jacksonian democracy as a political phenomenon have been delineated and brought into some appropriate perspective, certain questions still remain to be answered. Granted that the Jacksonian electorate—as revealed by the comparisons that have been set forth—was not really very large, how account for the fact that voter participation doubled between the elections of 1824 and 1828? It is true that the total vote soared from around 359,000 to 1,155,400 and that the percentage of voter participation more than doubled. Traditionally, students of the Jackson period have been impressed by this steep increase in voting and by way of explanation have identified the causal factors as the reduction of suffrage qualifications, the democratic influence of the West, or the personal magnetism of Jackson. The validity of each of these hypotheses needs to be reexamined.

In no one of the states in which electors were chosen by popular vote was any significant change made in suffrage qualifications between 1824 and 1828. Subsequently, severe restrictions were maintained in Rhode Island until 1842, when some liberalization was effected, and in Virginia down to 1850. In Louisiana, where the payment of a tax was a requirement, the character of the state tax system apparently operated to restrict the suffrage at least as late as 1845. Thus with the three exceptions noted, the elimination of suffrage barriers was hardly a factor in producing an enlarged electorate during the Jackson and post-Jackson periods. Furthermore, all but a few states had extended the privilege of voting either to all male taxpayers or to all adult male citizens by 1810. After Connecticut eliminated its property qualification in 1818, Massachusetts in 1821, and New York in 1821 and 1826, only Rhode Island, Virginia, and Louisiana were left on the list of "restrictionist" states.[16] Neither Jackson's victory nor the increased vote in 1828 can be attributed to the presence at the polls of a newly enfranchised mass of voters.

Similarly, it does not appear that the western states led the way in voter registration.[17] Prior to 1824, for example, Ohio, Indiana, and Illinois had never brought to the polls as much as 60 per cent of their adult white males. Most of the eastern states had surpassed that level by considerable margins. In the election of 1828 six states registered votes in excess of 70 per cent of their adult white male populations. They were in order of rank: New Hampshire, Maryland, Ohio, New Jersey, Kentucky, and New York. The six leaders in 1832 were: New Hampshire, Kentucky, Ohio, New York, New Jersey, and Delaware. It will be obvious that the West, however that region may be defined, was not leading the "mighty democratic uprising." Western influences, then, do not explain the increased vote in 1828.

There remains to be considered the factor of Jackson's popularity. Did Jackson, the popular hero, attract voters to the polls in unprecedented proportions? The comparisons that have already been made between the Jackson elections and other elections—state and national—before, during, and after his presidency would suggest a negative answer to the question. Granted that a majority of the voters in 1828 favored Jackson, it is not evident that his partisans stormed the polls any more enthusiastically than did the Adams men. Of the six highest states in voter participation in 1828,

16 There is no reliable study of suffrage qualifications, but the standard account is Kirk H. Porter, *A History of Suffrage in the United States* (Chicago, 1918). Porter erred in stating that New Jersey retained a property requirement until 1844; it was replaced in 1807 by taxpayer suffrage. See my *The History of Voting in New Jersey: A Study of the Development of Election Machinery, 1664–1911* (New Brunswick, N. J., 1953), 100. Porter's statement that a freehold property requirement existed in Tennessee under the 1796 constitution is based on a misreading of that document. Porter, *Suffrage*, 24, 80; Francis N. Thrope, *Federal and State Constitutions, Colonial Charters, and Other Organic Laws* (7 vols., Washington, D. C., 1909), VI, 3418.

17 See Table I.

three favored Adams and three were for Jackson, which could be interpreted to mean that the convinced Adams supporters turned out no less zealously for their man than did the ardent Jacksonians. When Van Buren replaced Jackson in 1836, the voting average increased slightly over 1832. And, as has been demonstrated, the real manifestation of the "new democracy" came not in 1828 but in 1840.

The most satisfactory explanation for the increase in voter participation between 1824 and 1828 is a simple and obvious one. During the long reign of the Virginia dynasty, interest in presidential elections dwindled. In 1816 and 1820 there had been no contest. The somewhat fortuitous termination of the Virginia succession in 1824 and the failure of the congressional caucus to solve the problem of leadership succession threw the choice of a President upon the electorate. But popular interest was dampened by the confusion of choice presented by the multiplicity of candidates, by the disintegration of the old national parties, by the fact that in most states one or another of the candidates was so overwhelmingly popular as to forestall any semblance of a contest, and possibly by the realization that the election would ultimately be decided by the House of Representatives. By 1828 the situation had altered. There were but two candidates in the field, each of whom had substantial sectional backing. A clear-cut contest impended, and the voters became sufficiently aroused to go to the polls in moderate numbers.

One final question remains. Why was the vote in the Jackson elections relatively low when compared with previous and contemporary state elections and with presidential votes after 1840? The answer, in brief, is that in most states either Jackson or his opponent had such a one-sided advantage that the result was a foregone conclusion. Consequently there was little incentive for the voters to go to the polls.

This factor can be evaluated in fairly specific quantitative terms. If the percentage of the total vote secured by each candidate in each state in the election of 1828 is calculated, the difference between the percentages can be used as an index of the closeness, or one-sidedness, of the contest. In Illinois, for example, Jackson received 67 per cent of the total vote and Adams, 33; the difference —thirty-four points—represents the margin between the candidates. The average difference between the candidates, taking all the states together, was thirty-six points. Expressed another way this would mean that in the average state the winning candidate received more than twice the vote of the loser. Actually, this was the case in thirteen of the twenty-two states (see Table III).[18] Such a wide margin virtually placed these states in the "no contest" category.

TABLE III

Differential between Percentages of Total Vote Obtained by Major Presidential Candidates, 1828–1844

State	1828	1832	1836	1840	1844
Maine	20	10	20	1	13
New Hampshire	7	13	50	11	19
Vermont	50	10	20	29	18
Massachusetts	66	30	9	16	12
Rhode Island	50	14	6	23	20
Connecticut	50	20	1	11	5
New York	2	4	9	4	1
New Jersey	4	1	1	4	1
Pennsylvania	33	16	4	1	2
Delaware	—	2	6	10	3
Maryland	2	1	7	8	5
Virginia	38	50	13	1	6
North Carolina	47	70	6	15	5
Georgia	94	100	4	12	4
Kentucky	1	9	6	29	8
Tennessee	90	90	16	11	1
Louisiana	6	38	3	19	3
Alabama	80	100	11	9	18
Mississippi	60	77	2	7	13
Ohio	3	3	4	9	2
Indiana	13	34	12	12	2
Illinois	34	37	10	2	12
Missouri	41	32	21	14	17
Arkansas	—	—	28	13	26
Michigan	—	—	9	4	6
Average Differential	36	36	11	11	9

A remarkably close correlation existed between the size of the voter turnout and the relative closeness of the contest. The six states previously listed as having the greatest voter participation in 1828 were among the seven states with the smallest margin of difference between the candidates. The exception was Louisiana, where restrictions on the suffrage curtailed the vote. Even in this

[18] The index figures in the table represent the difference between the percentages of the total popular vote secured by the two major candidates in each state. For the election of 1832, the figures represent only the difference between the votes obtained by Clay and Jackson.

instance, however, it is significant that voter participation in Louisiana reached a record high. In those states, then, where there was a close balance of political forces the vote was large, and conversely, where the contest was very one sided, the vote was low.

Most of the states in 1828 were so strongly partial to one or another of the candidates that they can be best characterized as one-party states. Adams encountered little opposition in New England, except in New Hampshire, and Jackson met with hardly any resistance in the South. It was chiefly in the middle states and the older West that the real battle was waged. With the removal of Adams from the scene after 1828, New England became less of a one-party section, but the South remained extremely one sided. Consequently it is not surprising that voter participation in 1832 failed even to match that of 1828.

Here, certainly, is a factor of crucial importance in explaining the dimensions of the voter turnout in the Jackson elections. National parties were still in a rudimentary condition and were highly unbalanced from state to state. Indeed, a two-party system scarcely could be said to exist in more than half of the states until after 1832. Where opposing parties had been formed to contest the election, the vote was large, but where no parties, or only one, took the field, the vote was low. By 1840, fairly well-balanced parties had been organized in virtually every state. In only three states did the margin between Harrison and Van Buren exceed twenty points, and the average for all the states was only eleven points. The result was generally high voter participation.[19]

When Jacksonian democracy is viewed from the perspectives employed in this analysis, its political dimensions in so far as they relate to the behavior of the electorate can be described with some precision. None of the Jackson elections involved a "mighty democratic uprising" in the sense that voters were drawn to the polls in unprecedented proportions. When compared with the peak participation recorded for each state before 1824, or with contemporaneous gubernatorial elections, or most particularly with the vast outpouring of the electorate in 1840, voter participation in

[19] Careful analysis of the data in Table III will suggest that there were three fairly distinct stages in the emergence of a nationally balanced two-party system. Balanced parties appeared first in the middle states between 1824 and 1828. New England remained essentially a one-party section until after Adams had passed from the scene; then competing parties appeared. In the South and the newer West, a one-party dominance continued until divisions arose over who should succeed Jackson. Sectional loyalties to favorite sons obviously exerted a determining influence on presidential politics, and consequently on party formation, in the Jackson years.

the Jackson elections was unimpressive. The key to the relatively low presidential vote would seem to be the extreme political imbalance that existed in most states as between the Jacksonians and their opponents. Associated with this imbalance was the immature development of national political parties. Indeed, it can be highly misleading to think in terms of national parties in connection with the Jackson elections. As balanced, organized parties subsequently made their appearance from state to state, and voters were stimulated by the prospect of a genuine contest, a marked rise in voter participation occurred. Such conditions did not prevail generally across the nation until 1840, and then at last the "mighty democratic uprising" took place.

6

PROBABLY no historian has more influenced the course of American historical writing than Frederick Jackson Turner. His essays on the influence of the frontier, which have been collected in his volume *The Frontier in American History* (1920), have spawned a small library of articles and books testing or supporting his views. Even in the 1960s, in a review of recent interpretations like John Higham's collection *The Reconstruction of American History* (London, 1962), no fewer than four of the essays found it necessary to relate their discussions to Turner's seminal ideas on the influence of the frontier on American social, economic, and political development. Among the several aspects of Turner's frontier hypothesis is the so-called "safety valve idea." Here is the way Turner phrased that idea in his essay "Contributions of the West to American Democracy" (1903):

> Most important of all has been the fact that an area of free land has continually lain on the western border of the settled area of the United States. Whenever social conditions tended to crystallize in the East, whenever capital tended to press upon labor or political restraints to impede the freedom of the mass, there was this gate of escape to the free conditions of the frontier. . . . Men would not accept inferior wages and a permanent position of social subordination when this promised land of freedom and equality was there for the taking.

In Turner's writings the safety valve idea received only passing reference; the above is one of the longest. Yet this aspect of his thought has been subjected to more analysis and criticism than any other. The principal reason, probably, is that it is the most precisely formulated of all Turner's speculations as well as the one most easily tested against empirical data. For more than a generation after Turner read his famous paper, the safety valve hypothesis was among the most widely accepted of his views. As Goodrich and Davison, at the close of their essay, admit, when they began their search for empirical verification of the hypothesis, they anticipated that a few weeks' work would be sufficient. Indeed, so widely accepted was the safety valve conception of the American frontier that Goodrich and Davison published a whole article "The Wage-Earner in the Westward Movement, I," *Political Science Quarterly*, L (June 1935), 161–185, delineating the history of the idea as an introduction to the article here reprinted.

The widespread acceptance of the safety valve hypothesis is not difficult to understand, for it seems to be almost self-evident. Everyone knew that much of the history of the United States was devoted to the settlement of the country and that this settlement was accomplished by the rapid movement of men and women into the empty lands. Did it not stand to reason that many urban workers would be a part of this movement, thereby escaping from the confines of the city, which in other, less favored lands tied them to the machines and factories of a rising industrial system?

While logic, though, has its place in history, the final test of any hypothesis is whether the logic is supported by the facts of the past. It was this test that Goodrich and Davison sought to apply. Their analysis assumed several steps. The first one was purely empirical. They examined the extant records of a well-known industrial town in the middle decades of the nineteenth century, Fall River, Massachusetts, for evidence of migration westward by industrial workers. When their search proved fruitless, they then turned to logic, which had been suggested to them by their historical evidence. They asked, was it realistic to expect urban workers to have sufficient wealth or income to undertake the costly movement to the West and the sustaining of life until farming could be gotten under way? Concluding that again the answer must be negative, they turned to a third approach. How successful were efforts to help penniless workers make the move to the free western lands? Here, too, their evidence failed to support the Turner hypothesis. As a final test, they turned to the West itself for evidence of a significant movement of workers out of the eastern cities.

As their analysis progresses, it should be noted that their definition of the problem narrows. At first they are looking for any signs of movement to the West on the part of industrial workers in the East. Then, as they turn to organized movements and studies of the western settlements, they emphasize the need to find large numbers of industrial workers who come from the big cities of the East.

This narrowing of the definition is demanded by the use to which the Turner hypothesis had been put. Usually it was used to explain the lack of class consciousness among American workers and the high wages which obtained in American industry. Only if numbers were large and derived from relatively big, industrial cities could the hypothesis explain what it was said to account for.

Hence, at the very close of their article, the authors are careful to notice that their evidence in no way affects the proposition that eastern workers may have migrated to western *cities,* or that the West may well have served as a safety valve for farmers, who otherwise would have flocked to eastern cities from their depleted farms in the East. In short, they admit that "there is nothing in the present study to cast doubt upon the doctrine that the growth of American industrialism was delayed and made difficult by the presence of the frontier alternative." In consequence, this article is a model of limiting to the immediate issue the conclusions to be drawn from a body of data and refraining from applying them to areas where applications are dubious or strained.

Perhaps more than anything else, this scrupulous refusal to leap beyond the evidence accounts for the rapid acceptance of the Goodrich-Davison conclusions. Soon after their publication, to be sure, there was a flurry of articles attempting to counter them. The principal opposing articles are Joseph Schafer's "Some Facts Bearing on the Safety-Valve," *Wisconsin Magazine of History,* XX (December 1936), 216–232, and "Was the West a Safety-Valve for Labor?" *Mississippi Valley Historical Review,* XXIV (December 1937), 299–314. But the weight of scholarship supported Goodrich and Davison. As they point out in a closing footnote, Fred A. Shannon's "The Homestead Act and the Labor Surplus," *American Historical Review,* XLI (July 1936), 637–651, arrived at their conclusion by a different path, but forsook their cautious approach to make the cities the safety valve of the country! A few years later, Clarence Danhof, in "Farm-making Costs and the 'Safety-Valve': 1850–1860," *Journal of Political Economy,* XLIX (June 1941), 317–359, picked up their cue about the high costs of farming and demonstrated the great difficulty of expecting urban workers to finance the move to the West. So completely has the narrowly conceived safety valve hypothesis been discarded by historians that when the editors of the distinguished Amherst Series of Problems in American Civilization published in 1956 a second edition of their volume dealing with the frontier thesis, they dropped the items relating to the safety valve.

In 1945 Fred Shannon, long an opponent of the safety valve

idea, which he considered a romantic approach to the westward movement in general, published "Post Mortem on the Labor-Safety-Valve Theory," *Agricultural History*, XIX (January 1945), 31–37. But the corpse has refused to stay in the grave. Several articles and even a book have been published since then, using some aspect of the safety valve hypothesis as an explanation for American economic development. Among these have been George G. S. Murphy and Arnold Zellner, "Sequential Growth, the Labor-Safety-Valve Doctrine and the Development of American Unionism," *Journal of Economic History*, XIX (September 1959), 402–421; Norman J. Simler, "The Safety-Valve Doctrine Re-evaluated," *Agricultural History*, XXXII (October 1958), 250–257; Ellen von Nardoff, "The American Frontier as a Safety-Valve—the Life, Death, Reincarnation and Justification of Theory," *Agricultural History*, XXXVI (July 1962), 123–142; and H. J. Habakkuk, *American and British Technology in the Nineteenth Century: The Search for Labour-Saving Inventions* (Cambridge, Eng., 1962).

The important point is that none of these studies really repudiates the work of Goodrich and Davison. Indeed, von Nardoff explicitly says it is absurd to talk anymore of industrial workers actually migrating to the West. Instead, these more recent studies now grapple with the qustions explicitly excluded from the Goodrich-Davison study, namely, the general effects of an empty frontier on wages, on the propensity to accept technological innovations, and on the resistance to unionization. This new approach is but another way of suggesting the completeness with which the Goodrich and Davison article shifted the direction of one aspect of American historical research. Probably no other piece of work has had such a sharp and lasting effect on the interpretation of one facet of the understanding of American economic and western history.

For many years Mr. Goodrich was professor of economics at Columbia University, from which he is now professor emeritus. Currently he is Andrew Mellon Professor of History and professor of economics at the University of Pittsburgh. Mr. Davison at the time he collaborated on this article was a graduate student at Columbia University; since then he has been a professional economist employed by labor organizations.

The Wage-Earner in the Westward Movement

BY CARTER GOODRICH AND SOL DAVISON

THE QUESTION AND THE SOURCES

AN EARLIER article has stated the question for investigation.[1] Accepted doctrines of the influence of the frontier in American history rest in part on the premise that substantial numbers of eastern wage-earners moved West and took up land. The frontier outlet is thus held to have served as a safety valve for industrial discontent. There was, moreover, a widespread belief in the reality of this movement long before Turner made it a part of his great synthesis. Edward Gibbon Wakefield erected a social theory on his disapproval of the process; Horace Greeley built one on its enthusiastic advocacy; and a long line of contemporary observers of varying opinions, from the earliest years of the Massachusetts Bay Colony to the last days of the frontier, recorded their belief that the movement was taking place. Yet in descriptions of the actual process of settlement there are very few references to the presence of former wage-earners among the pioneers. Here, it was suggested, is a significant discrepancy. If there was a substantial movement of industrial workers, it deserves fuller description than it has received. If not, the theories stand in need of modification.

The present paper, therefore, represents an attempt to discover

SOURCE: Reprinted with permission from *Political Science Quarterly,* LI:1 (March 1936).

[1] *Political Science Quarterly,* June 1935, pp. 161–185. As there indicated, the investigation was made possible by a grant from the Columbia University Council for Research in the Social Sciences. Interpretation and writing have been joint responsibilities, but it should be recorded that the collection of material has been almost entirely the work of the junior author. Use has been made of the libraries and collections of the historical societies of Wisconsin, Iowa, Minnesota, Montana, Nebraska, Kansas, Oregon, California, Missouri and New York, the public libraries of New York, Detroit, Boston, Lynn, Fall River, Portland (Ore.), and Tacoma, the Library of Congress, the Massachusetts State Library, the Columbia University Library, and the Meeker Memorial Museum of Greeley, Colorado. Special acknowledgment should be made of the courtesies extended by Messrs. T. C. Blegen and Arthur J. Larson of the Minnesota society, Mr. George Root of the Kansas society and Mr. A. B. Copeland of the Meeker Museum.

how much of a migration of wage-earners took place during the half-century or so in which there was at one end of the country a substantial factory population and at the other an actively advancing frontier. Since there are no comprehensive statistics available, it will be recognized that any estimates must be based on a sampling of the imperfect records surviving so long after the event. The two great sources that might have been thought serviceable, the Census and the records of the General Land Office, throw little light upon the precise question at issue. Though the former appears to approach it by giving both birthplace and occupation, it is clear that nativity does not show where the trade was first practised and that our problem cannot be solved without determining the relationship between the occupation at the time the count was taken and the previous occupation of the same individual. No direct use, therefore, can be made even of the manuscript Census; [2] and the records of applications and entries under the Homestead Act are even more disappointing. They contain no information as to occupations, unless casually mentioned in a character reference; and though the mailing address on the application might be thought of as a clue to previous residence, inspection indicates that the one usually given was not the old home but a place either on or near the homestead itself.[3]

Any attempt at an answer must, therefore, be built up from much more scattered and fragmentary sources of information. Of these, we have placed chief reliance on the files of contemporary newspapers. The press of the great cities and of the industrial centers gives clues to the kind of people who were leaving the East, and in these cases the impressions gained from the standard journals could often be checked against the views of a vigorous labor press. Again, the frontier papers frequently carried descriptions of the people who were arriving in the new country. State and county histories were a second resource, and a few of the more reliable

[2] At least short of the task of taking the names of individual wage-earners in a given Census and then searching for them in the haystacks of succeeding enumerations. Consider, for example, the problem of making use of the Census returns in a frontier state. The people in whom we are primarily interested will all be described there as farmers. But suppose there is the record of a "mechanic" born in Massachusetts. Even if we could be sure that he was a wage-earner rather than an independent artisan, there would still be no indication whether he had learned his trade in the state of birth or in the frontier state or in any one of a number of possible stopping places between. Of the latter there would, of course, be no record whatever unless, by chance, he had children born on the way.

[3] A collection of application forms from the various states which had large areas of public lands to dispose of indicates that the same limitations would apply to the use of their records also.

of these accounts provided information as to the origins of the settlers in certain western localities. There were cases in which hotel registers could be used to show where the migrants had come from, and others in which city directories could be used to trace the eastern occupations of people found in the West. Records of emigration societies throw considerable light on the status of the migrants who moved under their auspices. On occasion, also, memoirs and diaries and even the recollections of old settlers have been used as corroborative evidence.

In approaching so wide and heterogeneous a range of possible sources, it appeared both necessary and desirable to shorten the search by accepting certain limitations and by concentrating attention on particular times and places that were most likely to show evidence of the movement for which we were seeking. We have not believed that the early numbers of wage-earners were sufficiently large to require us to carry the inquiry back of the year 1830, and we have not in any case taken it further forward than the decade of the 1880's which Turner thought of as marking the end of the great frontier period. For obvious reasons, also, we have paid little attention to the Civil War years.

Within these broad limits, moreover, some further concentration seemed advisable. If the movement of workmen to the West was to be regarded as an escape from oppressive conditions, it might well be expected that the outlet would be sought most eagerly when wages were lowest and conditions the worst. Thus the logic of the safety-valve doctrine suggests that the movement would be particularly marked during industrial depressions, and the belief that migration was unusually active at such times finds frequent expression in contemparary writings and at least partial support in the statistics of land alienation. A pair of quotations from the depression of 1837 may serve to illustrate a point that was made no less frequently in later periods of distress. In May of that year a western paper records its anticipation of the movement:

> The troubles of the times are likely to increase the emigration westward this season. Besides mechanics and laborers, there are vast numbers who will seek in the rich regions of the West, to repair the ravages of the storm that has passed over them.[4]

Three years later the *New York Morning Herald* described the process as in full swing:

> The emigration from this city to the "Far West," is increasing tremendously. Whole squads of young men are preparing to emigrate in a few days to the fertile fields of the western states. . . . No wonder the rents and

[4] *Detroit Semi-Weekly Free Press,* May 5, 1837.

real estate fall in New York. There is a general movement in society, and where it will stop, the holy apostle Saint Peter, only knows.[5]

An attempt to check the validity of this supposition and these observations may be made by examining the relationship between the course of the business cycle and the sale and disposal of the Public Lands. On the opposite page, therefore, we present a chart on which are plotted three lines: an index number of wholesale prices as an indication of general business conditions, the acres of public land sold and—from 1863—the number of original homestead entries. The result of the comparison is an interesting one. In the earlier period, the amount of land disposed of tended to vary directly with wholesale prices. In the second period the opposite was the case and the number of homestead entries tended to vary inversely with the index of business conditions.[6]

It is the first of these results that seems to conflict with the hypothesis. If land sales fell during depressions, it would appear that the process of new settlement must then have been checked. But there is another possible explanation. It will be observed that public land sales reached their greatest heights just prior to the peaks in wholesale prices that preceded the depressions of 1837 and 1857. It is known that the lands in these periods were a great field of speculation and that, in each case, the breaking of the land bubble had much to do with the crash that followed. To a large extent, therefore, the figures measure speculation rather than occupation and it is quite possible that actual settlers found it easier to purchase the land in depressions than during the land booms. Thus the results for the first period do not necessarily conflict with the theory that the westward movement was intensified during depressions and the results for the second period seem definitely to confirm it. Apparently, then, we are justified in giving special, though by no means exclusive, attention to periods of depression.

A somewhat similar concentration of interests is possible with respect to the places of search. It is not hard to discover where most of the emigrants were going in any particular period. For a number of the western territories there are two dates that indicate when to look for great immigration. These are the times of the government survey and of the coming of the railroads. If we confine our principal attention to the North, people in the thirties thought mainly about going to Michigan and Illinois; in the forties, to Iowa and Wisconsin; in the fifties to Minnesota and eastern Kansas

5 April 23, 1840.

6 Hibbard makes the point for the first period in his *History of Public Land Policies* (New York, 1924), pp. 101–105.

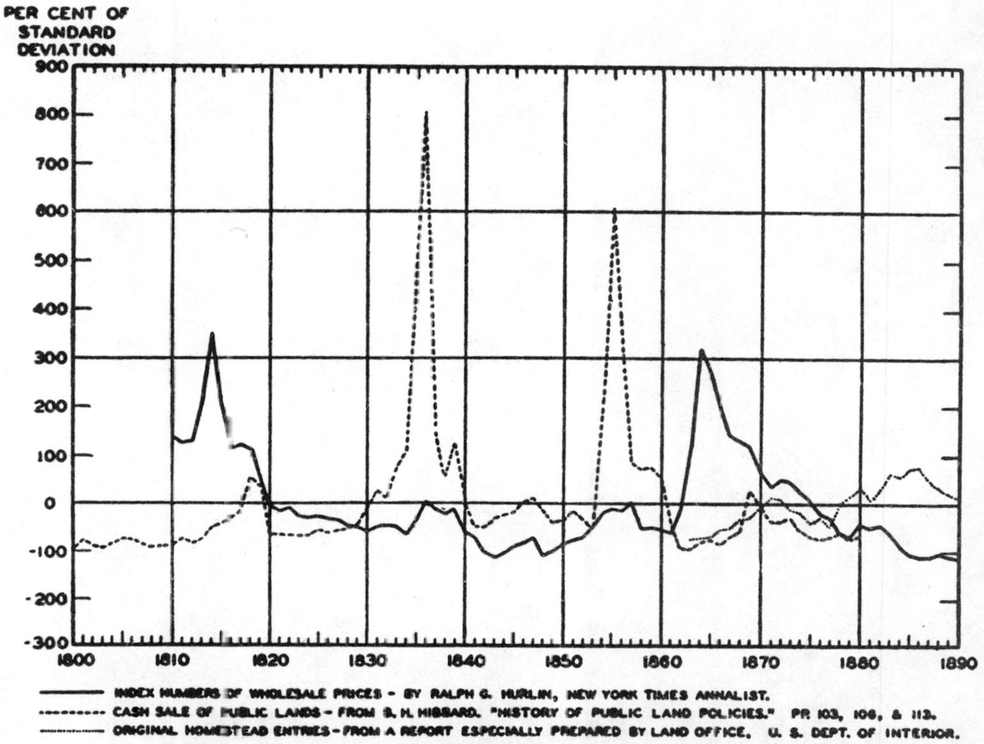

BUSINESS FLUCTUATIONS AND THE DISPOSAL OF PUBLIC LANDS

and Nebraska; and in the seventies to western Kansas, Nebraska and the Dakotas.[7] In examining the western material, therefore, this has made it possible to look into specific regions at specified dates. For the eastern material there was, of course, still more obvious reason for concentration upon the industrial regions.

No doubt the results would have been more satisfactory if our resources had made it possible to give an equally thorough examination to all periods and all parts of the frontier, but the selections made were those that appeared most likely to develop the evidence of working-class migration. To the extent, therefore, that these choices introduce an element of bias, it would appear to be in the direction of overestimating rather than of underestimating the relative importance of the wage-earners' share in the westward movement.

THE CASE OF FALL RIVER

In presenting the results of the investigation, it seems natural to begin with the evidence collected in those eastern centers from which the movement was presumed to start. At the beginning of our period there were few concentrations of wage-earners outside the great cities and a number of specialized manufacturing towns situated largely in New England. Among the latter we chose Fall River, Massachusetts, for special study because of the abundance of material. We found there a complete file of newspapers beginning at 1826 including for a short time a labor paper as well. The public library also possesses city directories for a good part of the period and these proved valuable in checking occupations.

The visitor to Fall River today finds what he may believe is visible proof of the migration of wage-earners. Standing adjacent to the City Hall on Main Street is a monument with a water fountain. On it is the following inscription:

PRESENTED
TO THE CITIZENS AND
MILL OPERATIVES
BY
HENRY D. COGSWELL, D.D.S.
OF SAN FRANCISCO
WHO IN 1833 AS A
FACTORY BOY MARCHED TO
THE MUSIC OF THE BELL

[7] We have determined these dates by what seemed to us to be the popular interest in the newspapers. Differing in some cases, and showing the movement more accurately, because based on Census records, are the maps in Thornthwaite and Slentz, *Internal Migration in the United States* (Bulletin No. I of the Study of Population Redistribution), (Philadelphia, 1934), Plates I and II.

Here indeed is the story of a wage-earner who made good in the West.

The first mention of westward migration discovered in the Fall River press speaks of a plan for a number of men from Pawtucket to settle in Illinois. Though the writer is himself hostile to the proposal, the way in which he relates migration to the spirit of discontent and the state of the cotton industry suggests that he is entirely familiar with the safety-valve doctrine:

> Emigration.—Several persons in Pawtucket, have associated themselves for the purpose of raising a company of one hundred able bodied men to make a settlement in Illinois. Is it the spirit of enterprise or the demoniacal spirit of discontent which renders our population so restless? One would think that Pawtucket offered as strong inducements, and as great facilities for industry as any place on the continent. . . . There is no doubt that the cotton manufacture on which Pawtucket chiefly depends, will, tariff or no tariff, go on to prosper. It is at this moment, the most profitable and safest business in the country; and it will continue to be profitable and safe, long after the prairie grass shall have grown over the heads of the emigrants. But if they must needs go, let success go with them. . . .[8]

The tantalizing thing is that we do not know whether these "hundred able bodied men" were wage-earners or whether or not they actually migrated. A similar item appeared the following month:

> A company is forming in Worcester county to establish a colony in the Valley of the Mississippi.[9]

Again there is no direct evidence of the character of the migration but it may be imagined that a Worcester county company was more likely than a Pawtucket one to be composed of farmers.

The first indication of a participation of Fall River people in the western migration appears, strangely enough, in a notice taken by the local paper from the *Pawtucket Chronicle:*

> Land Company—We notice in the Pawtucket Chronicle the articles of agreement entered into by a company of gentlemen in this town and vicinity, called the Fall River Western Land Company. The object of this company as we understand it, is to purchase a tract of land at the West, on which to settle—to divide the land into farms for individual purchasers, reserving a portion of it for a village or town. A committee, we learn, is to proceed to the Great Valley in the spring to select a suitable spot and purchase the land. The company, so far as we know its members, is composed of industrious and enterprising young men of this place, whose society we should regret to lose, but for whose prosperity and happiness whether here or elsewhere, we most heartily wish.[10]

[8] *Fall River Monitor,* August 7, 1830.
[9] *Ibid.,* September 25, 1830.
[10] *Ibid.,* February 11, 1837.

This seems to point to a group of similar character to the one formed in Pawtucket. But any doubt as to its composition is quickly dispelled by the following notice:

> The Fall River Western Land Company had a meeting on Monday last, when $13,000 was paid in for the purchase of land in the West. A committee is now traversing the Western country to select and purchase land for this company. The company is composed of a number of enterprising gentlemen, whom we shall regret to lose, but doubt not, they will make a profitable investment of their money.[11]

One could hardly expect a group of Fall River wage-earners, whose earnings were generally much less than $1.00 per day, to band together in sufficient numbers to raise $13,000.

For the next twenty years there is but scattered mention of direct migration from Fall River though there are frequent general references to the process of settlement. Often these appear as reprints from New York and Boston papers and occasionally from a western paper. Sometimes an item showed the demand for labor in the West:

> Laborers and Mechanics Wanted West.—Two hundred laborers are wanted within 12 miles of Michigan City (Indiana) to work on grading the track of the railroad. Also 100 carpenters are wanted at the beautiful and healthy town of Washington, at the mouth of the Sac River, Wisconsin Territory.[12]

Sometimes advertisements of western lands appeared, offering liberal terms and aid to settlers. Here, for example, is the appeal of the American Land Agency Association:

> To Persons removing to the West, this Association offers the greatest facilities for making a judicious selection of a location and property, adapted to their wants and circumstances; *because* we keep in all our offices a Register of Lands and Farms for sale, with a description of the improvements, surrounding circumstances and the price; and freely communicate to all inquirers information concerning the Soil, Climate, Productions, Roads, Population, Schools, and Religious Societies, and especially concerning the validity of the Title of any Property they be disposed to purchase. . . .[13]

There is, however, little to indicate whether or not these invitations were accepted.

The discovery of gold in California caused as much excitement in Fall River as it did everywhere else in the country. Many who had the means started out by boat to Panama or around the Horn or by wagons across the plains. The papers published the names of some of those who left. Unfortunately the city directory was not

[11] *Ibid.*, April 22, 1837.
[12] *Ibid.*, July 29, 1837.
[13] Advertisement in the *Fall River Monitor*, November 9, 1844.

printed at that time so it is impossible to determine their occupation; but where the news stories themselves provide the clues, the migrants were not wage-earners but prominent business and professional men.[14]

A railroad consolidation brought unemployment to Fall River in the fifties:

> Among the changes consequent upon the union of the Old Colony and Fall River Railroads, we learn that the machine and repair shops of the road, at Fall River, will be discontinued, and the works are to be removed to South Boston, and joined to those of the Old Colony, now in operation on Dorchester Avenue. The number of hands which this change will throw out of employment here, is somewhere about twenty. Two of them, we understand, intend to go to Kansas.[15]

A later section will indicate why it was of Kansas that they thought. The present point is that two of the twenty workers definitely looked to the West to relieve their economic distress. A little later a notice appears of some people who were planning to leave Fall River, but nothing is told to let us know whether they are wage-earners or not:

> The Western fever appears to have broken out again of late, and we hear of parties going from various places in New England to seek homes in the Far West. Quite a number of our citizens have recently removed to that section of the country, some to Illinois, some to Iowa, and some to Minnesota and Nebraska. Others are preparing to follow them soon. On Tuesday afternoon, in the Baptist Temple, Rev. A. Bronson delivered a solemn, affectionate address to a party (members of his church and congregation) who were about leaving for the West. . . .[16]

After the Civil War, there is constant mention of people leaving for the West. The two following items appeared in 1869.

> Mr. Frank McGraw, who lately left this city for Minnesota, in a recent letter to a friend here, expresses great satisfaction with his new home at Sauk Centre. He is now building a farm house, has 100 acres of timber and meadow land, 60 acres of Prairie, and 5 acres already under the plow.

> We have now received from Mr. E. F. Anthony a copy of Sauk Centre (Minnesota) Herald of Nov. 18th, from which we clip the following:
> "The family of E. F. Anthony arrived on Sunday evening from Fall River, Mass., accompanied by E. B. Anthony and wife, of the same place, Mr. James Brett of New Bedford, Mass., and Mr. A. B. Stinchfield of Lewiston, Me. Mr. E. B. Anthony and Mr. James Brett are interested in locating here. . . ."[17]

[14] See below, pp. 81–83, for somewhat more satisfactory information concerning the Lowell and Boston participants in the Gold Rush.
[15] *Fall River News,* October 12, 1854.
[16] *Ibid.,* April 26, 1855.
[17] *Fall River Daily Evening News,* November 25, 1869.

The Fall River directory for 1869 tells us that Frank McGraw was a bootmaker, E. F. Anthony a clerk, and E. B. Anthony a carpenter. This would seem to show that three wage-earners left Fall River for Minnesota. But, unfortunately, two items, one in 1870 and the other in 1871, seem to make their migration ineffective:

> Personal.—Mr. Enoch Anthony, who went from this city to Sauk Centre, Minnesota, last fall, with the intention of settling there, returned on Saturday evening, being unable to find employment.[18]
>
> Personal.—Mr. Frank McGraw, who left this city for Minnesota, some two years ago, has returned with his family once more to take up his abode in our city of spindles. He has seen the Western elephant—had his head in its mouth—and returns abundantly satisfied with his experiences. We are glad to learn that his health has been greatly improved by his sojourn in Minnesota.[19]

Thus, two out of three who went from Fall River returned again.

In 1870 the following item appeared:

> Personal.—Messrs. Henry Thomas and S. B. Chase, late clerks at the Merchants' Mill, George Holden, recently of the Day Police, Levi Greenwood and Edwin P. Elsree, all of this city, start to-night for the Far West, with a view, should matters seem favorable, of settling in that section of our country. Messrs. Thomas and Chase will probably proceed as far as Nebraska; Messrs. Holden and Greenwood turn their steps toward the healthy and growing State of Minnesota, while Mr. Elsree, having a roving commission, will probably make his *base* on the most advantageous portion of the field, and catch his claims "on the fly". We wish them all health and happiness, and just as much of this world's wealth as they can make use of.[20]

Fortunately, later issues enable us to trace all but one individual of this group. The first case is a success story, as the following items indicate:

> Personal.—Messrs. Henry Thomas and S. P. Chase, late clerks at the Merchants' Mill of this city, write home from Plattsmouth, Nebraska in glowing terms of the growth and prosperity of that locality. The Nebraska *Herald*, published at Plattsmouth, gives the young men the following friendly notice:
>
> 'Mr. Henry Thomas and Mr. S. P. Chase, of Fall River, Mass., arrived in our city last week with a view to establish themselves here. They were connected with the Merchants Manufacturing Company, and come well recommended to business men. We hope they will be able to suit themselves here, as they are the style of men we like to see commence business in our city."[21]
>
> Personal.—The Nebraska Herald of the date of July 18th, published at

[18] *Ibid.*, January 10, 1870.
[19] *Ibid.*, December 12, 1871.
[20] *Ibid.*, May 2, 1870.
[21] *Ibid.*, May 20, 1870.

Plattsmouth, contains the following notice of our young friends, Messrs. S. B. Chase and Henry Thomas, late clerks at the Merchants' Mill in this city.

"We would call attention to the advertisement of Chase & Thomas, commission merchants and dealers in grain. They have only been in our city a few months, but in that short time they have established a reputation for straightforward dealing that they may feel proud of. We learn that they intend making quite a specialty of selling grain on commission, thus giving the farmer the benefit of the market. They will advance money on consignment."[22]

If Messrs. Thomas and Chase succeeded, we find their success balanced by the failure of Holden and Elsree. Shortly afterwards, the ballplayer is back in Fall River:

Mr. Edwin P. Elsree the well known baseballer and bill poster who went out West on a "Fly" a few weeks ago, returned to his "home base" this morning. We are not "posted" as to the reasons for his return.[23]

A few years later, Mr. Holden of the Day Police also returns:

Personal.—Mr. George Holden, formerly of the police force of this city, and Mr. Joseph Borden, son of Dean Borden, both arrived here yesterday with their families, from Minnesota. Mr. Holden has been absent about four years, and Mr. Borden a somewhat longer period, we believe. Both have come back, we understand, with the intention of remaining East.[24]

Somewhat similar stories are found in the Fall River papers concerning the emigration from other New England communities of men who were either definitely or presumably wage-earners. Again, they appear in the news because they failed and returned home:

Several Wareham laborers who went West in search of employment have returned, wiser but sadder and poorer men.[25]

As is usual in the settlement of new regions, the emigrants to the Black Hills find it a hard road to travel. Of the party of twenty-three young men from New Haven, twenty have returned, some being compelled to travel the distance from Deadwood City on foot. By this time they ought to be expert pedestrians, and their experiences may deter future foolish romancers from trying a new rough country without capital, courage or that practical knowledge so necessary in fighting nature in her wild condition.[26]

Of the considerable group of migrants referred to in these items, a significant number of the wage-earners returned. On the other hand, in a contrast that may well have been typical, a story of success is told of two men who had money enough to open a busi-

[22] *Ibid.*, August 4, 1870.
[23] *Ibid.*, June 6, 1870.
[24] *Ibid.*, April 18, 1874.
[25] *Ibid.*, May 8, 1876.
[26] *Ibid.*, August 15, 1877.

ness and apparently the benefit of previous commercial experience.

A brief but significant notice appears in 1871:

> Chicago-Colorado Colony.—Mr. C. N. Pratt, agent of the Chicago-Colorado Land Company, will lecture at the Hall of the Y. M. C. Association this evening. An admission fee of ten cents will be charged to defray expenses.[27]

Fortunately the records of this colony have been preserved and published.[28] From them we learn that a number of Fall River people had joined the organization even before the occasion of Mr. Pratt's lecture. In the list of members that paid the first five dollar installment of a $155 fee are thirty names from Fall River; and the city directory indicates that most of these people were employees in the textile mills, though a few merchants and independent artisans were also included. This does not mean, however, that all of them succeeded in raising the rest of the money or persevered in the intention to move to Colorado. From the published extracts from the account books, it appears that only thirteen of the thirty either made further payment on their fees or actually arrived at the new settlement. In any case, the city directory shows that twenty of the original thirty, including no less than ten of the thirteen who really went, were again living in Fall River in 1878. A later section will discuss this sort of organized migration in some detail. Here it is essential merely to note that, though this is the largest movement to the frontier that we have found among the wage-earners of Fall River, yet only three men can be accounted for as having definitely remained in the West.

By contrast, the items regarding the migration of business and professional men have a very different ring, as the following examples indicate:

> Personal.—Milton Andros, Esq., formerly of this city, but for the last ten years a resident of San Francisco, where he is engaged in the successful practice of law, arrived here yesterday morning on a brief visit. Mr. Andros went to California some ten years ago for his health, with the intention of remaining there but a few months, but he liked the country and its climate so well that he concluded to make the land his permanent home.[29]
>
> Personal.—We are informed that Mr. J. Alsopp, late of the firm of Mather and Alsopp, will leave to-morrow for California.[30]
>
> Personal. We had a pleasant call this morning from Mr. A. N. Dix, formerly resident of this city, where he was well known as a wide awake

[27] *Ibid.*, March 16, 1871.

[28] *Experiments in Colorado Colonization*, edited by J. F. Willard and C. B. Goodykoontz, University of Colorado Historical Collection, vol. 3 (Boulder, 1926).

[29] *Fall River Daily Evening News*, July 19, 1875.

[30] *Ibid.*, April 10, 1874.

and popular clothing dealer. Mr. Dix has been residing for the last 18 years in Iowa.[31]

A later item tells us that Mr. Dix is engaged in the grocery business in Iowa.[32]

It would be possible to add many similar references but it is not with these classes that we are primarily concerned. On the other hand, we have presented every case between 1830 and 1880 in which wage-earners or those who might have been wage-earners are mentioned. It is, of course, entirely possible that poor and unknown mill workers might not have been considered worth mentioning so that their removal would have gone unnoticed. Such was the case of those who went to Colorado. Yet it seems unlikely that any important mass movement could have taken place without attracting some notice in the press. In particular we might expect that, if workers had withdrawn in sufficient numbers to have a marked effect upon the labor supply, some comment would have been made upon the fact in the discussion of labor controversies.

Here again Fall River provides a considerable body of evidence for testing the hypothesis. The town had a turbulent industrial history, with strikes every decade, and these received extended comment from diverse points of view. The *News* was friendly to the workers in the years preceding the Civil War, and a labor paper, *The Fall River Mechanic*, was published in 1844 and 1845. At the end of our period, moreover, Carroll D. Wright, then head of the Massachusetts Bureau of Labor Statistics, published an extensive report dealing with industrial relations in Fall River, Lowell and Lawrence. Yet neither these sources nor the more ordinary papers found any occasion for referring to the effects of the westward movement. A great variety of prescriptions were suggested for the ills of the workers but migration to the West does not appear among them. The nearest approach to it is a timid suggestion that farms in the vicinity might give employment to those thrown out of work by the depression of 1857. The *News* points out that the farmers might thus "relieve the city of at least five hundred of the unemployed, and by setting them to work in various ways, not only prevent much suffering and distress, but with actual and more equal benefit for themselves." [33] There was, however, no suggestion that the workers should go West and become farmers themselves.

A more typical article, which the *News* quoted with approval

[31] *Ibid.*, November 4, 1874.
[32] *Ibid.*, November 9, 1874.
[33] *Fall River News,* November 12, 1857.

from the *Worcester Palladium*, debates the issue between the appeal to the government for higher tariffs and the appeal to the employers for more enlightened policy:

The Whig manufacturers have revived the old game of cutting down the wages of the operative. The year of the Presidential election is always a terrible time with manufacturers, and with the cutting down of their wages the operatives have to take a substantial share of Whig admonition upon the subject of *political duty*. A paper in their employ sums it up homily thus:

"The long and short of the whole matter is, our government must protect our laborers, or they must make a government that will do it."

The *Palladium* continues by declaring that: "There is not, or rather, there ought not to be, the slightest necessity for cutting down the wages of the operatives in manufacturing establishments." Though business has its "ups and downs"; "a wise and prudent forecast, if exercised, would be always prepared." The employers, however, did not think of laying aside "a portion of their profits for a day like this"; instead they have in good years

not only made dividends from 10 to 25 per cent on their capital, but have expended all their surplus funds in extending and enlarging old establishments, and in erecting new ones. Avaricious, they have grasped all the profits, when they were enormous; and now they ought to be generous and share with their operatives the little burthens which a temporary pressure upon their business may impose.

As for the operatives, the moral is drawn that they "must look to their employers for a little more wisdom and prudence in their management, rather than to the government, for an improvement in their conditions." [34]

The labor paper, naturally, offers very different recommendations. If wages were lowered, the remedy was to strike. If the workers lost, as they often did, the thing to do was to go back to work and prepare for the next "campaign." The attitude is typified in a letter written to the labor paper after the loss of the ten-hour strike:

Perhaps some of your Association whose temperament is ardent, may feel discouraged because they have not gained their point before this time. What war ended in one campaign? Year after year they enter the battle field ere they win the laurels of victory. Are the mechanics of Fall River to expect victory without conflict? If they do, they have mistaken the character of the power, and the cunning of their opponents. One thing has been done, if nothing more, a faithful protest against oppression has been made. Some advantages have been obtained. Every artisan, if he knew his rights, would

[34] *The Worcester Palladium,* as quoted by the *Fall River News,* February 17, 1848.

nail the ten hour flag to the mast and not permit it to be taken away, until these hours were established as the hours of labor. Another advantage has been gained, the light has been shed abroad and those tools of the employers and those recreant to their pledges, *the long hour men* will feel the galling yoke of bondage which they have submitted to wear for a few cents. . . .

It strikes me that the influx of mechanics brought to this place through bribery, or misrepresentation, is another difficulty in the way of your success. There is nothing manly in these men who remain and labor long hours after they see what the mechanic has to contend with. They came to this town like a company of soldiers, to put down white niggers. Shame be to them! Without them the employers could not subdue us! When they leave town this fall, I would advise them to march to the steamboat headed by the Algerine deacon with the black flag, with the following motto upon it, "We, the long hour men, have crushed the ten hour system in Fall River." A drum and fife ought to lead the way, playing the dead march. If the ten hour system fails, it may be attributed chiefly to those mechanics who have come to this town and work long hours.[35]

Neither in this nor in other cases does the labor press refer to the possibility of movement to the West either as a threat to the employers or as a danger to the permanence of the trade unions. Men who spoke of themselves as "white niggers" did not seem to be writing like people with alternatives.

Carroll Wright's report is in large measure devoted to explaining the existence of this spirit. In trying to determine why the labor movement in Fall River was more violent than those of Lawrence and Lowell, he traced the industrial history of the three communities. He spoke of the differences in the kinds and qualities of the goods produced. He contrasted the degree of interest which the owners took in actual management in the three cases. He mentioned also the fact that some people in Fall River complained that foreigners were responsible for all their troubles; English weavers, they said, had come over with their strange notions of trade unionism and corrupted the native labor supply. But nowhere does Mr. Wright himself, nor anyone who was interviewed in the course of the investigation, speak of the presence or absence of westward migration as affecting the supply of labor or as accounting for these contrasts in industrial relations.

Whatever may be concealed in the gaps of the record, the available material from Fall River fails to disclose evidence of an extensive migration of wage-earners to the frontier. The little movement that can be traced, moreover, shows a somewhat unexpected result. If we include the "clerks at the Merchants' Mill" and other doubtful

[35] *The Fall River Mechanic,* June 29, 1844.

cases, we have the record of twenty men who might have been wage-earners and who went West in the period after the Civil War. Of these, at least fourteen returned like the "baseballer" to their "base" in Fall River. The grateful dentist succeeded, but of these others who also "marched to the music of the [factory] bell," seven out of ten appeared to have failed.

OTHER EVIDENCE FROM THE EAST

The material from other eastern cities is scantier than that presented from Fall River but is in general of much the same tenor. Even for Lowell, Massachusetts, the show town of the American industrial revolution so often described by contemporary visitors, both the newspapers and other accounts yield mainly negative evidence. When the *Lowell Mercury* in 1832 had occasion to compare conditions of mill workers in the United States and England, and praised the relative freedom of the American, it explained the difference not by the existence of an economic alternative but by the fact that the "workingmen, the mechanics can decide by their vote every question in town meeting." [36] There is, however, one item from the *Working Man's Advocate* which appears at first sight to give evidence both of the "escape" of wage-earners and of the resulting effect upon conditions in the mills:

> Raising of Wages—It will doubtless be recollected by most of our readers, that last March the wages of the Female Operatives in the factories at Lowell were reduced from 15 to 25 per cent. The consequence was that a large number of the old, experienced help left, and the owners were obliged to fill up their mill with raw hands from the country, many of whom had never seen a Cotton Mill before. All this was done during the "distressing times" last winter, when the stockholders of these monopolies were making a clear profit on the investment, of TWELVE per cent.
>
> We have been informed by a gentleman who resides in Lowell, that the owners have learned by trying the "experiment", the difference between old, experienced operatives and raw hands, and for the purpose of drawing them back have raised their wages up to the old standard.—(N. E. Art.) [37]

The last sentence suggests that these "female operatives" could not have gone very far away, and the question where they did go is in all probability answered by the fuller report of a later incident:

> Correspondence to the Tribune
> Lowell, Massachusetts, April 26.
>
> Messrs. Greeley & McElrath:
>
> The Directors of the Suffolk Cotton Mills in this city have decided to stop making cloth at the present ruinous prices, and have to-day given

[36] *Lowell Mercury,* March 20, 1832.
[37] *Working Man's Advocate,* October 11, 1834.

notice to 500 persons employed by the company that the services of one half their number must be forthwith dispensed with. It is stated, on good authority, that a similar disposition will be made of those employed by the "Boott", "Tremont", and "Massachusetts" Cotton Mills, which corporations employ 500 persons and represent a capital of $3,500,000. . . .

The stopping of so many mills will have a serious effect upon the business community and upon the dividends of such as are unfortunate enough to own stock in them, but there will be no suffering, no crime, no riots on the part of the discharged operatives. The females, a large part of whom are daughters of New England farmers, will quietly return to their country homes, and the men will seek employment elsewhere, some as farmers in New England; some will go West, and others will follow their numerous friends who have preceded them in California.[38]

If the women went home, there is nevertheless an indication that some of the men went West, at least in the California Gold Rush. During this time the Lowell papers, like those of Fall River, often give the names of the local emigrants but usually without indicating their occupations. One item describes a party which clearly contained no wage-earners:

The Magnolia . . . takes with her a full cargo of merchandise assigned to Messrs. Simmons, Hutchinson & Co., a house established at San Francisco for extensive brokerage and commission business by Capt. Simmons and Mr. Hutchinson. . . . The party is not a party of gold hunters; probably none of them will go to the diggings. Capt. Simmons is the owner of a large tract in and near the city of San Francisco, purchased on a former visit to that country. Dr. White has gone out to practice his profession of medicine, and Mr. Billings to establish himself in the practice of law in which he has been bred.[39]

An item reprinted in a western paper does give grim evidence that one employee of a Lowell mill did reach the mines:

Execution of a Lowell Immigrant in California.—We hear that accounts were received by the last mail from California of a lynching at the mines, in which Mr. Jonathan Pillsbury formerly employed by the Massachusetts and Appleton Corporation, in this city, and two others lost their lives. The three were charged with having murdered and robbed a man, and were summarily hung. Mr. P. was on the point of taking the steamer at San Francisco for home, when an officer arrested him, and took him back to the mines. . . (*Lowell Courier*).[40]

During this time it was "quite impossible," as a Lowell paper remarked, "to keep run of every company or association contemplating an expedition to the Pacific Coast. Every seaport and almost every city and town in New England, is sending out large num-

[38] *New York Tribune*, April 29, 1850.
[39] *Lowell Journal and Courier*, January 22, 1849.
[40] *Northwestern Gazette*, Galena, Ill., August 22, 1852.

bers."[41] It is, of course, harder to "keep run" of them today. A number of scattered bits of evidence, however, give indication of the variety of people who set out. A characateristic item refers to a Holyoke group which required $500 from each of its members. "The young men comprising the company," it is noted, "are of the first respectability and full of life and vigor."[42]

More comprehensive evidence on the composition of these companies is given in Octavius Thorndike Howe's *Argonauts of '49.* In one case he finds it possible to cite figures:

> The first vessel to sail from Boston with a regularly organized company was the ship *Edward Everett,* carrying the Boston and California Joint Stock Mining and Trading Company. About the middle of December, 1848, a number of young men met in a room in Exchange Street, Boston, and organized a company for the Gold Coast, with Henry Smith, of Boston as captain and president. They limited their number to one hundred and fifty and in a short time their ranks were full. The company was the best organized and most representative of any that left Massachusetts during the gold excitement. It consisted of one clergyman, four doctors, eight whaling captains, a mineralogist, a geologist, fifteen professional men, including medical and divinity students, a number of merchants, farmers, manufacturers, and seventy-six mechanics.[43]

Another passage describes the Bunker Hill Company which bought the ship *Paulina* "for four thousand dollars, fitted her up and provisioned her for eighteen months. They were mostly mechanics but not without means as their capital stock of fifteen thousand dollars was all paid in."[44]

These scattered items indicate that a considerable number of mechanics left New England for California during the Gold Rush. Yet it is significant to note that Mr. Howe speaks of the members of the Bunker Hill group as "not without means." We may suspect, therefore, that many of them were artisans or foremen of a higher "respectability" than the "run of the mill" wage-earners.

As for migration in less exciting times, the remaining evidence from the East gives little indication of wage-earner participation. Miss Vera Shlakman, who is preparing a history of the industrial town of Chicopee, Massachusetts, under the auspices of the Council of Industrial Studies of Smith College, has kept this question in mind during her researches. In addition to certain notices of the migration of people who were clearly not wage-earners, she finds references, without occupational identification, to nine persons leav-

[41] *Lowell Daily Journal and Courier,* February 2, 1849.
[42] *Ibid.,* January 18, 1849.
[43] Octavius Thorndike Howe, *Argonauts of '49* (Cambridge, 1923), p. 47.
[44] *Ibid.,* p. 63.

ing for Iowa in 1855,[45] and ten starting for California in 1865,[46] and also a statement that a party of eight or ten mechanics including two overseers left the neighboring city of Holyoke for Wisconsin in 1855.[47] In one case, there is even the record of a departure fittingly celebrated. According to the *Springfield Republican* of May 30, 1858, a man wh had worked for twelve years for the Dwight Manufacturing Company, proprietors of a Chicopee cotton mill, was presented with a telescopic rifle when he gave up his job to go West. But there is no indication, either in the local or Springfield papers, in the diary of a local resident, or in other contemporary records, of any westward movement of wage-earners substantial enough to have had any marked effect upon the industrial life of the area.

In the New York press, it is again possible to find fairly frequent reference to the emigration of classes other than eastern wage-earners. In the early thirties, for example, an extensive movement to Texas was reported, and the Texas and Rio Grande Land Company offered excellent terms in a series of advertisements in the New York papers:

> Terms (Cash) 200 acres of fine prairie land, $35, which will also include a passage for one individual; and any further quantity of land of the same character will be sold, until the end of January, at a rate of 10 cents an acre. Parties will have their lands surveyed and granted to them, by government commissioners and surveyors, without any charges.
>
> Families belonging to purchasers of the Company's lands are carried out in the vessels chartered by the Company at 15 dollars for a man; 10 dollars for a wife or sister; the same for boys under 14 years of age, and 5 dollars for all under that age (except infants.) Nothing charged for a moderate amount of freight. Parties find their own provisions.[48]

Yet a contemporary letter from Texas indicates that it was for the most part not wage-earners who were taking advantage of these opportunities: "In the first settlement of Texas, the population were mere adventurers—many seeking a residence as an asylum—at present the emigrants are wealthy, educated farmers and professional men, physicians and lawyers, affording in every neighborhood a circle of intelligence and decorum." [49]

A still more characteristic item mentions the departure of "a fine collection of Germans, men, women and children, who recently arrived in this country [and] who left this city for the West, some

[45] *Springfield Republican,* May 21, 1855.
[46] *Ibid.,* May 17, 1868.
[47] *Ibid.,* March 23, 1855.
[48] Advertisement in the *New York Commercial Advocate,* January 27, 1835.
[49] *New York Spectator,* November 27, 1834.

for Illinois, some for Missouri, and some for Wisconsin."[50] Quotation after quotation could be set down to illustrate the westward movement of foreigners, but no comparable collection could be made to illustrate any similar migration of American wage-earners. In spite of Horace Greeley's lifelong interest in promoting such a movement, a prolonged search through his writings in the *Tribune*, as the previous article pointed out, yielded definite mention of only one "industrious mechanic" who had actually gone to the West.

THE DIFFICULTIES OF MIGRATION

Though the eastern papers thus appear to contain relatively few direct references to the sources of the westward movement, they do nevertheless provide a considerable body of secondary evidence. In addition to their frequent declarations that workers should go West, which were illustrated at length in the preceding article, they contain also a lesser but still large number of statements to the effect that it was very hard or even impossible for workers to take this advice. These latter items are no more proof that the wage-earners did *not* go to the frontier than the former are that they *did* go. They are, nevertheless, worth citing as an introduction to a discussion of the difficulties in the way of working-class migration and of certain organized attempts to overcome these obstacles.

"The difficulty in thousands of cases," as a letter to the *Tribune* put it, "is that they cannot obtain the means of going West."[51] In the days before the passage of the Homestead Act, this complaint is naturally associated with demands for "a reform in the manner of disposing of the public lands."[52] A letter to *The Voice of Industry* lays the trouble to speculative prices:

> And what is the effect of this land speculation on the community? I hardly ever knew a journeyman or a day laborer to earn enough at any common business to buy a farm at speculative prices. There are thousands in want of profitable employment who have no way to procure an honest living, and cannot get money enough to pay for the privilege of using an acre of good, well cultivated land.[53]

Another item from the same paper repeats the complaint and adds the suggestion of a remedy:

[50] *American Sentinel* as quoted by the *New York Evening Post*, August 14, 1838.
[51] *New York Tribune*, April 26, 1847.
[52] *The National Laborer*, Philadelphia, August 27, 1836.
[53] *The Voice of Industry*, November 5, 1847.

It will do well for one who has the help of a few hundred dollars of capital in warding off starvation, to talk about the ease with which every man may get a good living in this country, and may earn a farm. But it is quite a different thing to have a family to support on the hand to mouth principle, and save the first hundred dollars. The chances are that the most frugal and industrious man, who has a family to rear on his own labors will grow poorer instead of richer in the struggle.—Why will it not be best to vote every such man at once a place to make such a farm on?[54]

At about the period of these last quotations, the *Tribune* tells the story of an enterprising group of workmen who proposed to overcome this difficulty for themselves by squatting on unsettled lands:

Westward Ho! A fine body of working Men in our city, mainly Germans by birth—but in part English and Americans, have united in an engagement to migrate together to some portion of the unsettled and probably unsurveyed public land of the Far West, (not being able to buy lands), intending to settle in a cluster, improve and cultivate until the not distant day, when it shall no longer be a misdemeanor to settle to live—if not where he happens to be, then somewhere else. They agree to have $100 each to start with, about half of which will be consumed by the expenses of the journey. Some who wish to join them are destitute, or have far less than $100, and an appeal is made to the philanthropic to aid them by gift or loan to get away, and thus relieve the pressure upon the Labor Market in our City. Whoever is disposed to aid them or to learn further of their plans, is earnestly solicited to call upon Mr. William Trautwein, 189 Bowery.[55]

It should be noted, however, that the necessity of raising money for even such a minimum of expenses appeared as a serious obstacle and as the occasion for a plea for philanthropic aid.

It is therefore not altogether surprising to find that references to the difficulties of the movement did not cease to appear even after the Homestead Act had removed the barrier of the price of land. One writer, indeed, made the flat statement after some twelve years of the law's operation that it had been "a failure and a delusion" and had done nothing to promote the movement of "the toiling masses":

Most prominent of the legacies bequeathed to the country by Mr. Greeley is the Homestead Law. But I must do his memory the justice of saying that in his zealous and persistent advocacy of the Homestead Law, he believed that he was serving the "toiling millions" for whose prosperity and elevation, he ever labored. And yet how few, how very few, of these "downtrodden millions" ever possessed themselves of what he regarded as the greatest boon and blessing. The Homestead Law, so far as its most popular feature is concerned, has proved a failure and a delusion. Things which cost nothing are slightly valued. There would have been a larger number of settlers growing up in industry and developing into usefulness and prosperity, as

[54] *Ibid.*, April 10, 1846.
[55] *New York Tribune*, April 26, 1847.

farmers, mechanics, and artisans, under the law which furnished lands from the public domain to actual settlers at $1.25 per acre, than has been secured under the plausible Congressional idea of "voting every man a farm." [56]

Although the paper that Greeley founded continued to insist that the legislation had solved the problem, and although an impassioned editorial inspired by the railroad strike of 1877 described the "Homestead Law" as "the imperishable barrier which the United States [had] raised between free labor and oppression" [57] at the very time that Samuel Gompers was expressing the new viewpoint of labor by "ridiculing the advice of engineers and firemen to go West," [58] the columns of the *Tribune* itself carried frequent references to the persistence of the difficulty. One vigorous statement of it appears as a direct answer to an editorial on the familiar theme:

To the Editor of the Tribune:

Sirs; In your issue of Saturday, the Editorial "The End of It", points the way, but where shall this "surplus population" get the means to go to farming? It is evident that could these congregated laborers be placed on farms of their own, or with farmers needing their labor, a vast amount of misery and vice could be prevented, and one phase of the labor question would be in a fair way of solution. But they have absolutely no way of paying for transportation to the government lands of the West, much less the necessary experience for even a brief stay after getting there.

In this vicinity are one hundred families (one eighth of the population), carpenters, masons, tinners and laborers who would gladly change a poorly paid, half employed, aimless life, for that one pointed out by you next door; but with no money, with less and less employment as weary months roll by, with children growing up to idleness, and with the hope of better times and steadier employment, longer and longer deferred, what is a man to do—and the pitiless winter neither so far away?

The "Go West" theory is good as far as a theory; that great empire has been developed by those who acted upon the advice of the Tribune's founder; but in practice here and now, it is the error of errors to offer it as the panacea for all the troubles under which the penniless mechanics and laborers of our land are struggling. Could not the problem be solved by an appropriation of Congress which would enable some thousands, even, of these sad faced men to locate on the cheap but fertile lands indicated by you? . . .

W. S. VINCENT.

Towanda, Pa.[59]

[56] *New York Tribune*, February 20, 1875.

[57] *Ibid.*, August 7, 1877. See also editorial of June 3 of the same year referring to the "thousands" of dwellers in eastern industrial centers who had "found homes, permanent labor and sure subsistence in these Western lands."

[58] *Ibid.*, July 27, 1877. "They were not farmers, but men who stuck to their engines and trains. All that they wanted was that they should have a voice in fixing the terms for which they should work, so as to obtain such wages as would enable them to support their families."

[59] *Ibid.*, August 18, 1877.

The final suggestion, moreover, had already been embodied in resolutions passed at workingmen's meetings during the preceding summer:

> A local meeting was held last night at No. 224 Grand-st., to make preparations for the mass meeting at Cooper Institute on Wednesday, and for the parade on the next day. . . . Resolutions offered by William West were adopted, demanding the opening of the public lands exclusively for the actual cultivator, and the loaning of the means for transportation and purchase of implements and provisions, and the passage of the Banks Bill for enlarging the scope of the Homestead Act. . . .[60]

These statements emphasized, and these proposals were intended to overcome, the obstacle of the expense of migration; but a number of other items suggested the presence of a further difficulty that would have been harder to remove by legislation. Again it is a letter to the editor that states the point most vigorously, and this time a man brought up in a pioneer community in western New York argues that a man who has worked all his life in a factory or shop is not likely to succeed in running a farm:

> Sir: I observe "C. H.'s" article in your issue of the 24th inst. in which he invites answers to his question about farming. He may think that farming may be carried out with all pleasantness, but he will learn a lesson that he has never experienced by trying it a few years. Farming to make a success of it needs experience as well as any other business. Farming on paper and book learning may seem pleasant and easy, but the reality to a means is experience, adaptability, proper care, good order, tools in all times in order, all things done in their proper time. . . .
>
> . . . This picture of a farm doubtless looks very pleasant to my city friend "C. H." for really to one not experienced it would seem that the farmer raised everything needed to make himself and family comfortable and happy. Does he think he could manage this farm successfully, stepping from city to farm? The experienced farmer only succeeds well. . . .[61]

In this case, the *Tribune* itself had shown its recognition of the difficulty. As early as 1857, an editorial writer had directed the following warning to a "Working-Man" who had some money and intended to turn farmer:

> Farming is a vocation, requiring knowledge, experience, and skill, like any other. No man born and reared in the city can remove to a farm at thirty or forty years of age and become immediately an efficient, thrifty, successful farmer. He will have much to learn and something to unlearn, and if he gets through his first year of farming without using up $500 of his capital, he may consider that he has done well.[62]

[60] *Ibid.*, August 8, 1876. A similar item appears the next day.
[61] *Ibid.*, March 10, 1877.
[62] *Ibid.*, April 8, 1857.

When an agricultural writer for the *Tribune*, George Geddes, looked back over the history of migration from the vantage point of 1878, this obstacle appeared to him to have been almost insurmountable:

> Very few cases can be shown of success in farming achieved by men who never lived on a farm, and who went directly from city life, depending entirely on the work of their hands, guided by uninstructed minds. Boys, brought up on a farm to the age of twelve or fifteen years, have gone to the cities, been successful there, and in after life have become successful and even model farmers. But they had the knowledge acquired in early life, and their capital derived from some other business, to pay for the mistakes they might make, while learning more. . . .[63]

Perhaps the fate of the fourteen migrants who returned to Fall River may be attributed to this difficulty, and a later section will provide what appears to be a further illustration.[64] As for the obstacle of cost, a well-known passage from Professor Paxson's *History of the American Frontier* lists the essential items involved:

> Every homeseeker needed means to get his wagon and team, to buy his simple outfit for operating the home and farm, and to maintain himself and his family while on the journey. . . . After raising funds to cover the cost of migration and to make the initial payment on the land, there still remained the necessity to support the family until the crops could be extracted from the reluctant soil. The first harvest can rarely have done this, for the number of acres that could be cleared, planted and cultivated in the first season was small. There are many estimates that show that the cost of getting a crop into the land for the first time might be twice or thrice what the land itself might bring when unimproved.[65]

Of these, the payment on the land might be avoided after the Homestead Act, though even then it was often wiser policy to buy better-situated land in private hands.[66] In some cases, contemporary statements make it possible to fill in approximate figures for certain of these expenses. A number of references specify the cost of transportation, and it seems probable that the average varied between $25 and $45 per person, depending on the period, the route, the presence or absence of rate wars, and the distance traveled.

Two contemporary estimates attempt to cover the entire range of items involved in the process of settlement. One is a calculation, published in 1843 by an English traveler named William Oliver, of the cost of making a start on the Illinois frontier. For the trip from

[63] *Ibid.*, "Farmer's Extra," Supplement, 1878, p. 7.

[64] See below, pp. 98–100.

[65] F. L. Paxson, *History of the American Frontier* (New York, 1924), p. 227.

[66] "Generally it was preferable to pay $400. or more for a quarter-section close to a railroad than go back into the hinterland and haul everything great distances over the worst of roads." F. A. Shannon, *Economic History of the People of the United States* (New York, 1934), p. 438.

New York to St. Louis, he stated the expenses as follows: by way of Philadelphia and Pittsburg, \$41.50 to \$58 with meals and \$13 to \$20 without meals; by way of Albany and Buffalo, \$16 to \$21 without meals.[67] For building and equipping the house and for buying and breaking in the land and stocking the farm, his estimates were as follows:

House	\$ 439.77½
Farm	1277.60
Total	\$1717.37½[68]

In spite of the half-cents, these are obviously figures of pioneering *de luxe*. Very likely the Englishman counted in items of equipment that would have appeared superfluous to the ordinary American, and the estimates include some \$1100 for the cost of labor, almost all of which the poorer settler and his family would perform themselves. Yet in this case they would need subsistence till the crops came in and certain additional equipment for clearing and breaking the land, which Mr. Oliver estimated as costing a further \$157.50. Thus it would be hard by any revision of the figures to reach a total below six hundred dollars.

A second estimate is for a more representative settler at a later period:

The cost of transportation for husband, wife, and say two children, will be at the minimum,	\$100.00
Two oxen, with yoke, at least,	100.00
One wagon, at least	100.00
Six months of provision, at 50 cents a day, to last until the first crops are gathered in, not less than,	90.00
Farming implements, necessary,	150.00
Seeds for first crop,	100.00
One cow,	50.00
	\$690.00[69]

Since this is after the passage of the Homestead Act, no item is included for payment on the land; but this estimate, nevertheless, like most of those that have been recorded, falls in the range between five hundred and a thousand dollars.

The figures as well as the complaints, then, suggest that the cost of settlement may well have been a serious obstacle to the migration of industrial workers even when land itself was free. Though Pro-

[67] William Oliver, *Eight Months in Illinois*, with *Information to Immigrants* (Chicago, 1924), pp. 224–228. (Original edition, Newcastle-upon-Tyne, 1843.)

[68] *Ibid*., pp. 243–247.

[69] *Experiments in Colorado Colonization*, edited by James F. Willard and Colin B. Goodykoontz (Boulder, 1926), p. 30.

fessor Paxson points out that many of those who went to the frontier must have made their way by borrowing, there can be little doubt that it was harder for wage-earners than for most other classes either to save the money themselves or to find "some obliging neighbor or relative" to take "their notes" and provide them with funds.[70] There were, however, certain definite attempts to overcome this difficulty and that of the workers' lack of farm experience through the resort to group colonization sometimes supported by philanthropic funds. The next section, accordingly, will examine the records of organized migration to see whether they yield evidence of a more extensive movement of wage-earners.

ORGANIZED MIGRATION

If distance and cost and unfamiliarity tended to check the movement of the eastern poor to the western lands, there were on the other hand, as has been pointed out, certain contemporary attempts to overcome these obstacles. Frequent letters to the *Tribune* suggested that philanthropy was needed to accomplish the transfer of the unemployed to the West, and the Citizens Association set up a Labor Bureau to direct them to the rural areas.[71] These intentions took more tangible form in the provision of charitable aid for the migration of certain classes of the population and in the organization of a number of colonies in which mutual aid—and sometimes philanthropic assistance as well—were to overcome the difficulties of settlement.

Direct aid to migration was apparently most often given to groups who were only potential wage-earners or on the borderline of wage-earning. In point of numbers, the most substantial activity was that of the Children's Aid Society in placing orphans or part orphans from the East in the homes of western farmers. Between 1854 and 1880, the Society sent out an average of over two thousand children a year to a total of 59,481; [72] and the bearing of this activity on our problem is suggested by a contemporary reference to these companies of "boys and girls, in need of homes, who will find good ones where they are going and eventually become farmers themselves, instead of beggars, or criminals, or poor mechanics out of work and suffering in the city." [73]

[70] F. L. Paxson, *op. cit.*, p. 227.
[71] *New York Tribune*, June 4, 1868; April 2, 1870.
[72] *Ibid.*, November 24, 1880.
[73] *Ibid.*, January 13, 1855.

Women, also, frequently went West under organized auspices. A notice in the mid-thirties indicates the nature of the movement:

> Female Emigration.—The St. Louis Daily Herald of the 10th, states that a company of "industrious, capable and intelligent" young women are about to start from Northampton, Mass. for the valley of the West. They are (says that Herald) needed as school teachers, to fill the various mechanical employments, which are the province of their sex, and above all, are needed as sweeteners of the toil and hardships of our young men, who now, in great numbers, are laboring in unblessed loneliness, over the vast domains of the West. These young women come out under the protection of a gentleman, and we do not hesitate, in the name of all that is pure and lovely, to promise them a hearty welcome from all classes of our fellow citizens.[74]

During the forties, Governor Slade of Vermont made a practice of conducting groups of New England girls to the West to become teachers. Thus one of many notices records his arrival at Buffalo "accompanied by twenty-three young ladies, whom he is escorting to the Western States, where they will be employed as teachers"; [75] and it is estimated that he brought about one hundred girls a year to the West. Another characteristic notice quoted from an Iowa paper describes the "arrival of forty-one ladies" as causing "a great sensation." "Many of our newcomers," it boasted, "are genuine Yankees." This item was headed "Welcome at the West," and the nature of that welcome may be made clear by one more quotation:

> Yankee Girls Out West.—Prentice complains, in the Louisville Journal, that the Yankee girls who came out West do very little teaching. Instead of teaching other people's chilren, they soon get to teaching their own.[76]

The children and most of these women were only potential employees of eastern industry, but the depression of 1857 brought about the organization of the Women's Protective Emigrant Society with the definite purpose of promoting the migration of unemployed wage-earners. Horace Greeley, in one of his best moods, explained the occasion and the need:

> On another page is an appeal of the "Women's Protective Emigrant Society" to which the generous attention of the public may be directed. This society is just organized for the purpose of sending destitute young women and girls who are deprived of the means of obtaining their daily bread, to the Interior or the West, where they may find employment. It is not intended to do this without ample precaution and regularity. Indeed, a system is already devised for the purpose of fully carrying out the object

[74] *New York Commercial Advertiser*, June 25, 1835.
[75] *Lowell Daily Journal and Courier*, May 4, 1850, citing *Buffalo Republican.*
[76] *Fall River News*, November 16, 1848.

as soon as means are obtained, the active promoters being likewise determined to go to work at once and do good in proportion to their limited means, trusting to the correct sentiment of the public to afford them rapidly an all-sufficient fund to perfect their scheme. No rhetoric can exaggerate the awful conditions of thousands, yes thousands—of respectable, industrious, virtuous girls in this metropolis whose wages are suddenly suspended, and who are left hopeless and helpless. It is estimated that there are no less than 7000 now ready to go West, because society has entirely withdrawn its succor from them. At best, they can earn but a pittance. A woman may be defined to be a creature who receives half price for all she does, and pays full price for all she needs. No hotel or boarding house here takes a woman at a discount of fifty per cent. Butchers, bakers, grocers, mercers, haberdashers,—all ask her the utmost penny. No omnibus carries her for a halfed sixpence. She earns as a child—she pays as a man. Besides her sex, if not barbarous custom, cuts her off from the best rewarded callings. . . . What, then, remains to be done? Simply individual action. Action prompt; action liberal, action abundant. There is no time to be lost. . . .[77]

The nature of the action is illustrated in the following item:

The Women's Protective Emigrant Society dispatched last evening a party of forty young women in charge of Miss Rich to Northern Indiana where Mr. Foster has procured good homes for them. The Society is now ready to receive others for Illinois, Indiana and other Western States, at its rooms, No. 29 Canal Street, where also contributions . . . will be thankfully received.[78]

Similar notices appeared, about two weeks apart, from November 10, 1857 to March 3, 1858; and during that time the Society appears to have sent out between 100 and 150 women a month.

A somewhat more substantial migration of wage-earners is indicated from time to time in the notices of the organized colonies and settlement associations which played an often forgotten part in the westward movement.[79] The course of one of these, which was organized by a New York City school teacher named Murphy, may be followed across the country in the papers of 1856. The *New York Tribune* records the plans for the start:

The Minnesota Settlement Association, now numbering 127 members, will leave New York about the 15th of April. They will settle on government land at $1.25 per acre, and have some years to pay for it. Meetings every

[77] *New York Tribune*, December 14, 1857.
[78] *Ibid.*, December 21, 1857.
[79] The Fourieristic or Associationist colonies, together with those founded on the basis of religious communism, have because of their intrinsic interest received more rather than less attention than their numerical importance would warrant. The reference in the text is to the more loosely organized bodies formed to overcome the difficulties of migration and settlement but with the ultimate intention of purely individual ownership. It should be added that the article does not attempt to deal with the Mormon migration.

Wednesday Evening at No. 163 Bowery. All members are notified to come forward and pay their last installment on shares.[80]

A St. Paul paper notes the arrival in Minnesota:

"Bound for Minnesota.—Monday evening's train from Chicago, brought three hundred men, women and children, from New York City to this place, bound for Minnesota Territory, where they intend to locate a town and make farm. The company is known as the Minnesota Settlement Association. They have among them farmers, mechanics, school teachers, printers and members of the theological and medical professions. Judging from their appearance, we should take them to be a very respectable and industrious class of men, amply supplied with the means to accomplish the objects they have in view.

"The male portion of the company met Tuesday in the third story of Robinson & Co.'s store to attend to the purchase of stock, farming implements, &c, prior to leaving for Minnesota." (*Dubuque Republican*).

The company referred to above arrived on Saturday last upon the City Bell, and they immediately took passage on the steamer Reveille for Mankato. They intend laying out a town in Blue Earth County, which under their auspices cannot fail hereafter to be of some importance.[81]

Further details and a conclusion may be found in the *History of Blue Earth County*. Each member, it appears, had been charged a fee of ten dollars, and the Association had promised "cheap transportation West, an opportunity to preempt 160 acres of the best farm land; one lot in the town site, which was to be plotted in the midst of the new settlement, which was certain of being a big town; and having a well settled community at once, instead of isolation incident to the ordinary pioneer life." But when the colonists arrived at the chosen site, and divided the land into claims of the promised size, they found that only 65 had sufficient timber. The sequel is told by the county historian:

Three of the head officers were allowed the first pick. The rest of the claims were numbered and divided by lot, but as there were 139 persons present entitled to claims, more than half the tickets were blanks. The result was a great dissatisfaction. Many who drew good claims were young men without families whose only purpose was speculation, while many heads of families drew blanks. A general row followed and much claim jumping. Most of the disappointed scattered. . . .

Soon after, the entire venture came to an ignominious end, for "the land was jumped in a short time by two enterprising claim hunters" and the section was finally settled by people from Wisconsin.[82]

[80] An advertisement in the *New York Tribune*, March 19, 1856.

[81] *Daily Pioneer and Democrat*, May 8, 1856.

[82] Thomas Hughes, *History of Blue Earth County, Minnesota* (Chicago, 1909), pp. 70–73.

Similar stories of disappointment appear frequently in the records, and one of the most significant is the case of another Minnesota colony in which it was specifically the urban workers that failed. In 1851 the *New York Tribunte* reported that Mr. William Haddock, "a printer of this city," had given a lecture on behalf of the Western Farm and Village Association, which was to enroll from 150 to 200 persons, embracing "a proportional number from each of the ordinary professions" and offering them—as in the case of Mr. Murphy's organization—the opportunity of pioneering with "all the comforts of civilization, which could only be realized by settling in close proximity." [83] A fuller notice appeared in the *Tribune* several months later, declaring that its object was

> to settle on our Government's Lands in the West in such a manner that farmers, mechanics, manufacturers and merchants may possess the advantages of the first purchase of the land, without paying the higher prices which a crowded population creates, and at the same time enjoy all the advantages of an intelligent and industrious community. . . .
>
> Young farmers, mechanics, manufacturers, machinists and millwrights, in every State, of good habits, are invited to send their names, stating their profession, the quantity of land they wish to obtain . . . also the probable amount of Capital they will possess. . . .
>
> It is often asked how much money will be required. The answer must be, the more the better. Yet it is plain that men of small capital possess more advantages in this Association, as one sustains another, like a bundle of sticks. . . .[84]

Two years after the original announcement, a correspondent reported on the progress of the colony in Minnesota. "It has a select population," he said, "having twice been sifted; in the first place none but reputable persons being admitted; and none but the persevering ones staying. . . . Most of those who left were mechanics and artisans, principally from New York City, who knew nothing about farming or the wants of a new settlement."

The history of this second sifting was fortunately recorded by one of the original settlers, and the typewritten manuscript is preserved in the archives of the Minnesota Historical Society. The author had been an Indiana farmer attracted, like the other settlers, by the proposals "to form a colony of several hundred and perhaps a thousand or more, taking none but those of good character and good citizens, and locate in the West, on government lands, in a body, on a good navigable stream, if possible. They would survey out a village lot and a farm of 160 acres, choice to be drawn by

[83] *New York Tribune*, July 24, 1851.
[84] *Ibid.*, October 24, 1851.

lots." For our purposes, the most significant sections of the narrative are those which deal with "the city members of the Association" who were, as he said, "nearly all mechanics, and knew little or nothing about the country. They had little idea how difficult it was to find a locality very much resembling the one pictured in their imaginations." [85] In the new location, their troubles began promptly:

> We had to have lumber. It seemed that no one had made any effort to get any. The Association had published in their papers that as soon as they got word where their location was, there was to be sent on what they called the "Pioneer squad," consisting of a dozen or more able bodied men, mostly carpenters, to put up buildings and have them ready for the temporary use of those coming. They came there. They were nearly all city chaps; didn't seem to have any leader; knew nothing of pioneering; though they could do nothing because they had no lumber, and it seems did nothing toward getting any. They sat around as though waiting for the lumber to come to them. They lived on mush and molasses. . . . The first arrivals of course found no shelter, and having women and children they had to leave, and naturally told hard stories about the place.

In this emergency, a neighbor of the author's went up the Chippewa River and floated down a load of lumber, and several other families from Indiana came to the settlement:

> We pitched in and put up a cabin for Iames on his lot, within a block or two of where Lord's lumber was landed. In a couple of days he was living in it. Wally Corywell had worked in a cooper's shop the winter before, and brought cooper's tools with him. Among those was a frow used to rive out barrel staves, shingles and shakes (long shingles). It came very handy. He rived out enough shakes to cover Iames' house, and they made a good, rain-proof roof. Those unsophisticated city chaps, "The Pioneer Squad," and others too, looked with wonder on those Indiana fellows as they called us, put up a comfortable house so quickly with material found right there on the ground. They could then see what they might have done had they known how.[86]

A similar contrast appeared in the first farming:

> We were the only men of the colony who went on to a farm, and I think we were the only ones who had any breaking done on a farm the first season. . . . Nearly everybody tried to grow something or other on their city lots. Those that did not plow or get plowing done used the spade. Many spaded up ground for a garden. Some had quite good sized patches. It seemed as if all those city chaps had bought new Ames spades and garden seeds. Second-hand spades, as good as new, were cheap the latter part of the

[85] *Experiences of E. M. Drew of the Western Farm and Village Association*, pp. 1–2.

[86] *Ibid.*, pp. 39–42.

season, 50 cents being the regular price, while new Ames spades retailed everywhere for $1.25. They had learned that a spade was not much account for farming in a new country.[87]

A final comment sums up the author's opinions of the "city chaps" as colonists:

A majority of the members of the "Western Farm and Village Association" were tradesmen, printers, tailors, lithographers, calico printers, designers of wall papers, etc. They knew very little else of work. Most of them, like Mr. Thorp, had some idea of gardening with a spade. As they had always lived in a city, they would get lost if they got out of sight of their shanties.[88]

If this story is a characteristic one, it tends to explain the cases of return from the West that were so conspicuous in the story of Fall River. In numbers, however, these early colonies were fairly insignificant; and the first case of large scale organized migration originated in the excitements of political history. When the Kansas-Nebraska Act applied to Kansas the doctrine of "squatter sovereighty." the anti-slavery advocates of New England determined to take matters into their own hands and fill the territory with settlers who would vote to make it a free state. Under the leadership of Eli Thayer, they organized the New England Emigrant Aid Company, to whose stock many clergymen and philanthropic individuals, including such men of wealth as A. Amos Lawrence, were subscribers.[89] Similar or affiliated groups, such as the New York Kansas League, were organized in other centers. The ends, however, were not exclusively political. Mr. Thayer himself hoped that the Company would make profits through the operation of various enterprises and the increase of land values, and there is ample evidence that the settlers themselves were as much interested in economic advantages as in the slavery question. Letter after letter preserved in the archives of the Kansas State Historical Society complains of poverty as both an obstacle and inducement to migration. The following is one of many examples:

Danby, Apr. 26, 56.

Mr. Barnes

Dear sir I write to you for informate & a circular in regard to Kansas. I have a strong desire to go West. I am a poor man & shall always be so here I am a miller by trade and am now receiving 30 dollars per month

87 *Ibid.*, p. 47.

88 *Ibid.*, p. 59.

89 The story of its organization is perhaps best told in an article by Mr. S. A. Johnson on "The Genesis of the New England Emigrant Aid Company" in the *New England Quarterly*, vol. 3, January 1930, pp. 95–122.

I would be very glad to go in May but dont know as I can as I have not the funds at present. . . .[90]

Another letter outlines the special advantages of settlement under the Company's auspices:

Allow me, Mr. Editor, to tell why I like the Company . . . and if I don't get it right, you or the agent here, can set me right. I like the Aid Company because under their auspices, a man can settle in Kansas with as little expense as he can settle himself upon the public lands of Illinois, Wisconsin, Iowa or Minnesota. . . .

Again, there are no other public lands where I can locate myself and enjoy the institutions I left in New England. The mill, the school the church are planted after settlement is made in other places, and then not until the population will warrant their erection, and often not then. But here, under the auspices of the Society, we have the mill, the receiving house, the school house, the church, and the Sabbath-School—all within the first three months of our prairie life.

If I left my Eastern home with sighs for anything, they were sighs for the institutions, the society, and friends of the East. But, to my surprise, I find the very institutions . . . which I left behind, already planted and maturing in our midst.[91]

The inducements were certainly substantial, and must have made a great appeal to people who could not or would not go under other conditions. By traveling in groups of thirty or more the settlers were able to obtain reduced railroad rates. Accommodations were to be provided for them while they selected their sites and built their new homes. Above all, they were to find at once a social life like that of their home communities, with churches, schools, stores and mills waiting for their arrival. No scheme of settlement offered more to overcome the obstacles that faced the city-bred wage-earner with little capital and without farm experience; it seemed, indeed, almost "tailor-made" to assist in his migration. News of the enterprise, moreover, was spread far and wide by the eastern press. If wage-earners ever went to the western lands, we should certainly expect to find them taking part in this movement. How many of them did so?

[90] From the Barnes papers in the collection of the Kansas State Historical Society.

[91] *Herald of Freedom* (Lawrence, Kansas), January 27, 1855. Compare also the Company's own statement of the advantages: "The emigrant suffers wherever he goes alone into his new home. He suffers from the fraud of others, from his own ignorance of the system of travel and of the country where he settles; and again from his want of support from neighbors which results in the impossibility of any combined resistance or of any division of labor."—"History of the New England Emigrant Aid Company, with a Report on its Future Operations", published by order of the Board of Directors, Boston, 1862.

In this case, something of a quantitative answer is made possible by the preservation of many of the original documents in the collection of the Kansas State Historical Society.[92] Thus the Barnes papers make it clear that almost all of the emigrants sent out by the New York Kansas League came from the smaller agricultural communities of the state.[93] The New England Company, on the other hand, drew a significant proportion of its settlers from the industrial centers; and its more elaborate records yield the materials for a statistical analysis. In the collection are five of the six or seven "emigrant books" which were kept by the secretary and which contained the names of all the people who settled under the auspices of the Company. In all, some 3000 heads of families or independent individuals went to Kansas under its direction, and in 727 of these cases there remain records of their occupations in the home community. One hundred and four different callings are listed, and these we classified into four major groupings: farmers, business men, professionals, and a last group which contained both independent artisans and wage-earners and in which all doubtful cases were placed. The resulting distribution follows:

	Number	Per cent
Farmers	239	32.9
Business Men	71	9.8
Professionals	61	8.4
Independent workmen plus wage-earners	356	48.9
	727	100.0

It was from the last group that we had to attempt to pick out the wage-earners. In many cases, as the detailed list of 61 occupations indicates,[94] the term used could refer either to an independent artisan or to a wage worker. Some light on the question, and on the general character of the migration, could be obtained by re-examining the list of occupations in terms of the communities in which they had been carried on. From this two obvious conclusions

92 Thanks must be given to Mr. S. A. Johnson of the Kansas State Teachers College at Emporia, who had gone through these papers, for pointing out to us those which would be most relevant to our study.

93 William Barnes was secretary of the League. His records contain names and addresses of many migrants, but in only 54 cases give both residence and occupation. Of this small sample, 18 appear to have been either independent workmen or wage-earners.

94 The following tabulation lists each of the occupations that is represented by four or more entries:

Blacksmiths	18	Carpenters	73	Coopers	4
Bootmakers	12	Carriage makers	4	Joiners	5
Butchers	4	Clerks	16	Laborers	13

emerged. In the first place, there is virtually no evidence of anything like mass migration from particular centers of labor unrest. In the total list, 283 communities are represented; and 171 communities, only seven of which provided more than ten emigrants each, contained members of the group of independent artisans plus wage-earners. Conversely, the 73 carpenters, for example, came from 51 communities, and the migration of six of them from Salem is actually the nearest approach to a mass movement of members of a particular trade from a single town. In the second place, it is evident that a very large proportion of the migrants came from very small places.[95] The table below gives their distribution by size of communities, for the cases in which this fact could be ascertained:

Lumbermen	12	Millwrights	4	Sailors	11
Machinists	29	Operatives	6	Shoemakers	33
Masons	4	Painters	11	Stone cutters	6
Mechanics	9	Printers	12	Tailors	5

The other occupations represented were bookbinder, bookkeeper, brass finisher, bridge builder, broom maker, chair maker, confectioner, currier, engineer, engraver, fireman, founder, gardener, gas (?), handle maker, pattern maker, rigger, sash maker, salesman, ship carpenter, ship joiner, shipwright, shoe fitter, slater, tanner, teamster, tin plater, tin worker, and toolmaker.

SIZE OF COMMUNITIES SENDING EMIGRANTS TO KANSAS UNDER AUSPICES OF NEW ENGLAND EMIGRANT AID COMPANY

Size Class [a]	Number of Communities	Number of Emigrants	Professionals	Farmers	Business	Mechanics and Wage-Earners
0– 1,000	18	22	4	10	1	7
1,000– 2,500	87	154	13	74	9	58
2,500– 5,000	60	136	11	38	14	73
5,000– 10,000	26	92	10	19	12	51
10,000– 25,000	14	85	4	18	10	53
25,000– 50,000	3	27	—	3	2	22
50,000–100,000	1	1	—	1	—	—
100,000–and over	2	53	8	2	14	29
Totals [b]	211	570	50	165	62	293

[a] From United States Census for 1850.

[b] The totals in this table are smaller than the numbers given previously since it was impossible to locate in the Census all the communities listed. Presumably the bias introduced by these omissions is in the direction of overstating the percentages of migration from the larger places.

[95] Katherine Coman in her *Economic Beginnings of the Far West*, vol. II, p. 337, says that these emigrants came from "the hill towns of New England, from the exhausted farms of New York and Pennsylvania, from the malaria haunted prairies of Illinois." She had evidently gone through the "emigrant

Thus half of all the Company's migrants, and 45% even of the mechanics and wage-earners, appear to have come from villages between 1000 and 5000 rather than from the larger manufacturing centers.

Even with these indications, the discrimination between wage-earners and workers on their own account remains a matter of doubtful and individual judgment. If we place in the former group every case that seems to us close to the borderline, we believe that some 221 out of the 727—or 30% of the total—may be regarded as wage-earners. If the same proportion holds for all the migrants who came out under the New England Company during the four years covered by the books, approximately 900 out of the 3000 were wage workers. Both the percentage, then, and the absolute numbers were substantial, though still small in relation to the total labor supply of eastern industry.

The migration of wage-earners never again received such a notable single stimulus, but the idea of organized migration persisted long after the fate of "Bleeding Kansas" had been decided. Greeley added it to his platform and expressed surprise that people moving to the West had not long before seen that there was "no comparison as to safety, comfort, usefulness of emigrating with a group of farmers, mechanics, teachers, and pastors, over that of going to a strange land alone." [96] When this type of migration revived after the Civil War, one of the most important of the new groups, Union Colony, located in Colorado and fittingly chose Greeley as the name for its settlement. This project received full publicity in the *Tribune*, the first notice appearing December 4, 1869; and a substantial part of the original records have been collected and published by the University of Colorado.[97] These provide lists of names and home addresses of 436 people who paid the $155 necessary for membership and also of 139 of the first settlers.

---

books". Our examination of them, however, revealed very little migration from Illinois; people from Illinois did go to Kansas but not under the direction of the New England Company. Apparently, Miss Coman's statement was based on an error from which we were saved by the intervention of an attendant at the library. In the old-fashioned handwriting in which the entries were made, the abbreviation for *Maine* (Me.) is very much like what one would expect for *Illinois* (Ill.).

[96] *New York Tribune*, May 24, 1859.

[97] *The Union Colony at Greeley, Colorado,* edited by James F. Willard, Colorado Historical Collection, vol. 1 (Boulder, 1918). Greeley today supports a coöperative retail which is described as the largest in the United States. Perhaps this may be thought of as indicating the survival of the spirit in which the original settlement was founded.

Unpublished papers in the Meeker Memorial Museum at Greeley contain application blanks filled out by 384 persons and giving not only home addresses but also occupations. The three lists do not contain identical names. Some who made applications did not become members, and some who became members apparently did not go West. Of the 73 applicants who were also listed among the early settlers, 17 may well have been wage-earners; and of the total of 384, some 74—or 19%—appear to belong in that category.

The geographical origins of the Colony may be examined by means of the longer list of those who paid their membership fees. Of the 436, New England, New York, New Jersey and Pennsylvania supplied 255, and the others were mainly from the West. New York leads with 101 entries, but the detailed list of communities dispels the notion that this indicates a preponderance of industrial wage-earners. These members came from 55 different communities, only 13 of which provided more than one entry apiece, and New York City and Brooklyn together furnished only 19. Again the origins seem to have been largely village and agricultural, and the suggestion that wage-earners played only a minor part in the enterprise is somewhat confirmed by an article in the *Nation* describing the settlers as "gentleman farmers."

The case of this Union Colony is apparently unique both in its high degree of success and in the fullness of the records that have been preserved. Its time, however, was one of very active experimentation in organized settlement. In the year of its origin, a Dakota paper linked the general movement with "scarcity of work," "increase of pauperism" and "the overcrowded condition of cities" and declared that "emigrant societies," often established "after the plan of Loan Associations," had provided "thousands of poor laborers, mechanics and tradesmen" with the means of coming West.[98]

With the depression of 1873 colony-building received renewed stimulus. At least two other organized bodies followed the Union to Colorado—the St. Louis Western and the Chicago Colorado colonies. The latter was organized by a group of German workingmen, and it was from this that a number of the Fall River wage-earners straggled back to their "home base." Kansas attracted a still larger number of organized groups, and Miss Weldron's dissertation mentions the formation during the seventies of the Chicago Workingmen's Colony and the Excelsior Company, which was made up of New York mechanics, as well as nine others which may well

98 *Union and Dakotaian*, Yankton, Dakota Territory, May 8, 1869.

have contained wage-earners—the Massachusetts, Bridgeport, New Haven, Syracuse, New York, Empire (also from New York), Brooklyn, Buffalo and Pennsylvania colonies.[99] Unfortunately there is little evidence of the fate of these ventures. We cannot tell, therefore, how many workmen they may have brought to the West, or how many they held there. In most cases, apparently, they did not last long, and it is probable that for many the end was similar to that described forty years later by the only couple remaining where the Syracuse colony had planted its settlement:

> All of the new settlers took claims and that spring planted their maize, which was promptly dried up by the drouth and blown away by the hot winds. They managed to skimp through the following winter and the next spring again planted their crops, but the season was only a repetition of the first, and by July, practically all of the little band was thoroughly disgusted and almost destitute. . .[100]

It thus appears that assisted and organized migration sometimes lessened but by no means eliminated the obstacles that stood in the way of the westward movement of wage-earners. The percentage of working-class participation in these group settlements may well have been higher than in the more individualistic movement to the West. It seems unlikely, however, that there could have been more than a year or two in which as many as five hundred wage-earners left the East for any or all of the colonies mentioned, and entirely improbable that the total movement of this sort was large enough to exert a marked effect upon the labor supply of the eastern factories.

OTHER EVIDENCE FROM THE WEST

Much of the evidence regarding the outcome of these organized ventures comes from western sources, and we may turn to similar materials for what indication they may give of the presence of wage-earners among the general body of settlers. On one point, the western papers of many localities and of all periods give unanimous testimony. Wage-earners were welcome and urged to come. "Good mechanics are much wanted," said a characteristic advertisement inserted on behalf of "the flourishing village of La Grange." [101] Western editors, moreover, took every depression and every instance of eastern distress as an occasion for pointing the moral of migra-

[99] Nell Blythe Weldron, *Colonization in Kansas, 1861–1890* (Ph.D. dissertation, Northwestern University), typewritten manuscript in the Kansas State Historical Society.

[100] *Topeka Capital*, Kansas, July 23, 1914.

[101] Advertisement in the *Democratic Free Press*, Detroit, March 22, 1832.

tion. According to the *Detroit Free Press* of 1837, "If the unemployed mechanics and laborers in the large cities at the East were informed of the prospects which are held out for them, they would be wanting in judgment, we think, if they did not immediately embark for the West."[102] Two decades later, the *Nebraska Palladium* made the inducements more specific and still more persuasive:

> Come where a man can earn from one to two acres of land every day he works, and where a female can earn a farm of from 80 to 100 acres besides supporting herself in a year's time. Better come where you can earn something for yourself and be of service to the community, than to stay where you can earn nothing and are a burden to the State.[103]

Letter-writing readers joined their editors in the plea. Thus an Indiana settler wrote to "the unemployed and hungry of New York": "Just move your families to the small villages of the West. Here is unlimited work to be done, and thousands of dollars to pay for it. . . . Who will not prefer this to the riots, starvation, insolence, suffering and crimes, which you report to be your present or approximate condition?"[104] Still more complacent is the advice from a Nebraskan in the seventies:

> It is with pleasure I read in a recent copy of a paper published in the mining districts of Pennsylvania of the continued dissatisfaction of the miners or at least a portion of them, and of their preparing to go West to take up public lands and each to go to work for himself.
>
> This is the wisest way of solving the trouble existing in the coal mining regions and everywhere, between employers and employed. . . . When the laboring men in any part of our country find themselves oppressed by capital, or embroiled in feuds with trade unions, they cannot do better than betake themselves to the primitive occupation of digging their living out of the generous earth.[105]

These comments show only that wage-earners would have been welcome. What we are more anxious to know is how many of them actually went West, and how large a part of the stream of migration they made. The records we have found, however, permit us to do no more than dip into the stream here and there at places and periods that we may hope were representative. In the case of Michigan, to which the *Free Press* urged the unemployed to go, we may make use of Mr. George N. Fuller's careful study of the origins of the population.[106] His observations for the state

[102] *Detroit Free Press,* (Weekly Edition) August 16, 1837.

[103] *Nebraska Palladium,* Belleview, Douglas County, Nebraska, January 24, 1855.

[104] *Ibid.,* February 21, 1855.

[105] *Syracuse Standard,* Syracuse, Nebraska, December 25, 1871.

[106] George N. Fuller, *Economic and Social Beginnings of Michigan,* Michigan Historical Publications, vol. I.

as a whole indicated that a very large proportion of the early settlers came from upper New York State. For Washtenaw County, which he considered typical both in physical features and in the sources of the people, he made an intensive study of the places from which the original purchasers of the land had come. Of those from outside Michigan, almost all were from New York State,[107] and this migration he analyzed as follows:

> By far the largest number of New York purchasers registered from Genesee, Monroe, Ontario, and Seneca counties; Cayuga, Livingston, Steuben and Wayne counties made up the next largest number; these eight counties, which made a fairly compact area, were in the northern and central parts of western New York. Four-fifths of these patents (183) name counties lying west of the meridian of Stony Point, which passes through the eastern end of Lake Ontario; and of these, seven-tenths (129) name these eight counties. Less than two-fifths of the whole number (89) mention counties bordering on Lake Erie and Pennsylvania, and purchasers were fewest in the latter. In both western and eastern New York they were most numerous in the area which was influenced directly by the Erie Canal.[108]

Mr. Fuller's general conclusion may be supported from another source. During 1836, the *Detroit Daily Advertiser* published a "Traveller's Register" giving the names and addresses of the people who came to the hotels of the city. In the period from June 11 to July 8, over two thousand names were published. Of these at least 958 came from New York State and by far the larger part from the Erie Canal region which Mr. Fuller describes. The city of New York, on the other hand, appears to have provided not more than fifteen or twenty of the migrants.[109] Both these sources, therefore, suggest the conclusion that wage-earners from the industrial centers did not form a large proportion of the early settlers of Michigan.

Similar evidence may be found for Minnesota. From a St. Paul newspaper, we took the names of 341 individuals who came to the state during May 1854 and April 1855.[110] More than three fifths of the total were contributed by the five states of New York (20%), Pennsylvania (13%), Maine (13%), Illinois (9%), and Wisconsin (7%). Thus two partly industrial states supplied much of the migration, but what evidence there is on the actual localities

[107] Of the total of 518, 212 were from Washtenaw itself and 41 from other counties in Michigan. Of the rest, 228 were from New York, 5 from other Middle Atlantic states, 3 from the West and 4 from abroad. *Ibid.*, p. 469.

[108] *Ibid.*, pp. 470–471.

[109] Some uncertainty arises from the possible confusion between state and city.

[110] *The Daily Minnesota Pioneer*, St. Paul.

suggests that for New York at least the migrants again came mainly from the smaller communities.[111]

Though the Gold Rush does not represent the type of pioneering on which the main emphasis of the Turner theory falls, it is nevertheless of interest to note certain evidence regarding the composition of the wagon trains that started across the Plains. The *St. Louis Republican* stationed a correspondent at Independence, and his reports make it clear that by far the greater part of the migrants that assembled there were from the farms and the small towns of the Middle West. A few came from the South and a few from the agricultural regions of the East; but the Pittsburgh and California Enterprise Company, of whose nearly 300 people 162 came from Pittsburgh, was an outstanding exception.[112] At the same time, moreover, another Missouri paper was deploring the effects of emigration from within the state. Farmers and farm laborers were being drawn away, and "many a broad acre of rich and improved land" would therefore lie idle.[113]

A final bit of evidence comes from the settlement of western Kansas during the eighties. One of the sections then receiving population was Greeley County with its appropriately named towns of Horace and Tribune. From July through December, 1886, the *Greeley County Gazette* mentions the names of 43 settlers who came to the community. Of these, 24 were from Kansas, 6 from Illinois, 4 from Missouri, 2 each from Kentucky and Indiana, and one each from Ohio, Pennsylvania, Wisconsin, New York and West Virginia. The known occupations included three lawyers, two doctors, a hotel keeper and merchant, a real estate dealer, a capitalist, a court clerk, and Land Office registrar, and a man engaged in the loan business. As for the other 32, most of them probably fitted the description given by the *Greeley Tribune:* "The immigration that is now pouring into Kansas is something to excite wonder and bewilderment. Thousands and thousands of intelligent farmers of the Eastern States are daily pouring into our Western counties in order to take

[111] Of the 27 people from New York State whose home towns were given, 9 came from Buffalo, only 2 from New York City, and the rest were scattered among the smaller communities. In Pennsylvania, however, 5 were from Philadelphia and 8 from Pittsburgh, among the 32 cases in which the localities were recorded.

[112] *St. Louis Republican*, April 12–22, 1849. One of the authors, in another connection, has devoted considerable time to reading the diaries and biographies written by people who had crossed the plains in the wagon trains. Though by no means having read all of the many such works published, he has found thus far not one case of an individual who had written such an autobiography or diary, who was not brought up in a rural community.

[113] *The Weekly Tribune*, Liberty, Missouri, June 21, 1850.

advantage of the low price of land."[114] Though the latter paper, in the spirit of its namesake, urged the disaffected laborer of the East that his strike would be victorious if only he would "strike for Tribune", there is no record that the advice was ever followed.

When the more general references to the origins of migrants can be found, their tenor is most often like that of the quotation from the *Greeley Tribune*. Some, to be sure, speak of the coming of business and professional men such as those listed in the *Gazette* or referred to in the Fall River papers. Thus the Commissioner of Immigration, maintained by the state of Minnesota in New York City, wrote hopefully to his Governor of the prospect of fifteen or twenty thousand settlers and added that "a fair proportion" would be "well-to-do-people, and persons with capital, who desire to enter and engage in different branches of manufacturing."[115] Many references, also, and a number of well-known monographs, deal with the settlement of immigrants from abroad. But a notice taken from the *Buffalo Democracy* represents an even more characteristic item: "The flux of Yankee immigration to the West, this season is entirely unprecedented; every propellor leaving this port is loaded down with emigrants, chiefly from New England States, and of the best class of sturdy farmers, bound for Wisconsin, Iowa and Minnesota."[116] Often also, it was the next previous frontier which supplied the settlers for the new. Thus a Minnesota land official made a trip through Michigan and Indiana early in 1855 and "heard of hundreds of families who designed removing the present season." "Multitudes poured in on him", he reported, "eager to learn particulars about the country."[117]

Again, the *Minnesota Pioneer* headed a note that "quite a large proportion of the passengers who arrived here Sunday were farm-

[114] *Greeley Tribune*, Tribune, Kansas, April 24, 1886.

[115] From a letter of E. Page Davis, Commissioner of Immigration for the State of Minnesota in New York, to Governor H. Austin of Minnesota, dated New York, December 8th, 1871. (In the collection of the Minnesota Historical Society.)

[116] Quoted in the *Daily Minnesota Pioneer*, St. Paul, April 30, 1855. Another reference to "New England farmers" settling in Iowa appears in the *New York Tribune*, December 2, 1851. This impression is confirmed by the results of conversations with a number of old-time Iowa settlers. It may be worth while to add that these surviving pioneers scoffed at the suggestion that eastern mill workers might have settled in their state. None could recall any of their neighbors who had come from the industrial centers, and their belief was that such people could not have succeeded on the land. Some of them thought that many of the mechanics and skilled artisans who had come to the state were of foreign origin.

[117] *Daily Minnesota Pioneer*, April 30, 1855. The official was G. W. Sweet, Register of the Sauk Rapids Land Office.

ers" with the caption: "The Right Kind of Men for a New Country,"[118] and returned to the same theme with greater eloquence in the following year:

> And the strangers coming amongst us are of precisely the right type. You see very few of those who look through the keen restless eyes, which mark the mere speculator; fewer still of the class which throws its "whole intellect" into the cultivation of mustachios, and contemplates with admiration the fit of Jenning's shortest waist and longest tail; but the great majority of the thousands are hard fisted, broad chested, open-faced, Middle States farmers, whose burden of inquiry is about the soil, and who look as if they intended to be at work on the day after they select a claim or enter it.[119]

From such sources, apparently, and not from the eastern mills, came the great majority of settlers of the western lands.

CONCLUSION

From this sampling of imperfect materials, we cannot claim the weight of conclusive proof. It is hoped that the question may receive further study and quite possible that such examination may disclose the existence of significant movements which our investigation has failed to uncover. There is, however, no mistaking the general tenor of what has been found. The bits of evidence drawn from widely scattered sources fit together into a pattern of unexpected consistency. In it, for example, workers' complaints of the difficulty of migration are matched by western figures of the cost of settlement. The return of Fall River wage-earners is made understandable by what happened to New York mechanics in the Farm and Village Association in Minnesota. Still more significantly, the lack of reference to wage-earners in western accounts of frontier origins appears consistent with what can be learned from the records of the industrial centers, and suggests that "the case of Fall River" was far from exceptional.

This cumulation of evidence thus points to the conclusion that the movement of eastern wage-earners to the western lands was surprisingly small.[120] Too few industrial workers reached the frontier to attract notice in the accounts of settlement. What is more

[118] *Ibid.*, October 24, 1854.

[119] *Ibid.*, April 25, 1855.

[120] "Surprisingly" at least to the investigators, of whom one had made use of the safety-valve doctrine for a number of years (e. g., in W. H. Hamilton, *Current Economic Problems*, Third Edition, 1925, p. 675, and the *Economic Record* of 1928, vol. IV, pp. 205-208), and the other began the work confident that a few months would be sufficient to demonstrate the existence of a substantial movement.

striking, too few wage-earners left the industrial centers to exert any marked effect on their labor situation. We could find no eastern paper showing any such concern over their departure as the Liberty *Weekly Tribune* expressed over the Missourians who were drawn into the Gold Rush. Even when the obstacles to working-class settlement were partially removed by assisted and organized migration, the numbers did not swell into a really substantial stream. Finally, one further corollary is suggested by limited but persuasive evidence. When eastern workers did attempt to take up land, they appear very frequently to have failed and returned home discouraged. To Professor Paxson's remark that "the city dwellers gave less than their share to the procession west; and more than their proportion of the pioneers that failed," [121] we may add that both statements seem to apply *a fortiori* to the urban wage-earners.

Since these findings run counter to an important element in the Turner theory, it is essential to indicate with care the boundaries of the disagreement. There is nothing in the present study to cast doubt upon the doctrine that the growth of American industrialism was delayed and made difficult by the presence of the frontier alternative. Nor has it attempted to examine the extent to which the growing industries of the Middle West recruited their labor supply from eastern wage-earners. The analysis confirms, moreover, rather than questions the opinion that the abundance of western land drew away many thousands of *potential* wage-earners who might otherwise have crowded into the factories "from the hill towns of New England" and "from the exhausted farms of New York and Pennsylvania." Though here the "safety valve" was the farmer's rather than the worker's, we need not doubt that its operation tended to hold up the level of industrial wages.

We cannot, however, accept the safety-valve doctrine in the direct and literal form in which it has been stated by Turner and his followers. This seems to have had no basis more substantial than the political debates over the homestead acts and the hopes and aspirations of Greeley and Evans, and can hardly be maintained unless new and concrete evidence is brought forward to its support. Once American industrialism was well established, it seems clear that the overwhelming proportion of its workers lived out their lives within its confines. It appears impossible to believe that any significant number of American wage-earners did in fact

121 F. L. Paxson, *When the West is Gone* (New York, 1920), p. 70.

"escape as individuals"—or in organized groups—"to lands that [were] free."

This conclusion, moreover, need not seem surprising if it is considered in the setting of the general development of the nation. In spite of the westward movement, the country throughout the period was steadily becoming more urban and less rural, and each Census recorded the relative gain of manufacturing as compared with agriculture.[122] The factories were thus drawing population from the countryside, and the presence of a reverse movement might be thought of as requiring more explanation than its absence. Again, the labor controversies of the time, as Professor Shannon has argued, were fought with a bitterness hard to reconcile with the doctrine that the workmen could escape "with a slight effort" to a life of independence on the western lands. If the American wage-earners of the period did in fact have broader opportunities than their fellows in other countries, it would appear that more of the explanation lies in the rapid growth of manufacturing employment than in the presence of a distant frontier.

[122] In a paper read last year before the Mississippi Valley Historical Association, Professor Fred A. Shannon pointed out that up to 1890 only 372,659 titles were granted under the Homestead Act. Allowing six persons to a family, this would have accounted for something over two million people, while at the same time the population of the United States increased well over twenty million. Even of these claims, a large proportion, as he points out, were commuted. In this valuable paper, which is as yet unpublished and which we have used by his kind permission, Professor Shannon arrived at much the same conclusion as that in the text, but by the use of entirely different evidence and procedure.

7

AMERICAN Negro slavery was many things, but in inception and throughout its history it was always an cconomic institution, a means of bringing labor to bear upon resources for the production of commodities. As an issue between the sections, slavery has long been recognized as influential in the political history of the United States. But the economics of slavery also has broad implications that transcend mere antiquarian interest in a defunct system of labor. For example, modern interpretations of the antislavery movement and the Civil War will differ according to one's conclusions about the economics of slavery. If slavery was unprofitable, then the antislavery crusade would appear to have been pointless, and even dangerous, because attacks on slavery might have given new life to a dying institution by provoking Southerners to defend it. Similarly, if slavery was unprofitable, then the war that abolished the institution at a frightful cost in property and blood appears as a needless tragedy.

As a result of the work of Ulrich B. Phillips, the unprofitable character of slavery became widely accepted among historians in the early years of the twentieth century. Among major modern historians, as Mr. Govan points out, only Lewis C. Gray disputed Phillips's view. Phillips spelled out his conclusions in a number of publications, all of which were models of close analysis and based upon an enviable familiarity with a wide range of primary sources. The most succinct and earliest presentation appeared in an article, "The Economic Cost of Slaveholding in the Cotton Belt," *Political Science Quarterly*, XX (June 1905), 257–275. More elaborate statements are continued in his later books, *American Negro Slavery* (New York, 1918), chapter XIX, and *Life and Labor in the Old South* (Boston, 1929), chapter X. As Mr. Govan shows in his article, other modern scholars like Charles S. Sydnor followed Phillips. Indeed, Mr. Govan's detailed criticism of Sydnor's work neatly summarizes and cogently exposes the illogicalities of many earlier analyses of slavery's alleged unprofitability.

The importance of Mr. Govan's article is that it initiated a reappraisal of Phillips's position which has ended in an almost complete reversal in the judgment of historians on the subject. His method of analysis is twofold. First he re-examines the definition of profit, for, as he says, the way in which that term is defined can make the difference between finding a low and a high return from the same set of plantation records. In general, those who argued that slave plantations were unprofitable usually used an unacceptable and outmoded definition of profit, thereby drawing misleading conclusions from their examination of the records.

Second, he analyzes fresh historical evidence with the new definition of profit in mind. This fresh evidence is of two kinds. The first is drawn from the census reports of 1850 and 1860 for thirteen of the slave states. All the selected figures he cites show an increase in wealth for the thirteen Southern states between 1850 and 1860. Perhaps the most striking and valuable comparisons are those of the total and the figures per capita for the "true value of real and personal property" in 1850 and 1860. The aggregate figure shows a more than 100 per cent increase while the per-capita figure records an almost 80 per cent rise in the ten years. Since these figures are for the South as a whole, they escape the charge of being unrepresentative or partial. In themselves they demonstrate that the Southern economy was growing in wealth at a rate of from 8 to 10 per cent a year—a very substantial increase for any economy. On the other hand, as a measure of the profitability of slavery, these figures are inconclusive because not all the wealth of the South was produced by slaves. For instance, it is possible, though not probable, that the unprofitability of slave labor was obscured by the high productivity of free white labor. But given the importance of the slaves in the production of the profit-making staple crops—slaves produced about 75 per cent of the cotton, for example—it is not likely that the wealth of the South could have doubled in ten years unless slave labor was producing at least some profit. This supposition is borne out by Herbert Weaver's investigation of Mississippi slaveholders, which Mr. Govan quotes.

Mr. Govan's second use of sources is to examine, from the standpoint of a modern definition of profit, the detailed records of three plantations. It is worth noticing that Mr. Govan does not rely solely upon the records, but points out that in totaling up the profit of the plantation, the style of life of the planter has to be taken into account, too. With their rather simple and haphazard accounting methods the planters often failed to include in their calculations their high style of living, though its luxuries and conveniences were obviously a part of income. Also to be noticed is that the three plantations whose records Mr. Govan analyzes were in the old South—South Carolina and Georgia—not in the new states of Mississippi or Alabama, where virgin lands were supposed to be the true source of profits in cotton cultivation. The glaring weakness in using only these three plantations is that they may not have been representative of the South as a whole. Consequently, Mr. Govan's conclusions are appropriately tentative.

Subsequent studies of the question of profitability from a broader range of sources, however, have sustained his conclusions with remarkable consistency. Kenneth M. Stampp in *The Peculiar Institution* (New York, 1956), for example, after examining the records of many more plantations, concluded that slaveholders were indeed getting a good return from their labor system. The strongest support for Mr. Govan's conclusions, however, came from A. H. Conrad and J. R. Meyer, "The Economics of Slavery in the Ante-Bellum South," *Journal of Political Economy*, LXVI (April 1958), 95–130. As economists, Conrad and Meyer approach the question as a problem of production, using aggregate figures for the whole South rather than individual plantation records. Furthermore, following a suggestion in Mr. Govan's article, they rightly include as a part of profit the gain to the planter from his rearing of slaves. This source of profit was particularly important for the planters in states like Virginia and Kentucky, where agriculture was depressed but where the sale of surplus slaves to the Deep South would often permit plantations to show a profit. That there was a surplus of slaves, it might be noted parenthetically, distinguished United States slavery from that of any other nation, either in antiquity or in nineteenth-century South America. No other slave system has been able to meet its needs for labor from natural reproduction alone. Cuba and Brazil, to take only two contemporary examples, were always dependent upon the international slave trade for the maintenance of their respective slave economies. Thanks to an efficient internal slave trade, as Messrs. Conrad and Meyer demonstrate, the slaveholders in the Southern part of the

United States were able to secure slaves at a reasonable price from internal sources almost entirely.

Once Conrad and Meyer have established the sources of planter income, they then compare the rate of return from investment with the return that would have been received if the same capital had been invested in Northern railroads or other non-Southern enterprises. The comparison reveals that the return was about the same for both, indicating that Southern slaveholders as a group realized as good a return from slavery as they could have received if they had placed their capital in nonslave labor enterprises.

Since the work of Conrad and Meyer was published, other investigations by economic historians have arrived at very similar conclusions. Among the most recent studies supporting the profitability of slave labor are Paul Wallace Gates, *The Farmer's Age: Agriculture 1815–1860* (New York, 1960), and Robert Evans, Jr., "The Economics of American Slavery, 1830–1860," in *Aspects of Labor Economics* (Princeton, 1962).

Mr. Govan's tentative conclusion has certainly been sustained by subsequent investigations, but there is still a danger that too broad inferences will be drawn from the apparent fact of the profitability of slavery. Some economic historians like Conrad and Meyer, for example, have gone beyond the conclusion of profitability to the additional and dubious point that slavery therefore constituted no obstacle to Southern economic growth. Slavery may have been profitable in agriculture, yet it still could have had the effect of preventing more advanced kinds of economic activity from developing. That slavery may have had a retarding effect upon the development of manufacturing in the South, for example, is the point made in Eugene D. Genovese, "The Significance of the Slave Plantation for Southern Economic Development," *Journal of Southern History*, XXVII (November 1962), 422–437. Genovese reminds us that because slaves were never consumers to the degree that free laborers were, their profit-making for the planter would not provide a market for Southern manufactures. Without a wide market, the South would lack an important precondition for the growth of manufacturing. Instead it secured what manufactures it needed from Northern factories or through Northern ports from abroad and remained largely an underdeveloped, agricultural economy. In brief, the part slavery played in retarding or shaping the Southern economy is not yet settled, even though the profitability of slavery in the Southern agricultural economy seems no longer in serious doubt.

Mr. Govan is Professor of History at New York University, where his special interests are economic history and the history of the American South.

Was Plantation Slavery Unprofitable?

BY THOMAS P. GOVAN

THE debate over the profitableness of slavery has been going on, in one form or another, for almost one hundred and fifty years.[1] It is, perhaps, too late for a definitive settlement of the question because of the destruction of so much of the evidence, but there can be an attempt at a reconciliation of the conflicting conclusions of the various students who have written about it.

The argument, too frequently, has been concerned with the question of whether or not slave labor was as profitable as free? Or, could a planter who made money with slaves have made more if he had employed free workers? These are interesting questions for speculation, but hardly more, because materials for a comparison do not exist. An experiment to test their truth or falsity probably could not have been made in the ante-bellum South where slavery appears to have been not so much an economic system as a social order to permit two unlike peoples to live together.[2] At least it does not seem to have been tried. Comparisons between free labor farms in the North and West and slave plantations of the South are of little value because of the widely varying climatic conditions, the nature of the crops, and other circumstances. Simi-

SOURCE: Thomas P. Govan, "Was Plantation Slavery Unprofitable?" *Journal of Southern History*, VIII (November 1942), 513–535.

[1] Research on this article was made possible through grants from the Julius Rosenwald Fund and the Social Science Research Council.

[2] E. Merton Coulter (ed.), Ulrich B. Phillips, *The Course of the South to Secession, An Interpretation* (New York, 1939), 152; Dwight L. Dumond, *Antislavery Origins of the Civil War in the United States* (Ann Arbor, 1939), 52; Clement Eaton, *Freedom of Thought in the Old South* (Durham, 1940), 174–75; Ralph H. Gabriel, *The Course of American Democratic Thought* (New York, 1940), 108–109.

larly profits of a plantation before and after emancipation could hardly be compared because of the vastly different conditions in the two periods.

But if the question is narrowed to the particular one of whether the planters of the Old South were making money from their operations, there is still no agreement to be found among the writers on southern agriculture. Ulrich B. Phillips concluded that by the close of the 1850's it was "fairly certain that no slaveholders but those few whose plantations lay in the most advantageous parts of the cotton and sugar districts and whose managerial ability was exceptionally great were earning anything beyond what would cover their maintenance and carrying charges." [3] Lewis C. Gray, expressly denying Phillip's conclusion, wrote, "Far from being a decrepit institution, the economic motives for the continuance of slavery from the standpoint of the employer were never so strong as in the years just preceding the Civil War." [4]

The same contradictions are to be found among ante-bellum observers. Solon Robinson, the noted agricultural reformer, published a report of his observations at the plantation of Colonel L. M. Williams of Society Hill, South Carolina. The profits of the plantation, according to this statement, were very low. But the editor of the Columbia *South Carolinian,* in complete disagreement, took the same figures and proved that the profits were very large.

Robinson, in his statement, valued the plantation's 4,200 acres (2,700 of which were in cultivation) at $63,000 or $15 per acre; 254 slaves at $88,900 or $350 each; and other assets including livestock, plantation tools, and equipment at $8,502; making a total of $160,402. Expenses amounted to $17,894.48 and included the following: interest at 7 per cent on the investment in land, slaves, and livestock (but not on the investment in tools and equipment), totaling $11,103; taxes on slaves and land; medical care; wages of three overseers; average expenditures for iron, tools, and equipment (the equivalent of depreciation); shoes, hats, and clothing; molasses, tobacco, and salt; and freight, commission, and other costs of selling and shipping cotton. The plantation produced 331,136 pounds of cotton. Its income from other sources amounted to $2,430, so that the average cost of a pound of cotton was 4.07 cents. Had this cotton sold at 6 cents, Robinson concluded, the profits would have been $1,973.68, at 7 cents, $5,385.04,

[3] Ulrich B. Phillips, *American Negro Slavery* (New York, 1918), 391–92.

[4] Lewis C. Gray, *History of Agriculture in the Southern United States to 1860,* 2 vols. (Washington, 1933), I, 476.

which was about what it brought, being a little more than 3 per cent.[5]

The editor of the *South Carolinian,* however, completely rejected Robinson's conclusions. First he protested against the uniform valuation of all land at $15 per acre when 1,500 acres were not in cultivation. The plantation did not need more than 750 acres of unimproved land for wood lot, grazing, etc., so that the remaining 750 acres were not, according to the writer, a legitimate part of the plantation. This reduced the real capital by $11,250 to $150,152. "But," continued the editor:

> the most glaring inconsistency which our agricultural tourist exhibits in calculating the profits of a business investment, is in adding the item of interest upon capital as expense. A person investing money in any enterprise is justly considered to be doing a fair business if he makes a small percentage over interest and expenses; and the statement which Mr. Robinson furnishes of Col. Williams's plantation, only proves that our fellow-citizen makes about 12½ per cent. on his capital, and that too with the price of cotton placed as low as six cents *in Charleston*—for freight and commission are included in the table of "expenses."
>
> . . . we deny the principle of adding interest on capital, as part of the expenses, when the object is to find out the profits upon that capital. . . . Mr. Robinson calculates interest upon the cost of the stock of the plantation, which is obviously fallacious and deceptive, where its natural increase must amount to more than the interest. . . . He omits to add to the income of the plantation the natural increase of the labor employed thereon—an item which is always prominent in the planter's calculation, and which would unquestionably amount to 5 or 6 per cent. per annum upon their original cost. And . . . he has certainly neglected the increased value arising from the yearly improvement of a well cultivated plantation. . . . The result then, according to our views, will be as follows:

Capital invested, $150,152.00
Income of the farm

331,136 lbs. cotton, at 6 cents	$19,868.16
Bacon and other provisions	2,430.00
Increase of negroes, say 5 per cent., set down as capital $89,000	4,495.00
	26,793.16
The annual expenses of the farm, as itemized by Mr. Robinson, a full estimate, including freight and commission,	6,791.48
Net profit of capital invested	$20,001.68

[5] James D. B. De Bow, *The Industrial Resources, etc., of the Southern and Western States,* 3 vols., (New Orleans, 1853), I, 161–64; D. Lee, "Cotton," in *Report of the Commissioner of Patents for the Year, 1849,* Part II, *Agriculture* (Washington, 1850), 307–13; Ralph B. Flanders, *Plantation Slavery in Georgia* (Chapel Hill, 1933), 221–22. There are several errors of calculation in the various reprintings of Robinson's report which account for the discrepancies in the figures used by different writers quoted here and subsequently.

These profits amount to over *thirteen per cent. per annum* over all expenses—the *Charleston* price of cotton being only put down at 6 cents. Suppose the crop averaged eight cents in Charleston, as it would do at the present time, the profits would be $26,614.40, or nearly 18 per cent.[6]

Thus, two contemporary observers, using essentially the same figures, arrive at quite different results. One said profit for the year was only $1,973.68, while the other was equally certain that it was $20,001.68. Paradoxically, both were essentially correct, because each meant something different when he wrote of profit. "Perhaps no term or concept in economic discussion is used with a more bewildering variety of well established meanings than profit," Frank H. Knight, a modern economist, has stated.[7]

Solon Robinson, probably following the definition of Jean-Baptiste Say,[8] the French nineteenth-century economist, apparently considered profit as mere wages of management. Almost all classical economists "recognized at least three elements in the income of the capitalist entrepreneur: one a payment for the bare use of the capital (equal to the interest rate); a second element representing payment for the entrepreneur's activities as manager; and a third connected in a rather vague way with the carrying of the risks or hazards of the enterprise." Most of them, however, continued to apply the term profit to the combination of the three elements of the proprietor's income. But Say insisted "on a separation between profit and interest and the treatment of profit as a species of wage."[9]

The editor of the *South Carolinian,* however, was not writing of economic profit. He was writing as an ordinary businessman or farmer according to the most generally accepted definition of profit, that of accounting. To him, the entire net income of the proprietor,

[6] De Bow, *Industrial Resources,* I, 163–64. Dr. D. Lee also questioned the validity of Robinson's calculations, saying, "The above estimates are defective and erroneous. . . . No allowance is made . . . for the increase in number and value of the slaves in the course of a year. If this is not equal to 7 per cent. on an average, it is to 3½ per cent., and sometimes reaches 8 to 10 per cent."

[7] Frank H. Knight, "Profit," in *Encyclopedia of the Social Sciences,* 15 vols. (New York, 1930–35), XII, 480–87.

[8] Jean-Baptiste Say apparently was widely read and very influential in the United States. His *A Treatise on Political Economy or the Production, Distribution, and Consumption of Wealth* was highly recommended by Thomas Jefferson, who edited the work for American publication in 1817. Five editions were printed and sold between 1817 and 1834, when the sixth edition was issued. Subsequently there was a new American edition in 1855. See Richard Hofstadter, "Parrington and the Jeffersonian Tradition," in *Journal of the History of Ideas* (New York, 1940–), II (1941), 396–97.

[9] Knight, "Profit," in *Encyclopaedia of the Social Sciences,* XII, 418.

after the deduction of all expenses, including depreciation and loss of value of assets, was profit.

Unfortunately, Robinson does not seem to have completely realized the meaning of his profit figure. He acted upon the definition of profit as wages of management, deducting interest upon investment as a cost of doing business, but he then assumed that there was a relation between the profit figure and the planter's investment. Actually there was no connection between the two. And when Robinson said that if the cotton were sold at seven cents, the profit would be $5,385.04, or about 3 per cent on the investment, he was merely saying that Colonel Williams' wages for managing the plantation were the equivalent of a 3 per cent return on his capital. The total income of Colonel Williams from the plantation during the year, by Robinson's statement, was $16,488.04, a 7 per cent return on his investment, or $11,103, plus $5,385.04, wages for management.

If this deduction or charge for "interest on investment" had been called "profit on investment," which would be equally accurate, Robinson's statement would not have been so completely misinterpreted by one modern student, who, in his rewriting of it, said, "The *cash expenditures* totalled $17,879.48, and included the following: interest on capital at 7 per cent."[10] This interest, it must be repeated, was not an expenditure of the planter, but was part of his income.

Most of the modern historians who deny the profitableness of slavery seem to confuse profit, as defined by Say and those who follow him, with the ordinary conception of profit used by businessmen and farmers. None of these historians, so far as can be ascertained from their studies, have used the rather elaborate financial statistics in the census of 1850 and 1860; or, at least, they have made no attempt to reconcile the conflict between their low estimates of profit from plantation operation and the overwhelming indication of a large increase of wealth in the South between 1850 and 1860.

Selected figures[11] for thirteen of the slave states, excluding rather arbitrarily Missouri and Delaware, show this increase very clearly:

[10] Flanders, *Plantation Slavery in Georgia*, 221. Italics mine.

[11] Compiled from: James D. R. De Bow, *Statistical View of the United States . . . Being a Compendium of the Seventh Census* (Washington, 1854), 82, 95, 169; *The Seventh Census of the United States, 1850* (Washington, 1853), xxxiii; *The Eighth Census of the United States, 1860*, 4 vols. (Washington, 1864–1866), II, *Agriculture* (1864), vii, 222, 247–48; Joseph C. D. Kennedy, *Preliminary Report on the Eighth Census, 1860* (Washington, 1862), 195.

	1850	1860
Number of farms	508,680	665,417
Total improved acres in farms	51,451,040	67,478,629
Average improved acres in farms	101.15	101.41
Total unimproved acres in farms	118,612,338	156,886,549
Average unimproved acres per farm	233.32	235.94
Average size of farms	334.47	377.35
Total cash value of farms	$1,035,544,075.	$2,228,179,125.
Average cash value of farms	$2,035.75	$3,438.71
True value of real and personal property	$2,809,875,462.	$6,245,129,163.
True value of real and personal property per capita—whites and free Negroes	$490.49	$878.08
Total number of slaveholders	326,054	358,728
Total number of slaves	3,110,652	3,833,782
Average number of slaves per slaveholder	9.54	10.69

Many objections to these figures can be raised. They were collected by the marshals of the various districts and many of them may be inaccurate. Some of these figures lump slaveholders and nonslaveholders together, while others combine rural and urban wealth without distinction. Nevertheless, they are the most complete and accurate now available. Fortunately, however, the manuscript returns of individuals for 1850 and 1860 have in many instances been preserved. From these Dr. Herbert Weaver has studied the individual fortunes of five hundred persons engaged in agriculture in Jefferson and Jones counties, Mississippi. Two hundred and three of these men were nonslaveholders, and the remainder slaveholders, in 1850. In reporting the results of his investigation, he stated:

> The only items checked were number of slaves, amount of improved and unimproved land owned, and the value of farms. By thus tracing individuals through a ten year period, the great prosperity enjoyed by all groups was established beyond all doubt. In practically every case there was an increase in every column. Slaveholdings, if they were slaveholders, showed a decided upward trend, and numerous nonslaveholders were found to own slaves in 1860. . . . Landholding increased . . . , but . . . it seems that the value of the land increased more than the acreage. A part of this was certainly due to a general increase in valuation of land, but the increase was too great to be attributed entirely to that fact. A great part of the increase in value represented increased acreage and improvements. Landholdings increased by about fifty per cent throughout the state, but the value of farms increased more than three fold.[12]

[12] Herbert Weaver, "The Agricultural Population of Mississippi, 1850–1860" (Ph. D. dissertation, Vanderbilt University, 1941), 121–25.

These figures from the census reports and the manuscript returns do not prove that slavery on southern plantations was profitable in its last decade but they do indicate this conclusion strongly enough to place the burden of proof upon those who deny that planters were making profits. Ulrich B. Phillips did not present any direct evidence on this problem but merely stated his own belief that slavery probably was not profitable in the late 1850's. He did not bear this out by citing figures based upon the actual experience of plantation owners, or upon contemporary estimates in newspapers or periodicals. Apparently his principal interest was not in the profits of the plantation owner but in comparing the cost of slave and free labor.[13]

The most complete and comprehensive attempt to estimate the profits of plantation slavery is to be found in *Slavery in Mississippi* (1933) by Charles S. Sydnor. In this he has prepared a profit and loss statement, based on average figures from a large number of plantations, which indicates a very small rate of return for plantation owners and advances Professor Sydnor's doubt of the profitableness of slavery. This statement, however, is open to so many objections and questions that a detailed and critical analysis seems appropriate. In his statement, Professor Sydnor said:

The chief source of income would be from cotton. Probably thirty of the fifty negroes worked in the field. If those produced 5¾ bales each, there would be a total of 158 bales which, at ten cents a pound, would be worth		$6,320.00
The expenses of the plantation would be as follows: 50 negroes at $600 each (in the late 'fifties the price was higher) represented an investment of $30,000. Calculating interest at 6 per cent, this amounted to	$1,800.00	
At least an equal amount should be added for depreciation in slave property by accidents, deaths, old age, etc.	1,800.00	
As the average hand worked about twelve acres, 600 acres would be ample for pastures and woodland as well as fields. Allowing $10 per acre, the investment in land at 6 per cent interest involved a yearly carriage charge of	360.00	
and it ordinarily depreciated at the rate of at least three per cent a year in value	180.00	

[13] Phillips, *American Negro Slavery*, 344–401; *id.*, "The Economic Cost of Slaveholding," in *Political Science Quarterly* (New York, 1886–), XX (1905), 257–75.

Annual hire of an overseer, at least	300.00	
Purchases from New Orleans or elsewhere of negro clothing, miscellaneous plantation supplies, etc. . .	1,000.00	
Without including various miscellaneous expenditures, such as the purchase of corn and pork, of which few plantations produced enough, the total of the expenses and interest charges was		$5,440.00
Profit of the planter		880.00[14]

From these figures Louis Hacker, in the *Triumph of American Capitalism* (1940), drew the conclusion that the hypothetical planter made only 2 per cent on his invested capital. By the same reasoning a man who lent money at 5 per cent would show a loss of 1 per cent because of the deduction of 6 per cent interest on investment.

Professor Sydnor, himself, understood that "interest on investment" was not an actual expense of the planter, because, as he said, the planter "was, of course, free to spend the interest on his investment in negroes and land, and this was the item that caused the profits from Mississippi plantations to appear high." He also stated that "the $880 might be considered the wages of the planter for managing the enterprise,"[15] but he never recognized that, according to many economists and the generally accepted definition of accountants and businessmen, profit is a combination of this interest on investment and wages for management.

Other objections must be made to the statement. In the chapter "Profitableness of Slavery," Professor Sydnor wrote, "Cotton, however, was not the only source of profit. A planter who barely made expenses by the sale of cotton might find his estate yearly increasing in value by the rearing of young negroes."[16] This certainly seems true because there was a steady natural increase in the slave population during the entire ante-bellum priod. In addition, the price of slaves tended generally upward except in years of financial crisis. Nevertheless, in his own estimate of plantation income, Professor Sydnor did not take this increase in value into account. Instead he deducted, as an expense, $1,800 "for depreciation in slave property by accidents, deaths, old age, etc." It hardly seems correct to consider a working force which not only reproduced itself but increased in number, skill, and price, as a source of expense to the planter.

Similarly the expense figure of depreciation of land seems diffi-

[14] Charles S. Sydnor, *Slavery in Mississippi* (New York, 1933), 195–202. The income figure was not printed in the statement.
[15] *Ibid.*, 197.
[16] *Ibid.*, 198.

cult to justify. At 3 per cent a year the land would be almost valueless after thirty-three years. But Mississippi land is still growing cotton. Unquestionably almost every crop takes something out of the land. But with equal certainty it can be said that the yearly work of the slaves, preparing the soil, ditching the fields, and clearing additional acres, aided fertility and increased value. This sometimes necessitated a cash expenditure for fertilizer or equipment, which would be a just charge to plantation expense; but it seems impossible now, with our limited and inadequate knowledge, to be certain whether there was a net gain or loss in value of land from the yearly plantation activity.

Professor Sydnor's estimate of the value of the planter's investment in land and slaves may also be questioned, because he seems to have assumed that the value of an asset is its market value at the particular moment.[17] Prices, however, are the result of so many complex and unascertainable factors that they rarely can be taken as the equivalent of actual value. It is only under ideal circumstances that classical economists accept price as equal to value, and most other economists look on price as one of the evidences of value, not its exact expression.

Neither can the accountant accept this, because it would mean that assets fluctuate in value annually, which would introduce into the profit and loss statement a variable figure unrelated to the activities of the particular enterprise. A profit or loss (the equivalent of an increase or decrease in value of an asset) is usually not considered by an accountant until it has been realized. Prices rise and fall for various reasons, and if these "paper" profits or losses from the unrealized increase or decrease of the market price of an asset were accepted as real, the actual profit or loss from operations during the accounting period would be obscured. For this reason an accountant usually values an asset at its cost, less depreciation, and not at its current market price.

Most of the land and slaves in the South did not change hands

[17] In another place Professor Sydnor says, "Since a fall in price of two dollars a slave would cause a drop of nearly a million dollars in the capital value of the slaves in the State, the profitableness of the institution depended largely on the price of slaves." This statement would not be accepted by an economist or an accountant, unless the owner was in the business of rearing slaves for sale, which few planters were; but, regardless of that, it has not even been considered by Professor Sydnor himself. If a fall in the price of slaves would result in a loss to the planter, then, in logic at least, an increase in price would give a profit to the planter. The price of slaves, according to Phillips, increased almost every year in the 1850's, but this profit, by Dr. Sydnor's own definition, is not included in the statement of plantation income. *Ibid.*, 201.

after 1849 and consequently the market price in the 1850's had little or nothing to do with their cost. Certainly a majority of the slaves had been reared by their owners, and their capital value as an asset was the cost of their rearing. There is no exact statistical information concerning the cost of rearing the slave, but it hardly could have amounted to Professor Sydnor's figure of $600, which was based on market price in the early 1850's. This arbitrary capitalization of all slaves at the current market price introduces another element of uncertainty into the statement—again because of the deduction of "interest on investment." For if investment increases each year, with the rise in the price of slaves, the deduction from profit of "interest of investment" is also larger. Consequently the planter shows a decrease instead of an increase in profit from the raised capital value of his assets.

This "interest on investment," some economists say, is a cost of doing business, to others it is a part of profit; and there is also disagreement about how it is to be figured and what rate is to be charged. Some define it as the current rate of return. If it is, no entrepreneur, according to theory, could be expected to make more without attracting competitive capital into the same enterprise. It is also a virtually impossible task to ascertain the current rate of return during this period. Others say it is the current rate of interest on borrowed money. But this figure fluctuated widely with various individuals and sections of the South, and the information upon which to base an average is lacking. Still others insist that it is the so-called "pure" interest rate, the one yielded by the safest investment, but this would be more difficult to ascertain than either of the others. Phillips recommended that such a charge be made in figuring the cost of slave labor, but he made no estimate as to what the rate should be. Sydnor who used 6 per cent and Robinson who used 7 per cent are alike in that they gave no reasons for their respective choices.

This difficulty in arriving at a satisfactory figure is one of the reasons why the financial accountant makes no use of interest on investment.[18] Another is the technical impossibility of handling a deduction from profit that is neither an expenditure nor the de-

[18] There is a serious debate among cost accountants as to whether interest on investment has a proper place in that limited and specialized field of accounting. Some argue, as does Ulrich B. Phillips in his analysis of the cost of slave labor, "that the provision of capital is a necessary expense of a business just as is rent, insurance, or wages, and that it should be treated in the same manner as these expenses." But the majority seem to believe that the return on capital is not an expense but a profit, and the business world is

crease in value of an asset. But the chief argument against its use, is that it gives no information. It is merely the separation of the proprietor's income into two parts, interest upon investment, and profit above that interest. This is of little or no importance to the owner or the accountant, and of interest only to the economist who, in reality, is forced to guess as to the proper apportionment between the two.

If these objections to Professor Sydnor's statement are valid, the hypothetical planter seems to be somewhat better off. The results from his operations would be something like this:

Income from Cotton		$6,320.00
Expenses:		
Annual hire of overseer	$ 300.00	
Plantation supplies	1,000.00	1,300.00
Gross profit		5,020.00

This is the total of the money income and expenditure, though it was stated that no provision had been made for "miscellaneous expenditures such as the purchase of corn and pork, of which few plantations produced enough," and no consideration has been given to the various selling and transportation charges such as freight, insurance, packing costs, and factor's commissions.

It is not, however, a complete statement of the financial condition of the plantation, but it is almost all that can be known with any certainty. If the increase or decrease in value of assets is taken into consideration, so many approximations have to be used that the resulting figures are virtually without meaning. Each acre of land would have to be valued separately; its original cost ascertained; the loss of fertility from the year's crop, the increase in fertility from the year's work, and expenditures for fertilizer and equipment, would have to be balanced against each other; and

accustomed so to consider it. As a result, to treat interest on investment as a cost of operation would produce financial statements which are misleading. William B. Lawrence, *Cost Accounting* (New York, 1925), 312–13; Roy B. Kester, *Advanced Accounting* (New York, 1933), 515–17; Phillips, "Economic Cost of Slaveholding," in *loc. cit.*, 268–69. Some cost accountants insist that interest on investment should be included "in order to determine what would be a fair profit in a given case," or "to determine whether it is better to manufacture or to buy goods in the open market, and whether it is better policy to manufacture by means of expensive machinery and other equipment or by manual labor." But even these suggest a technical arrangement whereby interest on investment is charged as a manufacturing expense to get manufacturing cost, but is then removed from the books before the net profit is arrived at, so that interest on investment is not shown in the financial statement at all. Jerome Lee Nicholson and John F. D. Rohrback, *Cost Accounting* (New York, 1919), 139–40; Kester, *Advanced Accounting*, 140.

the resulting figure be shown as income or expense, as the case might be. Obviously this could not be done with any degree of accuracy. Each slave would then have to be valued on the basis of his cost—the cost of rearing him to work age if born on the plantation, or his original purchase price—his physical condition, age, experience, and special training; and a balance struck as to his increase or decrease in value during the particular year. The totals of these increases or decreases in value would have to be added to or taken away from another figure which would show the net gain or loss from births and deaths of slaves. Only in this way could an accurate figure for a particular plantation be ascertained.

Most of this, however, is hypothetical, and cannot be ascertained from surviving records. It was seldom taken into consideration by the planters themselves who usually were content with the simplest records and figured profits or losses on the basis of cash income and expenditure. They, like the modern accountant, businessman, and farmer, considered their entire net income as profit, and made no attempt to divide it, according to classical theory, into interest on investment, wages of management, and compensation for risk.

If attention is turned to the actual results of plantation operations as they are to be found in some surviving account books and papers, and in reports of contemporary newspapers and periodicals, no consistent pattern of profits is to be found. Cotton, rice, and tobacco, the staples of the South, were such speculative crops that there were wide variations in profit from plantation to plantation, and from year to year. For instance, in 1846–1847 on an Alabama plantation owned jointly by Mrs. R. Brown and Franklin H. Elmore, working 108 slaves and having an estimated value of $70,000, the profits from the sale of 199 bales of cotton were $7,352.40, or 10.5 per cent, with no direct superintendence by either of the proprietors.[19] On the other hand, Farish Carter, one of the most successful Georgia planters, in 1851 made profits of $1,530 on a plantation valued at $150,000. This was a return of only 1¼ per cent on his investment.[20] In neither of these statements was credit taken or deduction made for the increase or decrease in value of slaves, the depreciation or appreciation of land, or any other intangible item.

Published estimates of the cost of growing cotton and of profits of plantations must be accepted with caution, particularly in the

19 Gilmer & Company, Montgomery, to Franklin H. Elmore, Charleston, March 18, 1847, in Franklin H. Elmore MSS. (Division of Manuscripts, Library of Congress).

20 Flanders, *Plantation Slavery in Georgia*, 222–23.

late 1840's and 1850's. During these years the merchants of Liverpool and the manufacturers of Manchester were protesting against the American monopoly of cotton production. The Cotton Supply Association was organized in Manchester with the openly avowed purpose of breaking the American domination of cotton supply by encouraging its growth in the colonies of the empire. Southern cotton growers and merchants, frightened by the possibility of increased competition, attempted to prove that the price of cotton was too low rather than too high, and that the profits from cotton planting had been grossly overstated.

One of these, who acknowledged his purpose, estimated that the gross profits from raising cotton on a well-equipped plantation with 100 slaves and valued at $100,000 would amount only to $1,750 with cotton selling at five cents a pound. But this, according to the writer, did not include anything "for the support of the planter . . . nor . . . to meet those contingent and incidental losses and costs . . . as the loss of servants from epidemics, the loss of *whole teams* from diseases, the frequent accidents to gins and houses from fire, losses from overflows, breaking of levees, &c." [21] Another, writing in the *Soil of the South,* also said that the profits of cotton planting were overestimated, but was forced to admit that "there are more fortunes made at planting than at any other business." His explanation of the paradox was that it was "attributable not to the supposed fact that there is more money made at the business than any other, but because planters are, as a class, more economical, and live more at home than any other." He estimated that the average cost of raising 2,000 pounds of ginned cotton was $160.16, or slightly over 8 cents a pound, but included, as part of cost, 7 per cent profit on the investment in slaves, land, and mules, or $105.76.[22]

One of the longest and most detailed records of a plantation which has been preserved is that of Hopeton on the Altamaha River in Glynn County, Georgia. This plantation was established before the War of 1812 by John Couper, a Scotsman, and remained in his possession until January 1, 1827. In a letter summarizing the results under his ownership, he said:

> You know I commenced planting without capital. Of course had to go in debt and 8 per cent compound interest I found to be the real perpetual motion. Though tolerable successful sometimes, yet I had sad reverses—Embargo, non-intercourse & War—interfered with my prospects, whilst

[21] De Bow, *Industrial Resources,* I, 150–52.
[22] "The Cost of a pound of Cotton," in *De Bow's Review* (New Orleans, 1846–1880), XVIII (1855), 468–70.

interest progressed—My loss of 60 prime effective negroes—carried off by the Enemy—lessened my annual income full $15,000—to supply their places *in part* I bt. 120 slaves for which I paid an average of 450$. Crops were not favorable. In the year 1824—I had *matured* a crop of 600 Bales cotton—which would have produced $90,000—This was lost in 12 hours by hurricane. In 1825 I again nearly lost my crop by caterpillar. Cotton then sunk in price, without any prospect of improvement. Lands were reduced to ⅓ of their value. Slaves to 250 or 200. In short I saw no hope of paying my debts and retaining my property—& tho not pushed—I thought best during my life to meet the storm. So to make a long story short—Mr. Hamilton being my principal creditor—on his agreeing to pay what other debts I owed—I surrendered to him all my property, debt, and dues of every description in a lump without valuation—except my lands on St. Simons and one hundred slaves—So on the 1st day of January 1827 I was thrown on the world without a dollar to support my people and family—Am glad to get off so well. Even though at a reasonable valuation the property I surrendered, was more than sufficient to pay my debts, yet had it been brought to a forced sale, it might have done less. I am satisfied and relieved from much anxiety. By this event neither my standing in society—nor my mode of living have suffered any change.[23]

This reads as a confession of failure, but though John Couper suffered many grievious misfortunes, he had, by his own statement, began planting without capital, and ended, after paying all his debts, with a plantation and 100 slaves, worth from fifty to a hundred thousand dollars. He had also, with a large family, lived in luxurious surroundings during most of the period, which is certainly no slight return from a lifetime devoted to planting.

John Couper had turned Hopeton over to his principal creditor, James Hamilton, a Scots merchant, and Hamilton in turn sold half of the plantation and 380 slaves to James H. Couper, son of John, for $137,000 to be paid over a period of fifteen years at 6 per cent interest. Couper was to have the entire management for which he was to receive $2,000 per year, the run of the plantation, and half the profits.[24] This arrangement continued until January 1, 1841, when Couper, to clear himself of debt, turned back his interest in the plantation to the Hamilton estate. After this, until 1852, Couper continued to manage the plantation for the estate. During the entire period of his management of the plantation from 1827 to 1852, he kept elaborate records of all phases of plantation operations including detailed financial information concerning receipts and expenditures.[25]

[23] John Couper, St. Simon's, to James Couper, Scotland, May 24, 1828, in John Couper MSS. (Southern Collection, University of North Carolina).

[24] *Ibid.*

[25] Hopeton Plantation Records (Southern Collection, University of North Carolina).

From these records it is possible to establish year by year the cost value of the investment in the plantation, the gross and net sales, expenditures, and net profit. As the rate of profit varied widely from year to year it has seemed clearer to present the results in tabular form.

Year	Capital	Gross Sales	Net Sales	Expenses	Profit	Rate of Profit
1827	$274,000.00	ns	$4,367.19½	$12,239.56¼	$7,871.76¾ [26]	
1828	294,895.22	ns	15,043.50	6,924.93	8,118.57	2.7%
1829	298,014.40	ns	11,707.08	9,021.95	2,685.13	.9
1830	298,014.40	ns	15,235.55	12,730.26	2,505.29	.8
1831	298,046.40	ns	22,482.34	16,949.10	5,533.24	1.85
1832	300,126,65	ns	17,030.23	10,910.86	6,119.37	2.
1833	302,617.07	ns	22,016.37	10,937.07	11,079.30	3.6
1834	302,617.07	ns	20,609.24	9,918.72	10,690.52	3.5
1835	302,617.07	ns	26,897.48	11,857.64	15,039.84	4.9
1836	302,617.07	ns	31,977.27	8,452.16	23,525.11	7.7
1837	302,617.07	ns	45.970.72	9,868.87	36,101.85	11.9 [27]
1938	302,617.07	ns	35,889.13	12,939.44	22,949.69	7.2
1839	302,617.07	$38,484.06	36,199.90	10,022.71	26,177.19	8
1840	302,617.07	26,476.34	24,288.01	11,276.11	12,951.90	4.2

The profits during these years were not large except in the years when the income from crops was supplemented by the hire of slaves to work on the Brunswick Canal. But the figures alone do not give the complete story.

As soon as James Couper took over the management of the plantation he began an experiment in sugar raising which turned out unsuccessfully. This not only caused an expenditure of $22,443.82 for machinery in the first six years but also diverted a part of the labor force from other crops. This was not a foolish or reckless experiment, because sugar planters, under not unsimilar conditions in Louisiana, were making great fortunes, but it, apparently, was chiefly responsible for the low profits in the first few years.

As the plantation was turned back to the established crops, rice and sea-island cotton, the rate of profit began to increase to a more satisfactory figure. The statement of plantation expenses also appears to contain a substantial amount—the exact figure cannot be ascertained—for the personal and household expenses of Couper

[26] Deficit.

[27] In the three years 1837–1839, inclusive, the income of the plantation was increased by hire of slaves to the contractors building the Brunswick Canal: 1837, $19,208.51; 1838, $15,010.75; 1839, $7,250.49.

and his family.[28] It is to be remembered that as part of his compensation for management he had the use of house servants, horses, and boats, as well as produce for his table from his plantation. This was no inconsiderable item if the report of Sir Charles Lyell was correct. He visited the plantation in 1845 when conditions were probably the same as between 1827 and 1840. He described the separate villa maintained for Couper and his family on nearby St. Simon's Island, the library containing "Audubon's Birds, Michaud's Forest Trees, and other costly works on natural history," and then added:

> Much has been said in praise of the hospitality of the southern planter, but they alone who traveled in the southern states can appreciate the perfect ease and politeness with which a stranger is made to feel himself at home. Horses, carriages, boats, servants, are all at his disposal. Even his little comforts are thought of, and everything is done as heartily and naturally as if no obligations were conferred. . . .
>
> The landed proprietors here visit each other in the style of English country gentlemen, sometimes dining out with their families and returning at night, or, if the distance be great, remaining to sleep and coming home the next morning. A considerable part of their food is derived from the produce of the land; but, as the houses are usually distant from large towns, they keep large stores of groceries and of clothing, as is the custom in country houses in some parts of Scotland.[29]

These were real profits and must be considered, even if it is not possible to set a figure for them. At the same time the plantation was increasing, not decreasing, in value. No charge for depreciation on lands, or slaves, or other capital assets, was placed on Couper's books. He had not even written off as loss the cost of the unsuccessful experiment in sugar, but there was no need to. The year by year increase in value of the plantation more than offset these losses.

When Couper turned back his half interest in the plantation to the Hamilton estate on January 1, 1841, three commissioners were appointed by the Superior Court of Glynn County. These commissioners estimated the value of the plantation to be $381,425, or an increase over original cost and additional investment of $78,807.93. This represented a net gain in value of 26 per

[28] Hopeton Plantation Records. Couper seems to have kept exact records of his income and expenditures, but his financial statements have not been preserved. In some instances it has been difficult to decide whether a given item should be charged as an expense or considered an increase of capital. It is not believed, however, that there were enough of these to affect the figures given above in any substantial way.

[29] Sir Charles Lyell, *A Second Visit to the United States of North America*, 2 vols. (New York, 1849), I, 244–46, 253, 254–55.

cent in fourteen years. This estimate, apparently, was too high for Couper and the trustees of the estate, and the actual transfer of title was made at a book value of $342,481.88. The increase in value was $39,864.81, or 13 per cent.[30]

During the twelve years from 1840 to 1852 the plantation was owned by the Hamilton estate but managed by Couper, at a salary of $5,000 a year for ten years and $6,000 a year for two. The same arrangement in regard to household expenses that had been true during the first period appears also to have been in effect during the second and must be remembered in connection with the actual figures of profits. The 1840's were probably the worst decade, economically, in the agricultural history of the ante-bellum South, but the results of Couper's management, after deduction of his and the overseers' salaries, were as follows:

Year	Capital	Gross Sales	Net Sales	Expenses	Profit	Rate of Profit
1841	$347,481.88	$30,470.58	$27,974.83	$16,821.98	$11,152.85	3.2%
1842	344,681.88	18,905.86	17,232.27	15,752.97	1,479.30	.43
1843	344,681.88	23,392.47	20,770.26	13,240.05	7,530.21	2.2
1844	344,181.88	30,411.03	27,699.58	17,259.71	10,439.87	3
1845	344,181.88	26,370.14	24,436.28	13,120.11	11,316.17	3.3
1846	344,181.88	41,161.97	37,602.85	13,685.68	23,917.17	6.9
1847	343,617.56	29,893.75	27,335.05	14,914.55	12,420.50	3.6
1848	343,617.56	30,807.12	27,810.52	16,397.00	11,413.52	3.3
1849	340,017.56	36,988.17	33,280.75	15,341.87	17,928.88	5.3
1850	342,017.56	35,795.48	32,571.73	16,583.30	15,988.43	4.7
1851	349,474.60	29,587.54	26,603.62	17,627.43	8,976.19	2.6
1852	349,474.60	39,761.40	35,268.04	17,938.93	17,329.11	5 [31]

The changes in capital from year to year were the result principally of purchases and sales of land and slaves. Land to the value of $8,789.58 was purchased, while $2,057.56 was received from sales of land, during the twenty-six years. In the same period seven additional slaves were bought and twenty sold. The land evidently had increased in fertility because the crops were larger and produced more income in the later years than in the earlier. The slave record for the plantation has not been located. But Sir Charles Lyell gave indirect evidence of an increase in the number of slaves when he wrote that in 1845 there were 500 at Hopeton, or an increase of 120 from the original 380.[32]

Another plantation for which an extensive record has been preserved is Gowrie, owned by Louis Manigault and located on

[30] Hopeton Plantation Records.
[31] *Ibid.*
[32] Lyell, *Second Visit,* I, 261–62.

the Savannah River. The sole money crop was rice. The original value of the plantation was $40,000, and on it were 220 acres of cleared ground, 80 acres uncleared, a fine rice mill, and 50 slaves. The plantation was gradually increased in size until finally it had 638 acres in cultivation, and from time to time additional slaves were purchased. The average value of the plantation during the first six years was approximately $42,115. Net proceeds of the crops of these years were $43,750, total expenses were $12,000, which made the average profit $5,095 a year or 12 per cent on the investment.[33]

There is a gap of sixteen years in the records; then for six years there is a detailed account of all receipts and expenditures. Manigault's investment, through the purchase of additional land and slaves, had increased to approximately $80,000 by 1857. The gross sales of rice for the six years from 1855 to 1861 were $103,739.55. Selling costs for the same period were $22,964.73, making net sales $80,774.82. Plantation expenses totaled $22,135.84, leaving as total net profits for six years, $58,638.98, or an average annual profit of $9,766.49. This amounted to a 12.2 per cent return upon the capital invested in the plantation.[34]

The profits from Gowrie were much higher than those from Hopeton. This may be accounted for in part by the difference in the years which the records cover, but probably more because Manigault did not make his home on the plantation, and no household expenses are included in the statement of plantation expenditures. It is certain, however, that Manigault did not consider these last six years to be extraordinarily successful ones. On the contrary he believed them to be particularly difficult.

The plantation had suffered epidemics of cholera in 1852 and 1854 in which twenty slaves, including "many of our *very best* hands," had died. There had been a destructive freshet in 1852, and a hurricane on September 8, 1854, both of which not only injured the standing crops but also strewed the entire plantation with loose rice "to the vast injury" of succeeding crops. Manigault's experienced overseer died in December, 1855, and it was not until April 8, 1859, that another capable man was employed. The overseers in the interim neglected the plantation and the slaves, and it took a year for the new overseer to repair injuries done by his predecessors.

[33] Statement of Louis Manigault, no date, pasted on flyleaf of "Statement of Sales—Gowrie Plantation—Savannah River," in Manigault Plantation Records (Southern Collection, University of North Carolina).

[34] Manigault Plantation Records.

This was satisfactory to the owner, who, in writing his report of operations during 1859–1860, said:

> Mr. Capers has not made a large crop but he says it was much on a/c of the bad condition in which he found the plantation, & I believe him, I am satisfied thus far with him, feeling that he has had no chance. We have bought two new Mules this winter, working in all six mules. During the past winter Mr. Capers has done much work. He has cut a new Canal through two squares, on the upper portion of the plantation, which I think will be of service. We have for the first time used the double horse ploughs, turning the lands much deeper than previously.

In spite of all these difficulties and neglect the land evidently had not deteriorated. The average production for the six years from 1833 to 1838 was 374 barrels of clean rice, while during the six years from 1855 to 1861 the crop averaged 843 barrels. There was, as said above, an increase in acreage devoted to rice from 220 to 638, or 190 per cent, but there was also an increase in production from a low of 220 barrels in 1833 to a high of 995 barrels in 1856, or 397 per cent.[35]

The plantation lost thirty-eight slaves in three cholera epidemics in 1834, 1852, and 1854, which forced Manigault to purchase forty-six slaves, between 1833 and 1861, in addition to the original fifty. This makes a total of ninety-six slaves brought to or purchased for the plantation; but there still were ninety-seven slaves on the plantation in 1857, the last year in which there is a record of the number of slaves. Consequently, it is not correct to charge any of this additional investment in slaves to expense. All that happened was that the natural increase in number and value was wiped out by the epidemics and the plantation neither made nor lost money on its working force.[36]

A third plantation for which there is record of capital, expense, and profits, is that of James H. Hammond of South Carolina, also on the Savannah River. Early in the 1850's Hammond offered his plantation, which he valued at $163,750, for sale. The plantation according to this offer consisted of the following:

1.	150 Negroes who shall constitute 80 task or effective hands and only 2 to 3 non-effective	$ 80,000.00
2.	630 acres . . . excluding . . . the Silverton Residence & tract of 280 acres & on the other side the Marsh & 1000 or 1500 acres as it may be, but including about 3000 acres of cleared land in good order—650 of it drained land—all except about 100 acres well marled, with mills, landing, etc. @ $12 per acre	75,600.00

[35] *Ibid.*
[36] *Ibid.*

3.	6000 bushels corn—60,000 pds. fodder	3,500.00
4.	30 mules & horse under 12 years mostly under 9 years	3,000.00
5.	5 fair Plantation Waggons. 3 ox carts. 4 Horse carts. 30 sets of gears. 60 ploughs, etc.	1,000.00
6.	100 head of hogs @ 1.50 & 40 head Cattle all ½ to Ayreshire with full blood bull and 10 oxen @ 10.00	650.00
		$163,750.00[37]

The detailed records of income and expenditure on Hammond's plantation do not appear to have been preserved but there is a memorandum in his papers which gives exact information for the five-year period from 1849 to 1853. During these years the total income from the sale of cotton, corn, rice, and fodder was $81,088.83. Plantation expenses amounted to $27,019.37, leaving a profit of $54,069.46, or an average annual profit of $10,813.89. Accepting his offer of sale as the total value of his investment, though its original cost to him probably was much less, Hammond had an average net annual return of 6.66 per cent.[38]

Unlike most planters, Hammond kept a separate record of his family expenses apart from the plantation records. In the same five years these expenses amounted to $31,913.55, which, if deducted from profits, gives him an annual net income over all expenses, business and personal, of $4,431.18, or 2.7 per cent.[39]

There seems to be no more justification for a depreciation charge against land or slaves on this plantation than there was at Gowrie or Hopeton, because, at least in Hammond's opinion, the plantation was gaining, not losing value. In 1859 he again wrote out an offer of sale, but this time he asked $175,000 and included only 140 Negroes comprising 70 full hands, 5,500 acres of land, fewer horses, mules, cattle, and pigs, and less corn and fodder.[40]

The records of these three plantations have been presented, not because they are considered to be typical of the plantation system, but merely because, through accident, they have been preserved in more detail than most others. Each was larger than the average plantation in the South, and all three were located in the older part of the South, where, incidentally, by common report, profits were lower than in the newer districts. They do indicate, however, that year after year, during periods of financial crisis or prosperity,

[37] Memorandum initialed J. H. H., no date, but probably 1852, in James H. Hammond MSS. (Division of Manuscripts, Library of Congress).

[38] Undated, unsigned memorandum in Hammond's writing, *ibid.*

[39] *Ibid.*

[40] Offer of Sale, July 19, 1859, *ibid.*

some plantations were making profits in the ordinary business sense of the term, and were increasing, not decreasing in value.

The evidence from these plantations, together with the overwhelming evidence of increase in wealth found in the census reports and in Herbert Weaver's study of the individual returns in two counties of Mississippi, all seem to point in a single direction. And that is to the tentative conclusion that the students who have stated that slavery was profitable are more nearly correct than those who deny its profitableness.

8

BY definition, historians write from hindsight. As a result they always run the risk of erroneously attributing to the men and events of earlier years attitudes and interpretations drawn from their own knowledge of subsequent history. Nowhere is this risk better illustrated than in the tendency of historians to characterize the ante-bellum South as undemocratic and outside the national drive to broaden the suffrage and to increase the participation of the common man in government. It seemed only logical to assume that a society which defended slavery, as the South did, should also resist the democratizing winds of the age. Even a southernborn historian like William E. Dodd in his *Cotton Kingdom* (New Haven, 1919) emphasized the political dominance of the big planters, leaving the impression of an oligarchic South confronting a democratic North in the years of sectional controversy.

But as Green points out in this article, the matter is not that simple. In the United States the question of who is to be included in the definition of "the people" has been an ever-changing one. It was quite possible for a society to be democratic for its time even though it defended Negro slavery, just as the North could be considered democratic while it rigorously denied the ballot to women. Yet for at least two generations after the Civil War, historians portrayed the ante-bellum South as outside the democratic upsurge of the first half of the nineteenth century.

This myth of the undemocratic South was wrong on two counts. The first error, as Green's article shows, was that the South participated vigorously and successfully in the movement to include the common man in the operations of the government. The second was that neither section, North or South, measured its commitment to democracy by its treatment of the Negro. Although the North by the 1830s had repudiated slavery, only five northern states permitted the free Negro to vote. And in all of them the Negro was discriminated against socially and in law. Recent research, like that of Leon Litwack in his *North of Slavery: The Negro in the Free States, 1790–1860* (Chicago, 1961), has reinforced Green's observation that in the North the Negro was never included in the great drive to political democracy.

Green's article demonstrates the politically democratic character of the Old South in three different ways. The first shows that the southern states abandoned or rejected property qualifications for voting about the same time and to the same extent as the northern states. He even notes that exceptions to this trend in the South, like South Carolina, were matched in the North in a state like Rhode Island.

But, as he rightly recognizes, constitutional change is only the formal basis of a movement to greater political democracy. A more profound question is whether the opportunities for democracy provided by the constitutions were in fact realized to the same extent as in the North. This is his second measure of democracy. Here the question is a quantitative one. Hence he compares the proportion of voters in the two sections to show that Southerners participated in their own governance and to the same degree as Northerners.

Democracy, though, is more than a matter of constitutional provisions and voting, important as these measures undoubtedly are. In the English-speaking nations democracy has also included a struggle between political parties for the favor of the electorate. For this competition to have meaning it is necessary that both parties have a reasonable possibility of winning elections; otherwise the struggle is more shadow than substance. Here, too, the question is essentially quantitative. His statistics on voting for the Whig and Democratic parties in the South constitute his third measure of a democratic polity in the southern states.

On the other hand, a further argument in behalf of democracy in the Old South that Mr. Green advances seems not germane. He regards the instructing of U. S. senators by state legislatures as to how the senators should vote in Congress as a measure of political democracy. But as Clement Eaton's "Southern Senators and the Right of Instruction, 1789–1860," *Journal of Southern History*, XVIII (August 1952), 303–319, points out, this device was hardly democratic. It gave the people no greater control over their senators; it only provided state legislators with more control. Therefore it was more a measure of southern concern for states' rights than for democracy.

To show that political democracy obtained in the South in the ante-bellum years is important enough. But Green in his article goes further than politics. He also offers suggestions that the South was democratic socially as well as politically.

One way in which he tries to demonstrate social democracy is to show that many political leaders were of humble social origin. The implication is that opportunities at the top of the political pyramid were open to all men, not simply to a small, hereditary, privileged elite. One of the staple ingredients of the myth of an undemocratic South was that such an elite dominated the political life of the region. Usually the dominance of the great planter class in the South was unfavorably contrasted with the opportunities open to men of lowly origin in the North, as exemplified in the career of Lincoln. Since the publication of Green's article, one of the important developments in the study of southern history is the recognition that society in the ante-bellum South was much less stratified than older historians had asserted. Although a book like Frank Owsley's *Plain Folk of the Old South* (Baton Rouge, 1949) goes too far in asserting the importance of the small farmer in southern society, its general point of the fluidity of class structure has been supported by other and later scholars. Clement Eaton, for example, in his recent book *The Growth of Southern Civilization* (New York, 1961) devotes a chapter, "The Discovery of the Middle Class," to documenting the upward social movement of many lower-class Southerners. One obvious reason for this social openness, as Green suggests, is that the Old South, far from being a land of settled and rigid class traditions, was in fact a frontier society, with all the opportunities as well as the limitations that empty land bestowed upon ambitious men in the better-known western frontier north of the Ohio River.

Other aspects of Southern social democracy advanced in Green's article, however, have not been upheld by more recent investigations. It is true that a number of southern leaders advocated public education as a part of the democratic movement of the 1830s and 1840s, just as was being done in the North. But the performance here was less successful than the movement to widen the suffrage. As late as 1850, for example, as J. D. B. DeBow, the Southerner who headed the U. S. Census, admitted, the South led the nation in illiteracy among whites. The South's illiteracy rate was twice that of the comparably rural Middle West and forty times that of the more urban New England. Moreover, prior to the Reconstruction period, no southern state could boast of a true system of public education such as in Massachusetts or New York. Finally, in the realm of social reform the southern states lagged far behind the rest of the nation after 1830. Part of the explanation for this lag was undoubtedly the South's consuming concern with the defense of slavery and its excessive commitment to agriculture, which retarded the growth of cities. But whatever the explanations, the fact remains that reform efforts were at best weak and at worst the object of southern popular ridicule and scorn. As chapters XII and XIII of Clement Eaton's *Growth of Southern Civilization* show, the South's record of concern for social change and improvement was not on a par with that in other sections of the nation.

But if more recent works have not sustained Green's efforts to demonstrate the social democracy of the South, virtually all writers have accepted his conclusion that the South fully participated in the movement toward political democracy in the years prior to the Civil War. (As the article by Richard McCormick makes clear, though, modern scholars would not connect this movement, as Green seems to do, with Andrew Jackson.) Charles S. Sydnor's *Development of Southern Sectionalism, 1819–1848* (Baton Rouge, 1948) documents the drive to expand the suffrage in a chapter appropriately headed "Movement Toward Political Democracy." In his textbook *History of the Old South* (New York, 1949), Clement Eaton has also followed Green's lead in a chapter entitled "The Two-party System of the Old South." Similarly, Dewey W. Grantham, Jr., in his recent survey of the literature entitled *The Democratic South* (Athens, Ga., 1963), emphasizes the South's participation in the democratic advances of the early nineteenth century.

Fletcher Green is Kenan Professor of History at the University of North Carolina and one of the "grand old men" of southern historical studies.

Democracy in the Old South[1]

BY FLETCHER M. GREEN

THE American dream of democracy and equality, based upon the philosophy of natural rights and popular sovereignty, found full, free, and adequate expression in such Revolutionary documents as the Declaration of Independence and the bills of rights of the state constitutions. "We hold these truths to be self-evident, that all men are created equal, that they are endowed by their Creator with certain unalienable Rights, that among these are Life, Liberty and the pursuit of Happiness." "All power is vested in, and consequently derived from, the people; . . . magistrates are their trustees and servants, and at all times amenable to them." "No man, or set of men, are entitled to exclusive or separate emoluments or privileges from the community but in consideration of publick services." These and similar expressions of democratic equalitarianism were familiar to the people in all the states of the American Union.

The mere declaration of these ideals did not insure their acceptance and enforcement; a vigorous and continuous defense of liberty is essential if it is to be preserved. Thomas Jefferson, spokesman for democracy, early observed that men were by their constitutions naturally divided into two classes: (1) those who fear and distrust the people and seek to draw all power into their own hands; and (2) those who have confidence in the people and consider the people the safest depository of public happiness and general well being. These two classes he called aristocrats and democrats. From the very beginning of American independence these two groups began a contest for control of the governments. This contest between the forces of aristocracy and democracy was one of the most important issues in the political development of the American nation

[1] This paper was prepared for presentation as the presidential address of the Southern Historical Association for 1945, but its delivery was prevented by the cancellation of the annual meeting.

during the first half century of its existence. In the northern states it was fought between the commercial-financial aristocracy and the working men, in the southern states between the aristocratic slaveholding planters and the yeoman farmers.

The first state constitutions were framed in an atmosphere of equality and the recognition of human rights, without hint of race or class distinctions, but they established property and freehold qualifications for voting and office holding, and a system of representation, that gave control of the state governments to the wealthy, conservative, aristocratic classes. The power and influence of the aristocracy were further enhanced by the victory of the conservative group that established the Federal Constitution. The Jeffersonian democrats, accepting, in theory at least, the doctrines of natural rights, popular sovereignty, government by compact and contract, and the perfectability of mankind, began a militant assault upon the strongholds of aristocracy. They demanded and obtained a bill of rights to the Federal Constitution, and an extended suffrage and a greater equality of representation in the state governments. Under their attacks the powers of aristocracy were gradually whittled away. Finally, with the accession of Andrew Jackson to the presidency in 1829, it seemed that democracy would certainly triumph. Most American people agreed with Alexis de Tocqueville that the democratic revolution was an irresistible one, and that to attempt to check it "would be to resist the will of God." [2]

As democratic reform moved into high gear under Jackson its forces were divided by the emergence of the bitter sectional controversy over slavery. The northern abolitionists saw in the institution of slavery the absolute negation of liberty and equality and they began to weigh and to find wanting almost every feature of southern society. In particular they condemned the southern state governments, declaring that in them political democracy was being overthrown by a slaveholding aristocracy. This change, said they, was the result not of caprice or political accident but of deliberate design on the part of the aristocracy; and it was succeeding because *"the non-slave-holding people of the South lacked the enterprise, intelligence and daring to demand and extract their democratic rights."* [3] In other words, they held that the masses of free whites were incapable of understanding or maintaining their rights, and that the

[2] Alexis de Tocqueville, *Democracy in America,* Translated by Henry Reeve, 2 vols. (Fourth edition New York, 1845), I, 1–2, 5.

[3] Thomas S. Goodwin, *The Natural History of Secession; or, Despotism and Democracy at Necessary, Eternal, Exterminating War* (New York, 1865), 40–41.

planter aristocracy was bitterly hostile to free institutions and the democratic theory of government universally.

By the time the sectional controversy reached the breaking point, the abolitionists had decided that the slaveholders had become a "DOMINANT CLASS, having positive control of the . . . political power of those States . . . the system of slavery concentrating, as it does all political influence in a few men who are virtually absolute in their respective States."[4] Contrasting the two sections, Richard Hildreth, the historian, declared: "The Northern States of the Union are unquestionable Democracies, and every day they are verging nearer and nearer towards the simple idea and theoretic perfection of that form of government. The Southern States of the Union, though certain democratic principles are to be found in their constitutions and their laws, are in no modern sense of the word entitled to the appellation of Democracies: They are Aristocracies; and aristocracies of the sternest and most odious kind."[5]

This interpretation of southern society and government was based upon moral hatred of Negro slavery, rather than a true knowledge of southern state governments or a philosophical or realistic understanding of democracy. Its appeal to the excited and hostile North was so powerful that most people accepted it as unquestionably accurate; and the general historians of the United States incorporated it into their writings. For instance, James Ford Rhodes says in his *History of the United States from the Compromise of 1850* that the "slaveholders, and the members of that society which clustered round them, took the offices. . . . The political system of the South was an oligarchy under the republican form." And Lord Acton, the British historian and publicist, wrote that "Secession was an aristocratic rebellion against a democratic government."[6]

The abolitionist promoters of the theory of the aristocratic nature of southern governments never attempted to define just what they meant by either artistocracy or democracy. Indeed democracy has always been difficult of definition. It is a relative term, and has had various meanings among different peoples and for the same people at different stages of their political development. In this paper it will be used in its general sense as a form of government in which

[4] Elhanon W. Reynolds, *The True Story of the Barons of the South; or The Rationale of the American Conflict* (Boston, 1862), 34–35.

[5] Richard Hildreth, *Despotism in America: An Inquiry into the Nature, Results, and Legal Basis of the Slave-Holding System of the United States* (Boston, 1854), 8.

[6] See also, Hermann E. von Holst, *The Constitutional and Political History of the United States*, 8 vols. (Chicago, 1876–1892), I, 348–349.

the sovereign power is held by the people and exercised through a system of representation in which the representatives are chosen by a fairly large electorate. The electorate has not been a fixed one in the United States. In the early days of the American republic the suffrage was bestowed upon adult male property owners; in the second quarter of the nineteenth century it was extended to all adult white males; during Reconstruction the Negro was given the ballot; and in 1920 women were permitted to vote in all elections. Recently, Georgia has given the ballot to youths eighteen years of age. No one would say that the state governments were undemocratic in 1850 simply because women did not vote; but they were *more* democratic in 1920 because women did vote. The same may be said in regard to Negro suffrage. Furthermore, up to the Civil War the emphasis on democracy was placed on *political* equality; since that time greater emphasis has been placed on social and economic equality. Modern thought presupposes that institutions, in order to be understood, must be seen in relation to the conditions of time, place, and thought in which they appear. It is difficult to look at democracy in this way, for one is prone to judge democracy of the past by the criteria of today. Yet the degree of democracy prevailing under the constitutions and governments of the Old South must be judged by the democracy of that era, not of the present. George Sidney Camp was but speaking for his generation when he wrote in 1840 that democracy "is not of an agrarian character or spirit. Its immediate object is an equal division of political rights, not of property. . . . But republicanism does aim a death blow at all those laws and usages the object of which is . . . to give it a particular and exclusive direction as a means of political power."[7]

As noted above, the Revolutionary state constitutions utilized to a large degree the framework of colonial governments and constitutional practices of the colonial period which had recognized and established a governing class of the wealthy aristocracy. Only eight of the thirteen states made any change in suffrage requirements; and these changes did not abolish the principle that only property holders should vote, they merely reduced the amount of property required. Property and freehold qualifications for voting and office holding meant that the governing class in the southern states was in large measure a planter aristocracy. The system of representation also favored the planter group of the eastern section. Though demo-

[7] George Sidney Camp, *Democracy* (New York, 1841), 155. Harper and Brothers were so anxious to spread the influence of this first general analysis of the principles of democracy by a native American that they brought it out in their Family Library.

cratic in form, these constitutions were certainly not democratic in fact. They did, however, lay the basis for the expansion of popular control, the chief element in a political democracy, to the majority of the people.

Hardly had the landed aristocracy established themselves in power when demands for revision and readjustment were heard in each of the states. Among the specific reforms called for were the disestablishment of the church and the abolition of religious qualifications for office holding; the abolition of the laws of entail and primogeniture; the broadening of the suffrage; the equalization of representation; and the reduction of property qualifications for office holding. All looked toward the curbing of the powers of the landed aristocracy. Piecemeal amendment and revision of the constitutions partially satisfied these demands.

In South Carolina the dissenting Presbyterians and Congregationalists, led by William Tennent, a Presbyterian minister, and Christopher Gadsden, prepared a memorial which was signed by thousands of people and presented a petition to the legislature in 1777 asking "free and equal privileges, both religious and civil" for all Protestants. Another group of reformers joined forces with the dissenters and demanded an elective upper house of the legislature rather than the appointive council. These changes were too democratic for the conservative and aristocratic element; but when the next elections showed a majority of the people favorable to the reform, and after the popular party had blocked an appropriation bill, the conservatives yielded. Even then Edward Rutledge and Arthur Middleton resigned the governorship rather than approve the changes. Maryland, too, modified her constitution in favor of Quakers, Mennonists, and other minor religious groups. Jefferson, Madison, and Richard Henry Lee succeeded in securing the disestablishment of the Episcopal Church in Virginia by legislative enactment.

South Carolina amended her constitution and joined Georgia and North Carolina in prohibiting entails and primogeniture. While no change was made in the Virginia constitution, the democratic element led by Jefferson forced measures through the legislature in 1786 abolishing entails and primogeniture. Jefferson believed that this legislation formed part of a system by which "every fibre would be eradicated of ancient or future aristocracy and a foundation laid for a government truly republican." The Virginia aristocracy never forgave him for this action.

The aristocracy made some slight concessions to the democrats in regard to suffrage and representation. South Carolina reduced the property requirements for voting from one hundred to fifty acres of land, and Georgia reduced it from ten pounds to the payment of all taxes levied by the state. Both states reduced considerably the property qualifications for office holding. And the up-country counties, inhabited largely by small farmers, were given a more nearly equal share of representation in the state legislatures. All efforts at change in these particulars failed in Maryland, Virginia, and North Carolina. In spite of the concessions granted, the conservative aristocracy was still in control of all five of the original southern states at the close of the eighteenth century.

The constitutions of the two new southern states added to the Union during this period of readjustment, Kentucky and Tennessee, show some influence of the frontier ideals of democracy. Kentucky gave the suffrage in 1792 to all free adult male citizens, but limited it to free white males in 1799. Representation was apportioned to free adult male inhabitants in 1792, and to qualified electors in 1799. No property or religious qualifications for office were prescribed, and the governor, after 1799, was to be elected by popular vote rather than indirectly by an electoral college as in 1792. Tennessee showed somewhat more aristocratic leanings in her constitution of 1796. Suffrage was limited to freemen possessed of a freehold; legislators and the governor were required to possess freeholds of two hundred and five hundred acres of land, respectively; representation was apportioned to the counties according to taxable inhabitants; and no person who denied the existence of God was eligible for any civil office. Though somewhat more democratic than the seaboard states, Tennessee nevertheless belongs with the group of older states controlled by the landed aristocracy. It should be pointed out, however, that in all these states there was much cheap land to be had; hence, it was no great burden to qualify for voting in any of these states.

The political revolution of 1800 which brought Jefferson and his party to power in most of the southern states, as well as in the federal government, led to the demand that the principles of the bills of rights be translated into realistic democracy rather than to stand as mere glittering generalities. In every state, democratic leaders condemned the discrimination made between those who had property and those who had none. They declared that where property had representation the people could not be free; and they were able to show that under the existing system of representation a minority of wealthy men of the east had absolute control of the state governments. They appealed to the philosophy of natural rights and demanded equality of political rights and privileges. This movement came largely from the small farmer or yeoman class concentrated in the newer counties of the up-country or the western parts of the states; hence it took on something of the nature of an intrastate sectional fight. It naturally involved social and economic issues as well as political rights.

The rapid settlement of the piedmont and mountain region of these states in the first quarter of the nineteenth century gave to the up-country a majority of the white population. These small farmers had somewhat different interests from the low-country planters. They desired internal improvements—roads, canals, and railroads—at state expense, in order that they might have an economic outlet for their farm produce, cattle, and domestic manufactures. A supporter of reform predicted that if the westerners were given their way roads and canals would be built, domestic manufactures would increase, wealth would multiply, and that the "Old Families . . . imbecile and incorrigible," would be replaced by a "happy, bold and intelligent middle class." [8] But the legislatures were controlled by the planter aristocracy of the east, who feared heavier taxation if the western farmers were given equal representation and resisted all change.

The yeoman farmers were joined by a small class of industrial laborers of the eastern cities. These people were smarting under the provisions of the constitutions that required a freehold for voting just as the yeoman farmers were smarting under the unequal system of representation. The laborers demanded manhood suffrage. The aristocratic planters feared to grant their demands lest the laborers join the small farmers in taxing the wealth of the east.

The democratic reformers demanded conventions fresh from the people with power to rewrite completely the constitutions. But since most of the constitutions left it to the legislature or made no provision for calling a constituent assembly, and since the artistocracy with their control over the legislatures could prevent a call through that body, the democrats were blocked at the very threshold of reform. The aristocratic minority fought doggedly to maintain its favored position, contesting every move of the democrats, and yielding only in the face of an open revolt. In Maryland they permitted a series of amendments between 1805 and 1810 that brought reorganization of the judicial system so as to bring justice closer to the people and make the courts more expeditious and less expensive. Property qualifications for officers were swept away; the suffrage

[8] *Niles' Register* (Baltimore, 1811–1849), XXXVII (1829), 145.

was extended to adult white males, the written ballot was required, and the plural vote was abolished; and some minor officials were made elective. In South Carolina representation was reapportioned in the house on the basis of white inhabitants and taxes combined. By this method the large slaveholding districts and parishes lost some of their representatives as allotted under the earlier constitutions. Suffrage was extended to include all white adult males who had resided in the state two years and were possessed of a freehold of fifty acres or a town lot, or who, if possessed of neither, had lived six months in the election district. This in reality meant white manhood suffrage. A series of amendments in Georgia between 1808 and 1824 made all officers from constable to governor, including judges of all the courts, elective by popular vote. These changes looked toward a greater participation in governmental affairs by the people and made the governments more responsive to the public will but, except in South Carolina, they did not appease the democratic reform spirit. The conservatives had prevented any change in North Carolina and Virginia.

Four new southern states, Louisiana, Mississippi, Alabama, and Missouri, were admitted to the Union during these years. Louisiana, admitted in 1812, fell to the control of the landed aristocracy. Only free white males were permitted to vote, and they were required to pay a state tax before qualifying. Members of the legislature and the governor were required to possess freeholds ranging in value from five hundred to five thousand dollars. Representation was apportioned according to qualified voters, or property holders. The governor and other officers were chosen by popular vote. Mississippi, too, was controlled by property holders. All officers were elected by popular vote; voting was limited to free white males who were enrolled in the militia or paid a tax; representation was based on white population; but members of the legislature and the governor were required to possess land ranging from fifty to six hundred acres, or real estate ranging in value from five hundred to two thousand dollars. Alabama greatly broadened the base of political power. Suffrage was granted to all adult white male citizens; no property qualifications were required for state officials who were elected by popular vote; and representation was according to white inhabitants. Both Mississippi and Alabama declared that freemen only were possessed of equal rights. Missouri required no property qualifications for voting or office holding, though members of the legislature must pay taxes. Only white could vote, and representation was based on free white male inhabitants.

Thwarted by the aristocratic minority in calling legitimate conventions, the democratic majority in the old states now threatened to take the matter in their own hands and call extra-legal conventions. Mass meetings were held in Georgia, North Carolina, Virginia, and Maryland; polls were conducted in various counties, all of which voted overwhelmingly for calling conventions; grand jury presentments called attention to the need for reform and recommended direct action if the legislatures failed to act; the voters in many counties instructed their representatives in the legislature to support a bill calling a constitutional convention; and hundreds of petitions went to the legislatures demanding relief. Typical of the sentiment for calling extra-legal conventions is the statement of a North Carolinian that if the legislature failed "to comply with the wishes of a great majority of the State," then "A convention will be assembled in the west, and the constitution amended without the concurrence of the east; and this being the act of a majority, and the legal act, will consequently be obligatory on the whole State. The constitution *will be amended*." [9]

A statewide reform convention assembled at Milledgeville, Georgia, on May 10, 1832, and issued a call for an election of delegates to a convention to meet at the capital in February, 1833, to alter, revise, or amend the constitution, or write a new one. It issued an address to the people in which it declared "that the people have an undoubted right, in their sovereign capacity, to alter or change their form of government, whenever in their opinion it becomes too obnoxious or oppressive to be borne. That crisis . . . has arrived, when the people should assert their rights, and boldly and fearlessly maintain them." [10] The legislature now capitulated and called a convention to meet at the same time and place as that called extra-legally. Comparable action took place in Maryland in 1836, but the legislature passed a series of amendments similar to those proposed by the reform convention and forestalled extra-legal action. In like manner the legislatures of Virginia and North Carolina capitulated to the reform party, and submitted the question of a "Convention or No Convention" to the voters. In both states the call was adopted by large majorities. Mississippi and Tennessee, too, at the demand of the people, called conventions to revise their constitutions. This was one of the most signal victories for majority or popular rule in American history. In these states the people without political voice had, by threat of appeal to numerical majority action, forced the landed aristocracy who possessed the legitimate and constitu-

[9] Salisbury *Western Carolinian,* July 17, 1821.
[10] Milledgeville *Southern Recorder,* May 31, 1832.

tional political power to submit the fundamental law to the scrutiny and revision of delegates elected from the people for that purpose alone.

Democracy had won a victory over aristocracy. The people had compelled the wealthy planter class in control of the legislatures to call conventions to revise the fundamental law of the states. Majority rule had exerted its power and justified its right. One democratic spokesman declared that the freemen had united their forces "to break to pieces the trammels of aristocracy, and show to the enemies of republican equality that the sons of freemen will still be free."[11]

John C. Calhoun, Abel P. Upshur,[12] and other aristocratic leaders of the South openly denied the Jeffersonian ideal of equality of all men and bitterly condemned majority rule as the tyranny of king numbers; and they had their supporters in the North among such men as James Kent, Joseph Story, and Orestes A. Brownson.[13] The less famous and little known leaders of democracy just as boldly proclaimed the doctrine of political equality. The views of the former have been given much attention by the historian; those of the latter have been generally ignored. The significant thing about the controversy, however, is that the views of the latter prevailed. The bills of rights remained unchanged and the majority forced the aristocracy to grant all white men an equal voice in the state governments. Charles James Faulkner, spokesman for the Virginia democracy in 1850, said that nothing short of a radical and fundamental change in the structure of the state constitution "could satisfy the progressive aspirations of a people who felt that their energies were held in subjugation by artificial restraints of republican freedom and equality." And, after the Virginia convention of 1850 had adjourned, he declared: "Its results was one of the proudest triumphs of popular government which the records of history attest. A revolution as decided in its results as any of those which for the last century have deluged the monarchies of Europe with blood, passed off under the influence of the acknowledged principles of popular supremacy as quietly and tranquilly as the most ordinary county election."[14]

The reform movement begun about 1800 now bore fruit in nu-

[11] Salisbury *Western Carolinian*, October 22, 1822.

[12] *Proceedings and Debates of the Convention of Virginia* (Richmond, 1830), 68–71, and *passim*.

[13] For Brownson's opposition to majority rule, see his "Democracy and Liberty," in *United States Magazine and Democratic Review* (Washington, 1837–1859), XII (1843), 374–87, and his "Unpopular Government," *ibid.*, XII, 529–37.

[14] *United States Magazine and Democratic Review*, XLI (1858), 227–28.

merous constitutional conventions,[15] and these conventions rewrote the state constitutions in line with the ideals of Jacksonian democracy. Many writers have attributed the democratic reforms of the 1830's to the influence of the western frontier. A study of the movement in the southern states gives an emphatic denial to this assumption. The people of the southern states were cognizant of what was going on in the West, but the demands for reform grew out of local conditions and would have arisen had there been no "New West" beyond the Appalachians. In fact, it would be more nearly accurate to say that many of the ideas and motives of Jacksonian democracy were southern in origin.

To what extent was aristocracy weakened and democracy strengthened by the work of the conventions of the 1830's? In the first place, property qualifications for voting were abolished in all southern states except Virginia and North Carolina, and with Louisiana still requiring the payment of taxes.[16] The last of the religious restrictions were also abolished. In a similar manner property qualifications for office holding were wiped out except for South Carolina and Louisiana, and age and residence requirements were reduced. A large number of officers heretofore selected by the legislature or appointed by the governor were now elected by popular vote. These include civil and militia officers, justices of the peace, superior court judges, and governors in all the states except Virginia and South Carolina. Rotation in office was generally applied through short terms and restricted re-eligibility. Progress was also made in the equalization of representation. There was no uniformity in the states, however. Some used white population, some qualified voters, some federal population returns, and some a combination of population and taxation. Those states that had heretofore granted special borough representation abolished it.

In still another way these changes broadened the base of democracy. For the first time the people had been consulted as to the revision and amendment of their constitutions. The conventions were

[15] Conventions were held in Virginia in 1829–1830, Mississippi in 1832, Georgia in 1833 and 1839, Tennessee in 1834, North Carolina in 1835, and an abortive or revolutionary one in Maryland in 1836. There is a close parallel in the action of the northern states. Beginning with Connecticut in 1818, Massachusetts, New York, Delaware, Vermont, and Pennsylvania, all held general constitutional conventions by the end of the 1830's; and in Rhode Island there was an unconstitutional convention in 1842 that went beyond the extra-legal action in the southern states.

[16] Among northern states, New Jersey and Rhode Island retained property qualifications, and Connecticut, Massachusetts, Pennsylvania, and Ohio retained the tax paying requirement.

called directly or indirectly by action of the people. The revised constitutions were in turn submitted back to them for ratification or rejection. In at least one state the people twice rejected the changes, and forced the desired forms through by legislative amendments. And the new constitutions provided for future amendment and revision.

In one matter there was a definite reactionary movement. This was the issue of free Negro suffrage. Virginia and North Carolina joined Maryland and Kentucky in taking from the free Negro the ballot he had heretofore possessed. In like manner all new states of the period, North as well as South, denied suffrage to free Negroes. The action of the old southern states was paralleled by that of the northern states. Delaware, Connecticut, New Jersey, and Pennsylvania took the ballot from the Negro. And New York in 1821 limited Negro suffrage by requiring that he possess a freehold valued at two hundred fifty dollars over and above all indebtedness. Hence only five of the northern states granted equal suffrage to Negroes. Whether or not Jefferson, Mason, and other Revolutionary proponents of natural rights philosophy intended to include Negroes in the statement that "all men are created equal and endowed with certain unalienable rights" is a debatable question: [17] but in actual practice the American people had decided by their constitutional provisions that Negroes were not included in the *political people*. From the very day of the Declaration of Independence the race problem had caused the American people to make an exception to the doctrine that "all men are created equal." But the partial exclusion of the Negro from the promises of democracy did not impair the faith of the whites in those promises.

The influence of the democratic reforms of the Jacksonian period were far-reaching. Evidence of this is to be seen in many phases of southern life—social, intellectual, economic, and political. But the people were not satisfied with their partial victory, and the signs of progress only made them more determined to complete the democratization of their state governments. Their increased political power made the task of securing additional amendments and revision of their constitutions easier than had been that of calling the conventions of the 1830's. In the first case, they had threatened extralegal action; in the second, they simply used the powers already possessed to put through additional reforms. This time they de-

[17] Samuel E. Morison and Henry S. Commager, *The Growth of the American Republic*, 2 vols. (New York, 1937), I, 82, state that "Jefferson did not mean to include slaves as men."

termined to take from the aristocratic class its last remnants of special political privileges. Important amendments in Georgia, Missouri, and North Carolina, and revision by convention in Louisiana, Kentucky, Maryland, and Virginia,[18] brought those states in line with the most democratic ones. Virginia in 1851 was the last state to provide for popular election of governor; and North Carolina in 1856 abolished the fifty-acre freehold required to vote for members of the state senate. The three new states, Arkansas, Florida, and Texas, all established complete equality of the whites in political affairs, and made all officials elective by popular vote. *The United States Magazine and Democratic Review*, analyzing the progress of constitutional reform in the nation, declared that the constitution of Louisiana showed "more political insight, and a more absolute reliance upon the principle upon which popular governments are based, than appears in the fundamental law of any other state in the Union." But the Missouri constitution "affords more efficient guarantees to individual rights, and leaves fewer opportunities for political corruption and for intercepting the fair expression of the wishes of the people" than that of any other state.

These changes left South Carolina the one remaining stronghold of the landed aristocracy in the South. While she had granted manhood suffrage in 1810, she continued to require her governor to possess a freehold until after the Civil War; the governor and presidential electors were chosen by the legislature; and representation was apportioned on a combination of white population and taxation. But among the northern states, Massachusetts continued to apportion representation in her senate on property until 1853; and Rhode Island continued to require voters and office holders to possess real estate valued at one hundred thirty-four dollars over and above all incumbrances, or with a rental value of seven dollars, until 1888.

The establishment of white manhood suffrage, the abolition of property qualifications for office holders, the election of all officers by popular vote, and the apportionment of representation on population rather than wealth, with periodic reapportionment, dealt a death blow to the political power of the landed, slaveholding aristocracy of the Old South. No longer could the members of that class dictate to the great majority of free white men. The aristocracy still had influence, as the wealthy merchant and industrialist of the northern states had influence, and as men of property in all times and places have influence, but they did not possess that influence because of special political privileges. Some southern planters pos-

[18] Louisiana in 1844 and 1852, Kentucky in 1849, and Maryland and Virginia in 1850.

sessed baronial wealth but this wealth no longer gave them political control. They constituted a social not a political aritocracy. "Such an aristocracy, although it may confer personal independence, cannot create political authority." [19]

If the landed aristocrat wished to sit in the seat of power and administer the affairs of state he must seek the support of the voter, his master. He must recognize every voter, however poor, as his political equal. And in the political hustings landlord and squatter, wealthy planter and poor white, did mingle as equals.[20]

The political revolution also meant that large numbers of the small farmer and yeoman classes began to enter politics, and win seats in legislature, Congress, and the governor's office. The first governor chosen by popular vote in Virginia, in 1851, was Joseph Johnson, whose childhood had been spent in abject poverty without the opportunity for formal schooling. Despite these handicaps he had served in the legislature and Congress, beating some of the most wealthy men of his district.[21] Indeed six of the eight men who served Virginia as governor in the years just prior to the Civil War came from the plain people; two began life as farm hands, one as a tailor, one as a mill hand, and another as a mail contractor. Henry County, Virginia, had the second highest percentage of large slaveholders in the state, yet only two justices of the peace, chosen between 1853 and 1858, possessed as many as ten slaves, while seven owned none and five owned only two each.[22]

Few studies of southern leadership have been made, but preliminary investigations suggest that a majority of the political leaders of the Old South between 1830 and 1860 came from the plain people rather than from the large planter class. Many such men received aid from wealthy planters to secure their education, as did George McDuffie and Alexander H. Stephens. The literary societies at the University of North Carolina paid all expenses of one "penniless student" each year. Several of these students rose to high rank in the state, one becoming a United States senator.[23] Dozens of the men who rank at the very top in political leadership

[19] Frederick Grimke, *Considerations upon the Nature and Tendency of Free Institutions* (Cincinnati, 1848), 311, 314; Camp, *Democracy*, 220–21.

[20] For descriptions of the equality of all classes at the polls, see Hamilton W. Pierson, *In the Bush; or, Old-Time Social, Political, and Religious Life in the Southwest* (New York, 1881), 131–46, and Lester B. Shippee (ed.), *Bishop Whipple's Southern Diary, 1843–1844* (Minneapolis, 1937), 22–23, 52.

[21] "Joseph Johnson" in *Southern Historical Magazine* (Charleston, W. Va., 1892), I (1892), 185–87.

[22] Gustavus W. Dyer, *Democracy in the South before the Civil War* (Nashville, 1905), 80–82.

[23] Kemp P. Battle, *Memories of an Old Time Tar Heel* (Chapel Hill, 1945), 93.

began as poor boys, and became planters and men of wealth by their own efforts. Let one of these men tell his own story. "When I was a boy—a very little boy—an honest but poor man settled (squatted is a better word) in a country where I yet reside. . . . Day by day he might have been seen following his plough, while his two sons plied the hoe. . . . The younger [of the sons] studies law and . . . was drawn into politics. He was elected to the State Legislature, to Congress, Judge of the Circuit Court, Governor of his State, to Congress again and again, but he never forgot that he was a squatter's son. He stands before you today."[24] Like Albert Gallatin Brown, many of the leaders of the Old South grew up on the frontier where free men could not and did not recognize any political superior. In fact much of the South was only one generation removed from frontier society in 1860. Aristocracy takes more time to establish itself than one generation.

One test of the effectiveness of democracy is the exercise of the suffrage by those qualified to vote. The southern states met this test to about the same degree that the northern states did. There was considerable variation from state to state in both the North and the South, but the percentage of votes cast, according to the voting population, in the southern states exceeded that of the North as often, and to about the same degree, as it failed to reach it. For instance, in the presidential election of 1828, Georgia with a white population of 296,806 cast 18,790 votes and Connecticut with a white population of 289,603 cast 18,277 votes; Alabama, however, with a white population of 190,406 cast 19,076 votes. Thus the vote of Georgia and Connecticut was 6.3 per cent of the voting people, but that of Alabama was 10.1 per cent. In the same election, Massachusetts with 603,351 free people cast 35,855 votes; Virginia with 694,300 whites cast 38,853 votes; but Tennessee with only 535,746 whites cast 46,330 votes. The percentages of these states were 5.9, 5.5, and 8.2, respectively. In the presidential election of 1860, Georgia with a white population of 595,088 cast 106,365 votes; Connecticut with 406,147 white people cast 77,146 votes; and Alabama with 529,121 whites cast 90,307 votes. The percentages for the three states were 18.0, 16.7, and 17.0, respectively. In this election, Massachusetts had 1,231,066 free people and cast 169,175 votes; Virginia had 1,105,453 whites and cast 167,223 votes; and Tennessee with 834,082 whites cast 145,333 votes. The percentages were 13.7, 15.1, and 17.4, respectively. A comparison of all the southern

[24] Albert Gallatin Brown, *Speech of . . . in the House of Representatives* (Washington, 1852).

with all the northern states shows a white population of 7,614,018 casting 1,260,509 votes and 18,736,849 people casting 3,369,134 votes, or a percentage of 16.6 for the South and 17.9 for the North. The western states gave the North the advantage in the over-all comparison. But if one uses adult white male population, which is more accurate for voting percentages, then the South had a percentage of 69.5 and the North of 69.7.[25]

The vote of the southern states was almost equally divided between the Whig and the Democratic parties in the presidential elections from 1836 to 1852 inclusive. In the five elections the total popular vote of the Whig candidates was 1,745,884, that of the Democratic was 1,760,452, or a majority for the Democrats of only 14,568. The Whigs had a majority in three elections, but in 1836 it was only 1,862 votes and its biggest majority was in 1840 with 52,851. The Democratic majority in 1844 was only 23,766, and in 1852, when the Whigs were weakened by the Compromise issue, it was 79,690. There was a total of twenty-seven states in the Whig column and thirty-seven in the Democratic column for the five elections, but except for the election of 1852 there was no overwhelming majority for either party; and in 1848 the parties divided the states equally. Such an equal division of party strength prevented any one group from dominating the political situation in the South. The states were shifting back and forth between the two parties so rapidly that no one could hope to retain power long enough to consolidate party, much less planter class, control. This situation also enabled the southern states to exert popular control over the United States senators who were elected by the state legislatures. With party changes in the states the senators were often instructed by the legislature how to vote on major issues in Congress. While the purpose of instruction was partisan it nevertheless resulted in the senators being made responsible to the majority will as expressed in state elections for many senators voted according to instructions and others resigned rather than do so.

With the coming of manhood suffrage came the demand for popular education so that the voter might cast a more intelligent ballot. It was recognized that democracy and republicanism could

[25] White population is used as a basis for all these calculations except that free population is used for the six states that permitted Negroes to vote. South Carolina is excluded, since the presidential electors of that state were chosen by the legislature. Population figures are taken from the United States Census reports; the votes from Thomas H. McKee, *The National Conventions and Platforms of All Political Parties, 1789–1900; Convention, Popular, and Electoral Vote* (Baltimore, 1900).

work effectively only with an educated electorate. Since "The chief object of constitutions and laws" is "to render its citizens secure in their lives, liberty and prosperity," the importance of "a good education to each individual, to every community, and to the State, cannot be too highly valued," declared a report of the Louisiana constitutional convention of 1844.[26] Popular education, wrote James M. Garnett of Virginia, "is of most importance in all governments. But it is indispensible in ours where all political power emanates immediately from the people, who must be themselves both intelligent and virtuous, or it will rarely happen that their public functionaries will be any better than themselves." [27] Even the aristocratic element recognized the principle that they must now educate their masters, although many did not wish to support education by taxation. One of them declared "that in adopting universal suffrage, we took necessarily the consequences that would flow from it were any portion of the people ignorant and debased. . . . Without you enlighten the sources of political power, we shall have no government. . . . You have adopted the principle of universal suffrage, but the basis is public education." [28]

Recognizing the need every southern state, with the exception of South Carolina where a system of poor schools existed, provided for the establishment of a public school system of education before 1860. North Carolina led off in 1839; the question had first been submitted to popular vote and carried by a large majority. In some states, Louisiana for instance, the constitution required the legislature to provide a state system and to support it by taxation. All the states except Virginia and South Carolina provided for a state superintendent of public instruction; in most states the superintendent was elected by popular vote. The system of public education in the southern states, in provisions for administration, support, and general results, compare favorably with those in the northern states in 1860.[29]

In like manner, popular control of southern state governments brought measures designed to minister to the economic wants of the people. In fact some leaders of democratic reform boldly proclaimed

[26] *Proceedings and Debates of the Convention of Louisiana, Which Assembled at the City of New Orleans, January 14, 1844* (New Orleans, 1845), 316–19.

[27] James M. Garnett, "Popular Education," in *Southern Literary Messenger* (Richmond, 1834–1864), VII (1842), 115.

[28] *Proceedings and Debates of the Convention of Louisiana* (1844), 909.

[29] Edgar W. Knight, *The Influence of Reconstruction on Education in the South* (New York, 1913), 94, 98.

that this was one of the major purposes of government.[30] Boards of public works, popularly elected, were created to supervise internal improvements and to further the economic progress of the states. They were interested also in the public utilization of the natural resources of the states. Imprisonment for debt was prohibited; banks were brought under state control; provision was made for chartering corporations; monopolies were prohibited; and provisions were made for uniform and equal taxation of property according to value. All these measures were included in the state constitutions. The states, too, safeguarded the rights and interests of the unfortunate classes. State asylums for the insane and schools for the deaf, the dumb, and the blind were established at state expense.

The history of the southern state constitutions and governments from 1776 to 1860 reveals a progressive expansion in the application of the doctrine of political equality. By 1860 the aristocratic planter class had been shorn of its special privileges and political power. It still gave tone and color to political life but it no longer dominated and controlled the political order. On the other hand, the great mass of the whites had been given more and more authority, and majority rule had been definitely established. The interpretation of the southern states as "political aristocracies of the sternest and most odious kind" had no basis in fact. With the exceptions already noted the southern state governments were as democratic in 1860 as their northern sister states. They had not attained the ideal goal of absolute equality, but in spirit and administration as well as in form they had progressively become more and more concerned with the rights and interest of the people.

[30] See, for instance, Charles J. Faulkner, "Speech," in *United States Magazine and Democratic Review*, XLI (1858), 218.
Canals and Railroads, 1800–1890 (New York, 1960).

9

ALTHOUGH the amount of attention that has been and is being lavished by historians and the public in general on the Civil War may seem excessive at times, the fact remains that after the War of the Revolution it is the most significant event in the history of the nation. For a century now historians have been analyzing and debating the constitutional, political, and cultural effects of the war that not only destroyed slavery but the old Union as well. Only in the twentieth century, however, have economic historians begun to explore the ramifying economic consequences of that struggle. As Cochran makes evident in his opening paragraphs, Charles Beard and Louis Hacker more than thirty years ago wove the economic impact of the war into the story of general American history. Since that time one of the standard interpretations has been to see the war as a great impetus to the American industrialization that astounded the late nineteenth-century world.

Actually, not all historians have followed the path cut by Beard and Hacker. As long ago as 1918 the noted economic historian Victor S. Clark concluded that the war was not a stimulus to economic growth at all, though he did not go so far as to call it a deterrent (see his "Manufacturing Development During the Civil War," *Military Historian and Economist*, III [1918], 92–100). And Fred Shannon, in his textbook *America's Economic Growth* (New York, 1951), also expressed doubt that the war stimulated economic expansion. In more recent years there has been a definite and systematic questioning of the war's positive effect on industrial growth. Douglass North's pathbreaking study *Economic Growth of the United States, 1790–1860* (Englewood Cliffs, N. J., 1961), although it does not deal directly with the war years, concluded that the war was an interruption of a long-term upward trend in economic growth. It remained for Cochran to present the evidence directly bearing upon the war years. His article, as he points out, is based upon the new series of production statistics recently compiled by the Bureau of the Census and by the National Bureau of Economic Research, the latter being the most respected private organization devoted to the collection and analysis of economic statistics. Indeed, until these new series were compiled, the whole question—which, after all, is a quantifiable one—could be little more than speculation.

Cochran's conclusions in this article are so sweeping and so divergent from the traditional view that it is not surprising that his work has evoked several very critical responses. Two should be mentioned, since some of their adverse criticisms are included in this introduction. They are Stephen Salisbury's "The Effect of the Civil War on American Industrial Development," in *The Economic Impact of the American Civil War*, edited by Ralph Andreano (Cambridge, Mass., 1962); and Pershing Vartanian's "The Cochran Thesis: A Critique in Statistical Analysis," *Journal of American History*, LI (June 1964), 77–89. Both these critics point to weaknesses in Cochran's evidence and argument; nevertheless the article remains a significant turning point in the evaluation of the economic impact of the Civil War.

One of the reasons Cochran's article attracted criticism is that it deals very broadly with a large question, namely, the causes of the great economic expansion in the last forty years of the nineteenth century. Moreover, by speaking of the retardation of industrialization, Cochran has not only called into question the conclusion that the war was a positive force but has gone to the other extreme in seeing it as a hindrance. After all, it is also possible to view the war as simply having little or no effect on industrial development.

Essentially his approach is to compare the rates of growth of production of selected commodities during periods before and after the war with those of the war years (1861–1865), or years as close to them as available statistics permit. In making these comparisons he finds that most of his war-year series show lower rates of production. Unfortunately he seems at times to overstate his case. Thus in accounting for the rise in the rate of wool production during the war, a contradiction to his argument, he says that the protective tariff on wool helps to explain this contrary development. Yet several pages later he turns agnostic about the tariff, stating that the actual effect of the tariff on industrial growth "will probably never" be settled. Sometimes he ignores other available data that seem to argue against his conclusion. For example, he fails to mention the tremendous increase in business incorporations that occurred during the war, notably in industrial states like Massachusetts and Ohio, as reported in *Business Incorporations in the United States, 1800–1943* by G. H. Evans, Jr. (New York, 1948). Yet certainly a spurt in business incorporations is a significant measure of industrial activity within the war period.

Despite this element of zealotry in presentation, though, Cochran's evidence makes it very difficult, if not impossible, to talk any longer of the war's stimulating effect upon economic activity. Mr. Cochran's position is in effect supported by the papers presented at a recent symposium on the economic impact of the Civil War that have since been published as *Economic Change in the Civil War Era* (Greenville, Del., 1965), edited by David T. Gilchrist and W. Davis Lewis. Most of the papers emphasize the prewar sources of American industrial growth, inferentially playing down the impact of the Civil War along the lines of Cochran's analysis.

Somewhat less incontrovertible, however, is Cochran's conclusion that the war retarded economic growth by interrupting the upward trend of the economy that had been evident in the preceding twenty years. There is less reason to accept Cochran's conclusion here simply because the contradictory evidence is stronger. We've already seen that business incorporations rose markedly during the war years. By Cochran's own evidence, another series of statistics, that of wool, also showed a stimulation of production between 1861 and 1865. Furthermore, two of his other series, those for agricultural implements and bituminous coal, were admittedly not retarded during the war period. In short, the retarding influence of the war needs further evidence for us to be as sure of it as we are of the lack of stimulating effects from the war.

The point that the Civil War did not have a stimulating effect on the American economy, which Cochran has now established, is only one of at least three rather basic questions that are involved in any assessment of the effects of the war on American industrialization. The second concerns Cochran's choice of years in which he seeks out signs of the war's economic effects. Although during the four years of the war the rates of production of certain commodities may well have fallen off, it is quite possible that during those four years new demands and new capacity were being developed that would give a spurt to the economy only *after* 1865. In a very real

sense this new demand and new capacity would also qualify as economic consequences of the war. In fact, many historians, like Beard and Hacker, for example, had in mind this consequence as much as the first. Recognizing this fact, Cochran in his obiter dicta has tried to meet the argument, though with considerably less authority than earlier. From his figures and method there is no conclusive way of knowing what long-range, deferred effects, if any, the war may have had on economic growth. Certainly there were some types of production facilities, built under the impetus of war demand, that would actually not begin to turn out commodities until after the war. Such production was obviously stimulated by the war, but by Cochran's method of measurement it would be counted as stemming from the postwar years simply because the production appeared then. A concrete example of this delayed production is the Union Pacific Railroad, which was chartered in 1862 but not completed until 1869. Cochran tends to discount the example of the Union Pacific by suggesting that it was a premature enterprise and therefore actually retarded the economy by using resources that might have been more efficiently employed by less "premature" enterprises. But Robert Fogel, in his *Union Pacific Railroad: A Case in Premature Enterprise* (Baltimore, 1960), has shown that the road in the ten years after it was completed added a very good measure of wealth to the economy.

Nor, it should be observed, can his method and data adequately deal with the third aspect of the question, namely, the nonquantifiable consequences of the war. These would include the new spirit of enterprise derived from a wartime boom, the effects of the new banking legislation, and the new and tighter organization of business activity, which the war mobilization demanded and ultimately produced. Yet these are important elements in any accounting for economic growth, especially in the light of current trends among experts in economic development, who emphasize the contributions of social and even psychological factors. See, for example, David McClelland's *The Achieving Society* (Princeton, 1961) for a thorough examination of psychological bases of economic growth and Robert Heilbroner's *The Great Ascent* (New York, 1963) for a general but penetrating study of the problems facing the new nations of the world striving for industrialization.

Although it might be said that Cochran's article establishes conclusively only a narrow point—namely, that the war was not a stimulant to economic expansion—that point nevertheless has important ramifications. For example, as a result of that factual

conclusion Cochran's attention was directed to making an enlightening comparison between the economic effects of the Civil War and those of the two world wars of the twentieth century.

Mr. Cochran is professor of economic history at the University of Pennsylvania. His many publications in economic history include *Railroad Leaders, 1845–1890* (Cambridge, Mass., 1953) and *The American Business System: A Historical Perspective, 1900–1955* (Cambridge, Mass., 1957).

Did the Civil War Retard Industrialization?

BY THOMAS C. COCHRAN

THE preceding chapter has given illustrations of the value of various social science methods. In this chapter a large historical question will be analyzed in some detail by the quantitative, statistical approach common to economists, with results that show how exciting events may obscure or wholly distort what is really happening.

In most textbook and interpretative histories of the United States the Civil War has been assigned a major role in bringing about the industrial revolution in America.[1] Colorful business developments in the North—adoption of new machines, the quick spread of war contracting, the boost given to profits by inflation, the creation of a group of war millionaires—make the war years seems not only a period of rapid economic change but also one that created important forces for future growth. The superficial qualitative evidence is so persuasive that apparently few writers have examined the available long-run statistical series before adding their endorsement to the conventional interpretation. The following quotations taken from

SOURCE: Reprinted by permission from the *Mississippi Valley Historical Review,* XLVIII (September 1961).

[1] This article is based on a paper presented by the author at the annual meeting of the Mississippi Valley Historical Association in Louisville in April, 1960.

the books of two generations of leading scholars illustrate the popular view.[2]

"The so-called Civil War," wrote Charles A. and Mary R. Beard in 1927, ". . . was a social war . . . making vast changes in the arrangement of classes, in the accumulation and distribution of wealth, in the course of industrial development." [3] Midway between 1927 and the present, Arthur M. Schlesinger, Sr., wrote: "On these tender industrial growths the Civil War had the effect of a hothouse. For reasons already clear . . . nearly every branch of industry grew lustily." [4] Harold U. Faulkner, whose textbook sales have ranked near or at the top, said in 1954: "In the economic history of the United States the Civil War was extremly important. . . . In the North it speeded the Industrial Revolution and the development of capitalism by the prosperity which it brought to industry." [5] The leading new text of 1957, by Richard Hofstadter, William Miller, and Daniel Aaron, showed no weakening of this interpretation: "The growing demand for farm machinery as well as for the 'sinews of war' led to American industrial expansion. . . . Of necessity, iron, coal, and copper production boomed during the war years." [6] A sophisticated but still essentially misleading view is presented by Gilbert C. Fite and Jim E. Reese in a text of 1959: "The Civil War proved to be a boon to Northern economic development. . . . Industry, for example, was not created by the war, but wartime demands greatly stimulated and encouraged industrial development which already had a good start." [7] In a reappraisal of the Civil War, in *Harper's Magazine* for April 1960, Denis W. Brogan, a specialist in American institutions, wrote: "It may have been only a catalyst but the war precipitated the entry of the United States into the modern industrial world, made 'the take-off' (to use Professor W. W. Rostow's brilliant metaphor) come sooner." [8]

In all of these reiterations of the effect of the Civil War on in-

[2] These particular authors are cited merely as examples of historical opinion, not because they are more in error than others. The reader needs only to take down other texts from his own shelf to find similar statements.

[3] *The Rise of American Civilization* (2 vols., New York, 1927), vol. II, p. 53.

[4] Homer C. Hockett and Arthur M. Schlesinger, *Land of the Free: A Short History of the American People* (New York, 1944), p. 355. Schlesinger wrote the section beginning with the Civil War.

[5] *American Economic History* (7th ed., New York: Harper & Brothers, 1954), p. 345. The same statement appears in a later edition (1960).

[6] *The United States: The History of a Republic* (Englewood Cliffs, New Jersey: Prentice Hall, 1957), p. 381.

[7] *An Economic History of the United States* (Boston, 1959), p. 284.

[8] "A Fresh Appraisal of the Civil War," *Harper's Magazine* (New York), CCXX (April 1960), p. 140.

dustrialism statistical series seem to have been largely neglected. None of the authors cited reinforce their interpretations by setting the war period in the context of important long-run indexes of industrial growth. Since 1949, series for the period 1840 to 1890 that would cast doubt on the conventional generalizations have been available in *Historical Statistics of the United States, 1789–1945.*[9] In 1960 a new edition of *Historical Statistics* and the report of the Conference on Research in Income and Wealth on *Trends in the American Economy in the Nineteenth Century* have provided additional material to support the argument that the Civil War retarded American industrial development.[10] These volumes give data for many growth curves for the two decades before and after the war decade—in other words, the long-run trends before and after the event in question. The pattern of these trends is a mixed one which shows no uniform type of change during the Civil War decade, but on balance for the more important series the trend is toward retardation in rates of growth rather than toward acceleration. This fact is evident in many series which economists would regard as basic to economic growth, but in order to keep the discussion within reasonable limits only a few can be considered here.

Robert E. Gallman has compiled new and more accurate series for both "total commodity output," including agriculture, and "value added by manufacture," the two most general measures of economic growth available for this period. He writes: "Between 1839 and 1899 total commodity output increased elevenfold, or at an average decade rate of slightly less than 50 per cent. . . . Actual rates varied fairly widely, high rates appearing during the decades ending with 1854 and 1884, and a very low rate during the decade ending with 1869." [11] From the over-all standpoint this statement indicates the immediately retarding effect of the Civil War on American economic growth, but since most of the misleading statements are made in regard to industrial growth, or particular elements in industrial growth, it is necessary to look in more detail at "value added by manufacture" and some special series. Gallman's series for value added by manufacture in constant dollars of the purchasing power of 1879 shows a rise of 157 per cent from 1839 to 1849; 76 per cent

[9] U. S. Bureau of the Census, *Historical Statistics of the United States: 1789–1945* (Washington, 1949).

[10] U. S. Bureau of the Census, *Historical Statistics of the United States: Colonial Times to 1957* (Washington, 1960); *Trends in the American Economy in the Nineteenth Century* (Princeton, 1960), published by the National Bureau of Economic Research as Volume XXIV of its *Studies in Income and Wealth.*

[11] *Trends in the American Economy,* p. 15.

from 1849 to 1859; and only 25 per cent from 1859 to 1869.[12] By the 1870's the more favorable prewar rates were resumed, with an increase of 82 per cent for 1869–1879, and 112 per cent for 1879–1889. Thus two decades of very rapid advance, the 1840's and the 1880's, are separated by thirty years of slower growth which falls to the lowest level in the decade that embraces the Civil War.

Pig-iron production in tons, perhaps the most significant commodity index of nineteenth-century American industrial growth, is available year-by-year from 1854 on. Taking total production for five-year periods, output increased 9 per cent between the block of years from 1856 to 1860 and the block from 1861 to 1865. That even the slight increase might not have been registered except for the fact that 1857 to 1860 were years of intermittent depression is indicated by an 81 per cent increase over the war years in the block of years from 1866 to 1870.[13] If annual production is taken at five-year intervals, starting in 1850, the increase is 24 per cent from 1850 to 1855; 17 per cent from 1855 to 1860; 1 per cent from 1860 to 1865; and 100 per cent from 1865 to 1870. While there is no figure available for 1845, the period from 1840 to 1850 shows 97 per cent increase in shipments, while for the period 1870 to 1880 the increase was 130 per cent. To sum up, depression and war appear to have retarded a curve of production that was tending to rise at a high rate.

Bituminous coal production may be regarded as the next most essential commodity series. After a gain of 199 per cent from 1840 to 1850 this series shows a rather steady pattern of increase at rates varying from 119 to 148 per cent each decade from 1850 to 1890. The war does not appear to have markedly affected the rate of growth.[14]

In the mid-nineteenth century copper production was not a

[12] *Historical Statistics* (1960 ed.), p. 402. "Constant" or "real" means dollars adjusted to eliminate price changes. It should be remembered that all series expressed in current dollars need to be corrected for rather violent price movements during these fifty years. Precise adjustments would vary with every series, and would involve many problems, but the movement of wholesale prices in general (Warren-Pearson Index) may be roughly summarized as follows. In 1850 prices were 12 per cent lower than in 1840, but by 1860 they were 11 per cent higher than in 1850. From 1860 to 1865 prices rose 99 per cent, but by 1870 the increase for the decade was only 46 per cent. By 1880 the decline for the decade was 26 per cent, and for the decade ending in 1890 it was 18 per cent. *Ibid.*, p. 115. In other words, current dollars are a very unreliable indicator, particularly as applied to wholesale prices.

[13] *Ibid.*, pp. 365–366.

[14] *Ibid.*, p. 357.

basic series for recording American growth, but since three distinguished authors have singled it out as one of the indexes of the effect of the war on industry it is best to cite the statistics. Before 1845 production of domestic copper was negligible. By 1850 the "annual recoverable content" of copper from United States mines was 728 tons, by 1860 it was 8,064 tons, by 1865 it was 9,520 tons, and by 1870 it was 14,112 tons. In this series of very small quantities, therefore, the increase from 1850 to 1860 was just over 1,000 per cent, from 1860 to 1865 it was 18 per cent, and from 1865 to 1870 it was 48 per cent.[15]

Railroad track, particularly in the United States, was an essential for industrialization. Here both the depression and the war retarded the rate of growth. From 1851 through 1855 a total of 11,627 miles of new track was laid, from 1856 through 1860, only 8,721 miles, and from 1861 through 1865, only 4,076 miles. After the war the rate of growth of the early 1850's was resumed, with 16,174 miles constructed from 1866 through 1870. Looked at by decades, a rate of over 200 per cent increase per decade in the twenty years before the war was slowed to 70 per cent for the period from 1860 to 1870, with only a 15 per cent increase during the war years. In the next two decades the rate averaged about 75 per cent.[16]

Next to food, cotton textiles may be taken as the most representative consumer-goods industry in the nineteenth century. Interference with the flow of southern cotton had a depressing effect. The number of bales of cotton consumed in United States manufacturing rose 143 per cent from 1840 to 1850 and 47 per cent from 1850 to 1860, but fell by 6 per cent from 1860 to 1870. From then on consumption increased at a little higher rate than in the 1850's.[17]

While woolen textile production is not an important series in the over-all picture of industrial growth, it should be noted that, helped by protection and military needs, consumption of wool for manufacturing more than doubled during the war, and then fell somewhat from 1865 to 1870. But Arthur H. Cole, the historian of the woolen industry, characterizes the years from 1830 to 1870 as a period of growth "not so striking as in the decades before or afterwards." [18]

Immigration to a nation essentially short of labor was unques-

[15] *Ibid.*, p. 368.
[16] *Ibid.*, p. 427–28.
[17] *Historical Statistics* (1949 ed.), p. 187. This table is not carried back to 1840 in the 1960 edition.
[18] Arthur H. Cole, *The American Wool Manufacture* (2 vols., Cambridge: Harvard University Press, 1926), vol. I, p. 392.

tionably a stimulant to economic growth. Another country had paid for the immigrant's unproductive youthful years, and he came to the United States ready to contribute his labor at a low cost. The pattern of the curve for annual immigration shows the retarding effect of both depression and war. In the first five years of the 1850's an average of 349,685 immigrants a year came to the United States. From 1856 through 1860 the annual average fell to 169,958, and for the war years of 1861 to 1865 it fell further to 169,345. In the first five postwar years the average rose to 302,620, but not until the first half of the 1870's did the rate equal that of the early 1850's. Had there been a return to prosperity instead of war in 1861, it seems reasonable to suppose that several hundred thousand additional immigrants would have arrived before 1865.[19]

In the case of farm mechanization the same type of error occurs as in the annual series on copper production. "Random" statistics such as the manufacture of 90,000 reapers in 1864 are frequently cited without putting them in the proper perspective of the total number in use and the continuing trends. Reaper and mower sales started upward in the early 1850's and were large from 1856 on, in spite of the depression. William T. Hutchinson estimates that most of the 125,000 reapers and mowers in use in 1861 had been sold during the previous five years.[20] While the business, without regard to the accidental coming of the war, was obviously in a stage of very rapid growth, the war years presented many difficulties and may actually have retarded the rate of increase.[21] Total sales of reapers for the period 1861–1865 are estimated at 250,000—a quite ordinary increase for a young industry—but the 90,000 figure for 1864, if it is correct, reinforces the evidence from the McCormick correspondence that this was the one particularly good year of the period. During these years William S. McCormick was often of the opinion that the "uncertainties of the times" made advisable a suspension of manufacturing until the close of the war.[22]

For a broader view of agricultural mechanization the series "value of farm implements and machinery" has special interest. Here the census gives a picture which, if correct, is explicable only on the basis of wartime destruction. Based on constant dollars the average value of machinery per farm fell nearly 25 per cent in the decade of the war and showed nearly a 90 per cent gain in

19 *Historical Statistics* (1960 ed.), p. 57.

20 William T. Hutchinson, *Cyrus Hall McCormick* (2 vols., New York, 1930–1935), vol. II, p. 67.

21 *Ibid.*, vol. II, pp. 67–95.

22 *Ibid.*, vol. II, p. 88.

the 1870's.[23] Differing from these census figures is a series prepared by Marvin W. Towne and Wayne D. Rasmussen based on the production of farm machinery. While this obviously does not take account of destruction of existing equipment or the rapid increase in the number of farms, the record of new production is hard to reconcile with the census figures. The production of implements and machinery reckoned in constant dollars is a sharply rising curve from 1850 on, with increases of 110 per cent from 1850 to 1860; 140 per cent from 1860 to 1870; and 95 per cent from 1870 to 1880.[24] Meanwhile the number of farms increased by about one third in each of the decades of the 1850's and 1860's and by one half in the 1870's.[25] Whatever interpretation is given to these figures, it does not appear that the war greatly increased the trend of agricultural mechanization. The series for gross farm product in constant dollars shows wide variations in increase from decade to decade, with the 1860's in the low group. The gains were 23 per cent, 1840 to 1850; 42 per cent, 1850 to 1860; 21 per cent, 1860 to 1870; 52 per cent, 1870 to 1880; and 20 per cent, 1880 to 1890.[26]

Much American business expansion was financed by short-term bank loans continuously renewed. Thus major increases in business activity should be mirrored in increases in bank loans, both for financing short-term transactions and for additions to plant and working capital that would, in fact, be paid off gradually. If there was a really great Civil War boom in business activity it should be indicated in the series "total loans" of all banks. But it is not. In constant dollars, bank loans fell slightly between 1840 and 1850, and rose nearly 50 per cent by 1860. It should be noted that none of these three decadal years were periods of high prosperity. During the war Confederate banking statistics were not reported by the comptroller of the currency, but by 1866 there is a comparable figure for the nation as a whole, and in constant dollars it is some 35 per cent below that of 1860. Even by 1870 the constant dollar value of all loans was more than 15 per cent lower than just before the war. If instead of examining loans one looks at total assets of all banks the decline in constant dollars from 1860 to

[23] *Historical Statistics* (1960 ed.), p. 285. For price index see note 12, above.
[24] *Trends in the American Economy*, p. 276.
[25] The percentage increases were 41 per cent (1860 over 1850); 30 per cent (1870 over 1860); and 51 per cent (1880 over 1870). *Historical Statistics* (1960 ed.), p. 278.
[26] *Ibid.*, p. 284.

1870 is reduced to 10 per cent, the difference arising from a larger cash position and more investment in government bonds.[27]

Net capital formation would be a more proper index of economic growth than bank loans or assets. Unfortunately, neither the teams of the National Bureau of Economic Research nor those of the Census Bureau have been able to carry any reliable series back of 1869. From colonial times to 1960, however, the chief single form of American capital formation has undoubtedly been building construction. Farm houses, city homes, public buildings, stores, warehouses, and factories have year-by-year constituted, in monetary value, the leading type of capital growth. Gallman has drawn up series for such construction based on estimating the flow of construction materials and adding what appear to be appropriate mark-ups.[28] Admittedly the process is inexact, but because of the importance of construction in reflecting general trends in capital formation it is interesting to see the results. The rate of change for the ten-year period ending in 1854 is about 140 per cent; for the one ending in 1859 it is 90 per cent; for 1869 it is 40 per cent; and for 1879 it is 40 per cent. Taking a long view, from 1839 to 1859 the average decennial rate of increase was about 70 per cent, and from 1869 to 1899 it was about 40 per cent.[29] The rate of advance in construction was declining and the war decade added a further dip to the decline.

Since the decline in rate is for the decade, the exact effect of the war years can only be estimated, but the logic of the situation, reinforced by the record of sharp cut-backs in railroad building, seems inescapable: the Civil War, like all modern wars, checked civilian construction. The first year of war was a period of depression and tight credit in the Middle West, which checked residential and farm construction in the area that grew most rapidly before and after the war. In both the East and the West the last two years of the war were a period of rapid inflation which was regarded by businessmen as a temporary wartime phenomenon. The logical result would be to postpone construction for long-term use until after the anticipated deflation. The decline in private railroad construction to a small fraction of the normal rate exemplifies the situation.

Lavish expenditure and speculation by a small group of war

[27] *Ibid.*, p. 624. The reader is again warned that deflation of current dollar values for this early period is an inexact process.

[28] *Trends in the American Economy*, pp. 60–64.

[29] *Ibid.*, p. 24. Gallman has two alternate series which I have averaged. For the purposes of this paper either series leads to the same conclusions.

contractors and market operators gambling on the inflation seem to have created a legend of high prosperity during the war years. But the general series on fluctuations in the volume of business do not bear this out. Leonard P. Ayres's estimates of business activity place the average for 1861 through 1865 below normal, and Norman J. Silberling's business index is below its normal line for all years of the war.[30] Silberling also has an intermediate trend line for business, which smooths out annual fluctuations. This line falls steadily from 1860 to 1869.[31] Much of Silberling's discussion in this chapter "Business Activity, Prices, and Wars" is in answer to his question: "Why does it seem to be true that despite a temporary stimulating effect of war upon some industries, wars are generally associated with a long-term retarding of business growth. . . ?"[32] He puts the Civil War in this category.

Collectively these statistical estimates support a conclusion that the Civil War retarded American industrial growth. Presentation of this view has been the chief purpose of this article. To try to judge the non-measurable or indirect effects of the war is extremely difficult. But since further discussion of the conventional qualitative factors may help to explain the prevailing evaluation in American textbooks, it seems appropriate to add some conjectural *obiter dicta*.

Experience with the apparently stimulating effects of twentieth-century wars on production makes the conclusion that victorious war may retard the growth of an industrial state seem paradoxical, and no doubt accounts in part for the use of detached bits of quantitative data to emphasize the Civil War's industrial importance.[33] The resolution of the paradox may be found in contemporary conditions in the United States and in the nature of the wartime demand. The essential wastefulness of war from the standpoint of economic growth was obscured by the accident that both of the great European wars of the twentieth century began when the United States had a high level of unemployment. The immediate effect of each, therefore, was to put men to work, to increase the national product,

[30] Leonard P. Ayres, *Turning Points in Business Cycles* (New York, 1939), p. 14; Norman J. Silberling, *The Dynamics of Business* (New York, 1943), p. 50.

[31] Silberling, *The Dynamics of Business,* p. 61.

[32] *Ibid.,* p. 66.

[33] Ayres, Silberling, and some other students of economic activity such as Herbert Hoover, however, blame the breakdown of the 1930's on the dislocations caused by World War I. *Ibid.,* pp. 65–66. See also *The Memoirs of Herbert Hoover: The Great Depression, 1929–1941* (New York, 1952), p. 105.

and to create an aura of prosperity. Presumably, the United States of the mid-nineteenth century tended to operate close enough to full employment in average years that any wasteful labor-consuming activities were a burden rather than a stimulant.

By modern standards the Civil War was still unmechanized. It was fought with rifles, bayonets, and sabers by men on foot or horseback. Artillery was more used than in previous wars, but was still a relatively minor consumer of iron and steel. The railroad was also brought into use, but the building of military lines offset only a small percentage of the over-all drop from the prewar level of civilian railroad construction. Had all of these things not been true, the Confederacy with its small industrial development could never have fought over four years of increasingly effective blockade.

In spite of the failure of direct quantitative evidence to show accelerating effects of the war on rates of economic growth, there could be long-run effects of a qualitative type that would gradually foster a more rapid rate of economic growth. The most obvious place to look for such indirect effects would be in the results of freeing the slaves. Marxists contended that elimination of slavery was a necessary precursor of the bourgeois industrialism which would lead to the socialist revolution. The creation of a free Negro labor force was, of course, of great long-run importance. In the twentieth century it has led to readjustment of Negro population between the deep South and the northern industrial areas, and to changes in the use of southern land.

But economically the effects of war and emancipation over the period 1840 to 1880 were negative. Richard A. Easterlin writes: "In every southern state, the 1880 level of per capita income originating in commodity production and distribution was below, or at best only slightly above that of 1840. . . . [This] attests strikingly to the impact of that war and the subsequent disruption on the southern economy."[34] In general, the Negroes became sharecroppers or wage laborers, often cultivating the same land and the same crops as before the war. In qualification of the argument that free Negro labor led to more rapid industrialization it should be noted that the South did not keep up with national pace in the growth of non-agricultural wealth until after 1900.[35]

Two indirect effects of the war aided industrial growth to degrees

[34] *Trends in the American Economy,* p. 85.

[35] Simon Kuznets, ed., *Population Redistribution and Economic Growth: United States, 1870–1950* (2 vols., Philadelphia, 1957–1960), vol. I (Methodological Considerations and Reference Tables), pp. 729–32; vol. II (Analysis of Economic Change), p. 109.

that cannot accurately be measured. These were, first, a more satisfactory money market, and secondly, more security for entrepreneurial activity than in the prewar period. The sharp wartime inflation had the usual effect of transferring income from wage, salary, and interest receivers to those making profits. This meant concentration of savings in the hands of entrepreneurs who would invest in new activities; and this no doubt helps to explain the speculative booms of the last half of the 1860's and first two years of the 1870's which have been treated as the prosperity resulting from the war. Inflation also eased the burdens of those railroads which had excessive mortgage debts. But a great deal of new research would be needed to establish casual connections between the inflationary reallocation of wealth, 1863 to 1865, and the high rate of industrial progress in the late 1870's and the 1880's.
for interstate operations, has been hailed as a great aid to business expansion although it would be hard to demonstrate, aside from a few weeks during panics, that plentiful but occasionally unsound currency had seriously interfered with earlier industrial growth.[36] The existence of two and a half billion dollars in federal bonds also provided a basis for credit that was larger than before the war. This led to broader and more active security markets as well as to easier personal borrowing. But two qualifications must be kept in mind. First, local bank lending to favored borrowers had probably tended to be too liberal before the war and was now put on a somewhat firmer basis. In other words, since 1880 a multiplication of banks had made credit relatively easy to obtain in the United States, and in the North this continued to be the situation. Second, the southern banking system was largely destroyed by the war and had to be rebuilt in the subsequent decades. It should also be remembered that by 1875 some 40 per cent of the banks were outside the national banking system.[37]

Because of a few colorful speculators like Jay Gould, Daniel Drew, and Jim Fisk, and the immortality conferred on them, initially by the literary ability of the Adams brothers, the New York stock exchange in the postwar decade appears to have mirrored a new era of predatory wealth. But one has only to study the scandals of the London and New York stock exchanges in 1854 to see that there was little growth in the sophistication or boldness

[36] See Bray Hammond, *Banks and Politics in America: From the Revolution to the Civil War* (Princeton, 1957), pp. 663–67, 670.

[37] *Historical Statistics* (1960 ed.), pp. 628–638.

of stock operators during these fifteen years.[38] In any case, the exploits of market operators were seldom related in a positive way to economic growth. Even a record of new issues of securities, which is lacking for this period would chiefly reflect the flow of capital into railroads, banks, and public utilities rather than into manufacturing. Very few "industrial" shares were pubicly marketed before the decade of the 1880's; such enterprises grew chiefly from the reinvestment of earnings.

There was strong government encouragement to entrepreneurial activity during the Civil War, but to ascribe to it unusual importance for economic growth requires both analysis of the results and comparison with other periods. Government in the United States has almost always encouraged entrepreneurs. The federal and state administrations preceding the Civil War could certainly be regarded as friendly to business. They subsidized railroads by land grants, subscribed to corporate bond issues, and remitted taxes on new enterprise.[39] Tariffs were low, but railroad men and many bankers were happy with the situation. Whether or not American industrialism was significantly accelerated by the high protection that commenced with the war is a question that economists will probably never settle.

The building of a subsidized transcontinental railroad, held back by sectional controversies in the 1850's, was authorized along a northern route with the help of federal loans and land grants when the southerners excluded themselves from Congress. Putting more than a hundred million dollars into this project in the latter half of the 1860's, however, may have had an adverse effect on industrial growth. In general, the far western roads were built for speculative and strategic purposes uneconomically ahead of demand. They may for a decade, or even two, have consumed more capital than their transportation services were then worth to the economy.

To sum up this part of the obiter dictum, those who write of the war creating a national market tied together by railroads under-estimate both the achievements of the two decades before the war and the ongoing trends of the economy. The nation's business in 1855 was nearly as intersectional as in 1870. Regional

[38] See James K. Medbury, *Men and Mysteries of Wall Street* (Boston, 1870), pp. 319 ff.; Margaret G. Myers, *The New York Money Market* (2 vols., New York, 1931), vol. I, p. 140.

[39] Myers, *New York Money Market,* vol. I p. 296; National Bureau of Economic Research, *Capital Formation and Economic Growth* (Princeton, 1955), p. 382. See also Carter Goodrich, *Government Promotion of American Canals and Railroads, 1800–1890* (New York, 1960).

animosities did not interfere with trade, nor did these feelings diminish after the war. By the late 1850's the United States was a rapidly maturing industrial state with its major cities connected by rail, its major industries selling in a national market, and blessed or cursed with financiers, security flotations, stock markets, and all the other appurtenances of industrial capitalism.

But when all specific factors of change attributable to the war have been deflated, there is still the possibility that northern victory had enhanced the capitalist spirit, that as a consequence the atmosphere of government in Washington among members of both parties was more friendly to industrial enterprise and to northern-based national business operations than had formerly been the rule. It can be argued that, in spite of Greenbackers and discontented farmers, legislation presumably favorable to industry could be more readily enacted. The Fourteenth Amendment, for example, had as a by-product greater security for interstate business against state regulation, although it was to be almost two decades before the Supreme Court would give force to this protection. By 1876, a year of deep depression, the two major parties were trying to outdo each other in promises of stimulating economic growth. This highly generalized type of argument is difficult to evaluate, but in qualification of any theory of a sharp change in attitude we should remember that industrialism was growing rapidly from general causes and that by the 1870's it was to be expected that major-party politics would be conforming to this change in American life.

Massive changes in physical environment such as those accompanying the rise of trade at the close of the Middle Ages or the gradual growth of industrialism from the seventeenth century on do not lend themselves readily to exact or brief periodization. If factory industry and mechanized transportation be taken as the chief indexes of early industrialism, its spread in the United States was continuous and rapid during the entire nineteenth century, but in general, advance was greater during periods of prosperity than in depressions. The first long period without a major depression, after railroads, canals, and steamboats had opened a national market, was from 1843 to 1857. Many economic historians interested in quantitative calculations would regard these years as marking the appearance of an integrated industrial society. Walt W. Rostow, incidentally, starts his "take-off" period in the 1840's and calls it completed by 1860.[40] Others might prefer to avoid any

[40] W. W. Rostow, *The Stages of Economic Growth* (Cambridge, Eng.: The University Press, 1960), p. 95.

narrow span of years. Few, however, would see a major stimulation to economic growth in the events of the Civil War.

Finally, one may speculate as to why this exaggerated conception of the role of the Civil War in industrialization gained so firm a place in American historiography. The idea fits, of course, into the Marxian frame of revolutionary changes, but it seems initially to have gained acceptance quite independently of Marxian influences. More concentrated study of the war years than of any other four-year span in the nineteenth century called attention to technological and business events usually overlooked. Isolated facts were seized upon without comparing them with similar data for other decades. The desire of teachers for neat periodization was probably a strong factor in quickly placing the interpretation in textbooks; thus, up to 1860 the nation was agricultural, after 1865 it was industrial. Recent study of American cultural themes suggests still another reason. From most standpoints the Civil War was a national disaster, but Americans like to see their history in terms of optimism and progress. Perhaps the war was put in a perspective suited to the culture by seeing it as good because in addition to achieving freedom for the Negro it brought about industrial progress.

10

ONE of the significant questions involved in explaining the success of the North in the Civil War is why the British government, which was frankly friendly to the South, did not intervene in the struggle against the Union government. For in addition to their general friendship toward the South the British depended heavily upon importations of southern cotton to keep their textile mills operating. So great was this dependence that Southerners before and after the outbreak of hostilities freely predicted British intervention on the ground that "cotton was king." Prior to the twentieth century the most common explanation for the failure of the British to intervene was that friends of the United States in Parliament and among the English public stressed the antislavery aspect of the Union cause. Since Britain had long since abolished slavery in its own colonies and strongly opposed the slave trade on the high seas, so the argument went, the government could not risk violating its antislavery principles by supporting a frankly proslavery government like the Confederacy. In short, the economic interest of England, it was said, was being ignored in the interest of an idealistic principle.

By the early years of the twentieth century, however, such an approach smacked too much of sentimentality and lack of realism. By then the economic interpretation of historical events was receiving a more favorable reception among historians. As early as 1906, for example, Emerson D. Fite in an article, "Agricultural Development of the West During the Civil War," *Quarterly Journal of Economics*, XX (February 1906), 259–278, pointed out that newspapers of the time reported that imports of northern wheat into England were the real reason why the British government remained neutral. In short, King Cotton was beaten by King Corn.

Fite's suggestion received a full-dress scholarly analysis and defense twelve years later in Louis B. Schmidt's "The Influence of Wheat and Cotton on Anglo-American Relations during the Civil War," *Iowa Journal of History and Politics,* XVI (July 1918), 400–439. By an examination of the Parliamentary debates and the statistics of trade in both wheat and cotton, Schmidt argued that it was a Northern economic factor, not a matter of principle regarding slavery, that preserved British neutrality. His argument is summarized in more detail in the beginning of Ginzberg's article here.

As Ginzberg points out, the wheat thesis of Schmidt was quickly accepted by a number of historians and soon passed into textbooks and other general treatments of American history. Curiously enough, despite the general persuasiveness of Schmidt's thesis, two authorities, E. D. Adams and Frank Owsley, who had made the closest studies of Civil War diplomacy, rejected the wheat thesis. Part of Adams's reason for rejection was weak, if not invalid, as Ginzberg makes clear in showing that cotton was available from producers other than the American South.

The real issue, though, breaks down into two parts. Was northern wheat indispensable to Britain? This question is a quantifiable one, that is, it can be answered by statistics of trade, which Ginzberg supplies. But as Ginzberg admits, the statistics do not settle the question. For it is altogether possible that British officials may have believed that wheat importations were crucial for their economy, regardless of our analysis of the figures today. Thus what British officials *thought* about the importance of wheat is the second part of the question. It was on this second part of the question that Adams and Owsley concentrated and concluded that Schmidt was wrong. The merit of Ginzberg's article is that he has, unlike either of his predecessors, dealt with both parts of the question. Hence he has decided the issue as conclusively as it can be, given the limitations of all historical inquiry about the dead.

This judgment about the merits of Ginzberg's conclusion has been sustained by subsequent examinations of British neutrality. See Martin P. Claussen's "Peace Factors in Anglo-American Relations, 1861–1865," *Mississpipi Valley Historical Review,* XXVI (March 1940), 511–522, and Robert H. Jones, "Long Live the King?" *Agricultural History,* XXXVII (July 1963), 166–169.

One term used by Ginzberg in his article may require definition.

In writing of E. D. Adams's analysis, Ginzberg refers to the "absolute inelasticity of the supply of cotton and the relative elasticity in the supply of wheat." Elasticity is an economist's term expressing the relationship between price and supply. Perfect elasticity exists when the production of a commodity increases proportionately with an increase in price, that is, if price doubles, for example, supply doubles. Absolute inelasticity exists when even the greatest increase in price cannot call forth even the smallest increase in production. Relative elasticity occurs where an increase in price calls forth an increase in production but not in as large a proportion as the increase in price.

Mr. Ginzberg is professor of economics at the Graduate School of Business, Columbia University. Although for many years he was concerned with economic history, of late his interest has shifted to current problems of manpower, resulting in studies like *The Negro Potential* (New York, 1956) and *Human Resources* (New York, 1958).

The Economics of British Neutrality During the American Civil War[1]

BY ELI GINZBERG

HISTORY, like the other social studies is subject to powerful fashions. Factors once completely ignored may suddenly be overemphasized. Criticism presages the eclipse of prevailing theories, and research the emergence of the novel. Such is the dynamics of scholarship. In the past, the economic interpretation of history was wantonly neglected; at present, it is in its heyday; tomorrow its star will probably shine more dimly.

1 The basic draft of the present article was completed several years ago. The author is indebted to Professor Harry J. Carman of Columbia University for having called his attention to the subject as one worthy of investigation and to Everett E. Edwards of the U. S. Department of Agriculture for valuable assistance in preparing the manuscript for publication.

Professor Louis Bernard Schmidt, in a paper presented at a session of the American Historical Association, meeting at Philadelphia in 1917, examined the economics of British neutrality during the American Civil War, especially the data relating to the major staples of the contestants, namely, wheat and cotton.[2] His study was in part precipitated by the increased interest in international relations incident to the entrance of the United States into the World War. Professor Schmidt observed that the influence of wheat "seems to have been consistently overlooked by all students of Anglo-American relations" during the Civil War and concluded that "Northern wheat . . . may well be regarded as the decisive factor, counterbalancing the influence of cotton, in keeping the British government from recognizing the Confederacy." So impressive was the evidence presented in support of this wheat vs. cotton thesis that a considerable number of American historians appear to have accepted it.[3] Although criticism and skepticism have not been completely absent they have been infrequent and inconclusive. As late as 1932, a specialist wrote that "Probably more evidence than has yet been collected is needed to settle this point." [4]

The present reëxamination of the economics of British neutrality during the American Civil War includes an analysis of the data originally presented in substantiation of the wheat thesis as well as an evaluation of the criticisms levied against it. Study of the thesis and these criticisms should throw light on the broader problem of historical method, especially on the interrelation of theories and facts.

The evidence presented to show that wheat from the northern and western sections of the United States was a factor of major

[2] L. B. Schmidt, "The Influence of Wheat and Cotton on Anglo-American Relations during the Civil War," in *Iowa Journal of History and Politics*, 16:400–439 (July 1918). The article is reprinted with omissions in L. B. Schmidt and E. D. Ross, editors, *Readings in the Economic History of American Agriculture*, 304–321 (New York, 1925). The original version has been used in the preparation of the present article, and all quotations and data not otherwise documented are from this source.

[3] J. T. Adams, *The March of Democracy*, 2:20–22, 82 (New York, 1932); C. A. Beard and M. R. Beard, *The Rise of American Civilization*, 2:82, 84 (New York, 1927); H. U. Faulkner, *American Economic History*, 391–394 (New York, 1929); and William Trimble, "Historical Aspects of the Surplus Food Production of the United States, 1862–1902," in American Historical Association, *Annual Report* (1918), 1:224 (Washington, 1921). Cf. Edward Channing, *A History of the United States*, 6:340–341 (New York, 1925), and E. D. Fite, *Social and Industrial Conditions in the North during the Civil War*, 1–2, 17 (New York, 1910).

[4] M. B. Hammond, in *American Economic Review*, 22:704 (December 1932).

importance in committing British foreign policy to neutrality may be subsumed under four heads:

1. Great Britain had become a great wheat-importing country by 1860. During the preceding five years, it consumed an average of 21,000,000 quarters per annum, of which 16,000,000 were produced at home. Hence, it imported between 25 and 30 percent of its annual supply. During the years 1860–62, the harvests were exceedingly poor and its annual production averaged only 12,000,000 quarters, thus necessitating a doubling of imports if consumption were not to be curtailed.

2. Russia, Prussia, France, and the United States were Britain's principal sources of supply. In 1861 and 1862, France suffered severe crop failures and was forced to curtail its exports of grain. The English imports from Russia and Prussia remained steady during the war years; these countries "were unable to respond to Great Britain's greatly increased demands."

3. In 1860, the United States was an important wheat-producing country. The outbreak of hostilities cut off the Southern market for Northern wheat, thereby releasing supplies for England in this hour of need. The United States exported 2.1 million quarters to the United Kingdom in 1860, 3.6 million in 1861, and 5.0 million in 1862. At a time when imports were mounting rapidly, the United States supplied an ever larger percentage of the total—11.2 percent in 1858–59; 29.2 percent in 1860; 41.5 percent in 1861; 43.5 percent in 1862; and 38.4 percent in 1863.

4. Speeches in Parliament and articles in periodicals during the war show that English public opinion was conscious of the dependence of the British Isles on American wheat, a dependence well recognized by those who formulated British foreign policy.

The late Professor Ephraim Douglass Adams, a leading authority on Anglo-American relations during the Civil War, did not accept the view that the need of American wheat was a factor determining British neutrality.[5] He disposed of the wheat thesis on three counts: 1, By midsummer of 1863, British intervention was no longer a real threat; the danger had passed by January of that year; 2, It is a mistake to equate cotton and wheat for "the former could not be obtained in quantity from *any* source before 1864" but increased imports of the latter were solely a matter of price; 3, The Governmental memoranda are absolutely silent on the question of wheat.

The thesis is damaged but not demolished by the fact that a

[5] E. D. Adams, *Great Britain and the American Civil War*, 2:13, footnote 2 (New York, 1924).

majority of the references to wheat in Parliament date from the Roebuck Resolution of June 1863, at which time intervention was already a forlorn hope. British dependence on grain from the American Middle West had previously been discussed in the House of Commons, and the argument was known and respected, at least by a few if not by many.[6] Furthermore, Professor Adams's contrast between the absolute inelasticity of the supply of cotton and the relative elasticity in the supply of wheat is not well supported by factual evidence. With the drastic decline in the cotton imports from the United States, there occurred a steady and progressive increase in imports from other countries.[7] In the light of Professor Adams's

Year	*United States*	*Other Countries*
1860	2,580,700 bales	785,000 bales
1861	1,841,600 "	1,194,000 "
1862	72,000 "	1,445,000 "
1863	132,000 "	1,932,000 "
1864	198,000 "	2,587,000 "
1865	462,000 "	2,755,000 "

intimate acquaintance with the British state papers, his third criticism, which he believed to be "conclusive in negation" of the thesis, is highly significant.

In discussing "the influence of wheat in keeping John Bull on his good behavior with the United States" Professor Frank Lawrence Owsley, in his book on *King Cotton Diplomacy*, places himself at the forefront of the critics of the thesis.[8] He holds, however, that the "complete silence on the subject . . . in the cabinet circles . . . would not be conclusive were there not other evidence of a more positive character which corroborates this negative evidence." His position may be summarized thus: 1, The "wheat famine" idea can be traced from John Bright and William E. Forster back to Charles Francis Adams and thence back to William H. Seward and Abraham Lincoln; in short, it was a piece of Federal propaganda. 2, The British press commented on the idea from time to time, but almost without exception sneered at it. The large importations from the

[6] *Ibid.*; Schmidt, 436–437; F. L. Owsley, *King Cotton Diplomacy; Foreign Relations of the Confederate States of America*, 450–488 (Chicago, 1931).

[7] Schmidt, 416–420. He points out that the British need for cotton was further modified by the spinning of finer fabrics and by the expansion of the woolen and linen trades which helped materially in taking up the slack due to the depression in cotton. F. L. Owsley, *King Cotton Diplomacy*, 572.

[8] *Ibid.*, 567–568. Owsley's interpretation of British neutrality is based largely on the economics of war profits. The evidence presented (569ff.) is impressive. His interest in the subject, like Schmidt's, was due to reflections on the World War.

United States were a matter of price, not of necessity. 3, "Most important of all . . . England took this wheat in payment for the countless millions of dollars' worth of rifles, cannon, powder, and other munitions of war which she was selling the United States . . . in 1864 and 1865, after the United States became practically self-sufficient in the production of war supplies and no longer made large purchases from England, the latter country turned abruptly away from America to Russia and East Europe for her wheat supply." Professor Owsley concludes that all the evidence tends "to demonstrate that wheat had little if anything to do with preventing English intervention in the American Civil War."

The famine bogy may have been Federal propaganda, and the wheat exports from the North probably helped to pay for much-needed imports of munitions; yet, if England were truly dependent on American wheat and if informed and influential groups really believed in this dependence, the arguments relating to propaganda and balance of trade are beside the point. The wheat thesis, as originally presented, includes a careful review of the relevant statistics and an analysis of the allusions to dependence on American wheat in the press and the debates in Parliament. Professors Adams and Owsley have contributed greatly to our understanding of the economics of British neutrality, but neither reviewed the basic data offered in support of the wheat thesis. To these we now turn.

At the time of the American Civil War, Great Britain imported from 25 to 50 percent of its annual supply of wheat, and the United States contributed from 30 to 45 percent of this importation.[9] Yet, these figures do not in themselves establish the *strategic* importance of American wheat. It was strategic only if other countries could not meet the demand, and only if the states of Britain were cognizant of this fact and acted accordingly.

The crop failures of the early sixties affected not only England but also France which in normal years was an important source of supply for English imports. For the years 1858 and 1859, France supplied England with over 1.5 million quarters of wheat and flour, or 35 percent of the total imported. During the crucial years, 1860–1862, French exports dropped to an average of less than 600,000

[9] The statistics used in the original version of the wheat vs. cotton thesis as well as in the present article are drawn primarily from two excellent articles: J. B. Lawes and J. H. Gilbert, "On the Home Produce, Imports, and Consumption of Wheat," in the Royal Agricultural Society, *Journal* (ser. 2), 4:359–396 (London, 1868); and H. Evershed, "Variation in the Price and Supply of Wheat," in *Ibid.*, 5:153–262 (London, 1869). Hereafter, these articles are cited as Lawes and Gilbert, and Evershed. There are eight bushels in a quarter.

quarters.[10] These data show that France failed John Bull at a crucial time.

What of the other sources of wheat? In 1858 and 1859, England annually received approximately 700,000 and 750,000 quarters from Prussia and Russia respectively. The corresponding figure for the three following years is an average annual import of over 1.2 million quarters for each of these countries. The supply from these countries was assuredly elastic; it increased 70 percent within three years. The statistical data relating to imports from "Other Countries" show an annual average of slightly less than one million quarters for 1858 and 1859—an increase of 100 percent for the following three years.[11] The data relating to the wheat exported from the United States are much more erratic: 1,099,000 quarters in 1858; 99,000 in 1859; 2,143,000 in 1860; 3,602,000 in 1861; and 5,022,000 in 1862,—the annual average for the last three years being 3.6 million.[12] When England needed to increase substantially its imports, all of its major sources of supply, with the exception of France, were able to respond, and the United States most easily. To understand the significance of the American response, the question must be asked: What would have been the predicament of Great Britain if Northern wheat had been withheld?

In 1858–60 there was available annually 5.0 bushels of wheat per capita for the population of the United Kingdom, and the average price was 5s. 10d. The corresponding average for 1860, 1861, and 1862 was 5.7 bushels, and the price approximately 6s. 9d. If Great Britain had not imported a single quarter of wheat from the United States during the critical years, the supply would have permitted the per capita consumption to remain at the same level as in 1858–60. That the price would have risen is beyond dispute, but it probably would not have approached the high level of 1854 when wheat sold for more than 10s. per bushel.[13] In this connection, it is important to recall that the exportation of wheat from the Continent depended "on the temptation to sell. A sudden rise on our markets has a singular effect in wringing wheat out of poor countries."[14] As we have already seen, there was wheat to be wrung.

[10] Evershed, 196. The year 1860 is included because of the significance of surplus stocks. Schmidt also included it. The data relate to the United Kingdom.

[11] Evershed, 196. Cf. Schmidt, 426, which reads: "these two countries were unable to respond."

[12] Evershed, 196. The decline was likewise rapid: 2,739,000 in 1863; 2,325,000 in 1864; 945,000 in 1865; 227,000 in 1866.

[13] Lawes and Gilbert, 361, 392, 396.

[14] Evershed, 158.

The analysis of the statistical data casts the most serious doubt on the contention that Northern wheat was of strategic importance for Great Britain during the early 1860s. It suggests that the comparatively low price of wheat and flour was the result of ample stocks available in the United States. The wheat thesis would, therefore, retain part of its validity if it could be proven that English statesmen emphasized the significance of American exports. Despite the statistics, it would remain practically intact if it could be proven that this overemphasis helped to shape the policy of British neutrality. Such a claim was originally made by Professor Schmidt and denials were entered by Professor Adams and Professor Owsley. What is the evidence?

The original statement of the wheat thesis frequently cited the *Economist* and the Parliamentary Debates to substantiate the claim that informed opinion was fully cognizant of the importance of Northern wheat for the British Isles and that the responsible members of the Government acted in the light of this consciousness. Throughout the two or more years when British intervention was a live issue, the *Economist,* though opposed to any overt recognition of the Confederacy, failed to advance the wheat argument, although so doing would doubtless have strengthened its advocacy of noninterference. In fact, it devoted remarkably little space to the grain trade in any of its manifold aspects,—a truly unusual fact when we recall the poor harvests of 1860 and 1861. Early in 1862, it included a series of letters that discussed whether or not the grain shortage was acute.[15] Toward the end of the year, it printed a long and informed article on important phases of the contemporary wheat trade, especially its relation to the English corn grower, the merchant importer, the money market, and the welfare of the masses.[16] The author made no reference to Northern wheat, nor did he express anxiety over Britain's dependence on imports. In short, this well-informed journal did not comprehend the strategic importance of Northern wheat.

A review of the Parliamentary Debates is not quite so barren of results. On July 18, 1862, William S. Lindsay, in urging his motion for British mediation, read a letter from America which contained the following: [17]

[15] *Economist* (London), 20:33, 61, 90–91, 145 (Jan. 11, 18, 25, Feb. 8, 1862).

[16] *Ibid.,* 20:1173–1180 (Oct. 25, 1862). Its discussion of the relation of the grain trade to the money market supports Owsley's explanation of the large exports of American wheat.

[17] *Hansard's Parliamentary Debates* (ser. 3), 168:521.

> Is she [England] afraid for her Northern supplies of bread stuffs? Let her consider that her demand for them is the lifeblood of our agricultural States. They must sell to her. The probable loss of her custom alone would secure her from any danger on our part.

Speaking on the same motion, W. E. Forster pointed out: "We had a cotton famine now; but if we did that [intervened], we should stand in danger of a corn famine."[18] In the course of the same debate, Seymour Fitzgerald contrasted these two famines: [19]

> A cotton famine was not like a corn famine. When the potato crop failed one year in Ireland or the wheat crop in England, there was always the prospect and the hope that in the year following the kindly fruits of the earth would be enjoyed in due season. But it was not so with the cotton crop.

Lindsay was an avowed agitator for the South, and Forster for the North. The wheat argument as presented by the former was expounded in a letter from a Northerner propagandizing for the cessation of hostilities. Forster, an equally rabid partisan for the Union, placed little emphasis on wheat. Fitzgerald refused to be impressed, though he considered it worthwhile to point out the grounds for his skepticism. Viscount Palmerston spoke for the Government, and though his speech was in accord with the best tradition of English diplomacy—platitudinous, sonorous, and obscure—it did not contain the slightest reference to wheat.

About a year later when the Roebuck Resolution was before the House of Commons, Lord Robert Montagu referred to the wheat argument while speaking against mediation. He held that the distress in England would doubtless be aggravated if the Northern States ceased to export grain. What is more important, he asserted that such a cessation would lead to a substantial impairment of the economic and political relations then existing between the Middle West and Canada, as Northern grain frequently, and in large quantity, passed through Canada.[20] In the course of the debate, Forster returned to the wheat argument: "... unless the harvest were better than it promised, the sufferings of the countrymen of the hon. Member [Mr. Maguire] would be great indeed if they were deprived of the American corn crop of this year." [21] Montagu emphasized the lucrativeness of Canadian trade and pointed out that war with the North might lead to the loss of those important colonies. Even

[18] *Ibid.*, 536.
[19] *Ibid.*, 575.
[20] *Ibid.*, 171:1795.
[21] *Ibid.*, 1813.

Forster was not eschatological, and John Bright, who also joined in the debate, failed to mention the wheat argument.[22]

The members of Parliament were not completely ignorant of the rôle that Northern wheat was playing, and more important, might play if Britain failed to remain neutral. It is, however, extremely doubtful that a small minority, not to mention a responsible majority, considered this rôle important, much less strategic. The argument was most respected by agitators, but even they failed to consider it worthy of more than passing comment.[23]

The review of the statistical data suggests that the figures by themselves do little to support the wheat thesis. Likewise, the literary data do not withstand careful scrutiny and therefore fail to supply the necessary substantiation. Thus ends a cycle. A historical factor "consistently overlooked by all students" is finally discovered; then others acknowledge it, although a few remain skeptical. Slowly their skepticism is transformed into criticism, and eventually the discovery must give way.

Historians frequently fail to realize that the economic interpretation of history is impossible,—that economic interpretations are as manifold as economic factors.[24] Furthermore, interpretations must differ with the length of the cross-section. An economic factor may be of strategic importance in explaining broad movements—the Decline of Rome, the Rise of the British Empire, the Abolition of Slavery in the United States—but it cannot be relied on primarily, not to mention solely, in analyzing the outbreak of a war, or the neutrality of an interested party. To do so is clearly fallacious. Factors other than economic are most frequently catalytics. Man individual differs from man collective, and history is concerned with man collective. It is indeed doubtful whether rational calculation explains much of individual behavior; clearly it explains almost nothing of the behavior of groups.

22 *Ibid.*, 1826–1838.

23 Cf. Owsley's discussion of the genesis of the thesis.

24 Cf. V. G. Simkhovitch, *Marxism vs. Socialism, passim* (New York, 1913), and "Approaches to History," in *Political Science Quarterly*, 44:481–497; 45:481–526; 47:410–439; 48:23–61; 49:44–83; 51:117–151 (1929ff.).

Selected titles: Revised June, 1966

harper torchbooks

HUMANITIES AND SOCIAL SCIENCES

American Studies: General

CARL N. DEGLER, Ed.: Pivotal Interpretations of American History TB/1240, TB/1241

A. S. EISENSTADT, Ed.: The Craft of American History: *Recent Essays in American Historical Writing* Vol. I TB/1255; Vol. II TB/1256

MARCUS LEE HANSEN: The Atlantic Migration: 1607-1860. *Edited by Arthur M. Schlesinger. Introduction by Oscar Handlin* TB/1052

MARCUS LEE HANSEN: The Immigrant in American History. *Edited with a Foreword by Arthur M. Schlesinger* TB/1120

JOHN HIGHAM, Ed.: The Reconstruction of American History△ TB/1068

ROBERT H. JACKSON: The Supreme Court in the American System of Government TB/1106

JOHN F. KENNEDY: A Nation of Immigrants.△ *Illus.* TB/1118

RALPH BARTON PERRY: Puritanism and Democracy TB/1138

ARNOLD ROSE: The Negro in America TB/3048

American Studies: Colonial

BERNARD BAILYN, Ed.: The Apologia of Robert Keayne: *Self-Portrait of a Puritan Merchant* TB/1201

BERNARD BAILYN: The New England Merchants in the Seventeenth Century TB/1149

JOSEPH CHARLES: The Origins of the American Party System TB/1049

LAWRENCE HENRY GIPSON: The Coming of the Revolution: 1763-1775. † *Illus.* TB/3007

PERRY MILLER & T. H. JOHNSON, Eds.: The Puritans: *A Sourcebook* Vol. I TB/1093; Vol. II TB/1094

EDMUND S. MORGAN, Ed.: The Diary of Michael Wigglesworth, 1653-1657 TB/1228

EDMUND S. MORGAN: The Puritan Family TB/1227

RICHARD B. MORRIS: Government and Labor in Early America TB/1244

WALLACE NOTESTEIN: The English People on the Eve of Colonization: 1603-1630. † *Illus.* TB/3006

American Studies: From the Revolution to 1860

JOHN R. ALDEN: The American Revolution: 1775-1783. † *Illus.* TB/3011

MAX BELOFF: The Debate on the American Revolution: 1761-1783 TB/1225

RAY A. BILLINGTON: The Far Western Frontier: 1830-1860. † *Illus.* TB/3012

GEORGE DANGERFIELD: The Awakening of American Nationalism: 1815-1828. † *Illus.* TB/3061

JOHN C. MILLER: Alexander Hamilton and the Growth of the New Nation TB/3057

RICHARD B. MORRIS, Ed.: The Era of the American Revolution TB/1180

R. B. NYE: The Cultural Life of the New Nation: 1776-1801. † *Illus.* TB/3026

A. F. TYLER: Freedom's Ferment TB/1074

LOUIS B. WRIGHT: Culture on the Moving Frontier TB/1053

American Studies: Since the Civil War

MAX BELOFF, Ed.: The Debate on the American Revolution, 1761-1783: *A Sourcebook* TB/1225

A. RUSSELL BUCHANAN: The United States and World War II. † *Illus.* TB/3021

EDMUND BURKE: On the American Revolution. † *Edited by Elliot Robert Barkan* TB/3068

THOMAS C. COCHRAN & WILLIAM MILLER: The Age of Enterprise: *A Social History of Industrial America* TB/1054

WHITNEY R. CROSS: The Burned-Over District: *The Social and Intellectual History of Enthusiastic Religion in Western New York, 1800-1850* TB/1242

FOSTER RHEA DULLES: America's Rise to World Power: 1898-1954. † *Illus.* TB/3021

W. A. DUNNING: Reconstruction, Political and Economic: 1865-1877 TB/1073

HAROLD U. FAULKNER: Politics, Reform and Expansion: 1890-1900. † *Illus.* TB/3020

FRANCIS GRIERSON: The Valley of Shadows TB/1246

SIDNEY HOOK: Reason, Social Myths, and Democracy TB/1237

WILLIAM E. LEUCHTENBURG: Franklin D. Roosevelt and the New Deal: 1932-1940. † *Illus.* TB/3025

ARTHUR S. LINK: Woodrow Wilson and the Progressive Era: 1910-1917. † *Illus.* TB/3023

JAMES MADISON: The Forging of American Federalism. *Edited by Saul K. Padover* TB/1226

ROBERT GREEN MCCLOSKEY: American Conservatism in the Age of Enterprise: 1865-1910 TB/1137

ARTHUR MANN: Yankee Reformers in the Urban Age TB/1247

GEORGE E. MOWRY: The Era of Theodore Roosevelt and the Birth of Modern America: 1900-1912 † TB/3022

R. B. NYE: Midwestern Progressive Politics TB/1202

FRANCIS S. PHILBRICK: The Rise of the West, 1754-1830. † *Illus.* TB/3067

JACOB RIIS: The Making of an American. ‡ *Edited by Roy Lubove* TB/3070

CHARLES H. SHINN: Mining Camps: *A Study in American Frontier Government.* ‡ *Edited by Rodman W. Paul* TB/3062

PHILIP SELZNICK: TVA and the Grass Roots: *A Study in the Sociology of Formal Organization* TB/1230

† The New American Nation Series, edited by Henry Steele Commager and Richard B. Morris.
‡ American Perspectives series, edited by Bernard Wishy and William E. Leuchtenburg.
* The Rise of Modern Europe series, edited by William L. Langer.
¶ Researches in the Social, Cultural, and Behavioral Sciences, edited by Benjamin Nelson.
§ The Library of Religion and Culture, edited by Benjamin Nelson.
Σ Harper Modern Science Series, edited by James R. Newman.
° Not for sale in Canada.
△ Not for sale in the U. K.

TIMOTHY L. SMITH: Revivalism and Social Reform: *American Protestantism on the Eve of the Civil War* TB/1229

IDA M. TARBELL: The History of the Standard Oil Company. *Briefer Version.* ‡ *Edited by David M. Chalmers* TB/3071

GEORGE B. TINDALL, Ed.: A Populist Reader ‡ TB/3069

VERNON LANE WHARTON: The Negro in Mississippi: 1865-1890 TB/1178

Anthropology

JACQUES BARZUN: Race: *A Study in Superstition. Revised Edition* TB/1172

JOSEPH B. CASAGRANDE, Ed.: In the Company of Man: *Portraits of Anthropological Informants* TB/3047

W. E. LE GROS CLARK: The Antecedents of Man: *Intro. to Evolution of the Primates.* °△ *Illus.* TB/559

CORA DU BOIS: The People of Alor. *New Preface by the author. Illus.* Vol. I TB/1042; Vol. II TB/1043

DAVID LANDY: Tropical Childhood: *Cultural Transmission and Learning in a Puerto Rican Village* ¶ TB/1235

EDWARD BURNETT TYLOR: The Origins of Culture. *Part I of "Primitive Culture."* § *Intro. by Paul Radin* TB/33

EDWARD BURNETT TYLOR: Religion in Primitive Culture. *Part II of "Primitive Culture."* § *Intro. by Paul Radin* TB/34

W. LLOYD WARNER: A Black Civilization: *A Study of an Australian Tribe.* ¶ *Illus.* TB/3056

Art and Art History

EMILE MÂLE: The Gothic Image: *Religious Art in France of the Thirteenth Century.* § △ *190 illus.* TB/44

MILLARD MEISS: Painting in Florence and Siena after the Black Death. *The Arts, Religion and Society in the Mid-Fourteenth Century. 169 illus.* TB/1148

ERICH NEUMANN: The Archetypal World of Henry Moore. △ *107 illus.* TB/2020

DORA & ERWIN PANOFSKY: Pandora's Box: *The Changing Aspects of a Mythical Symbol* TB/2021

ERWIN PANOFSKY: Studies in Iconology: *Humanistic Themes in the Art of the Renaissance* △ TB/1077

ALEXANDRE PIANKOFF: The Shrines of Tut-Ankh-Amon. *Edited by N. Rambova. 117 illus.* TB/2011

OTTO VON SIMSON: The Gothic Cathderal △ TB/2018

HEINRICH ZIMMER: Myths and Symbols in Indian Art and Civilization. *70 illustrations* TB/2005

Business, Economics & Economic History

REINHARD BENDIX: Work and Authority in Industry TB/3035

GILBERT BURCK & EDITORS OF FORTUNE: The Computer Age: *And Its Potential for Management* TB/1179

THOMAS C. COCHRAN: The American Business System: *A Historical Perspective, 1900-1955* TB/1080

ROBERT DAHL & CHARLES E. LINDBLOM: Politics, Economics, and Welfare TB/3037

PETER F. DRUCKER: The New Society: *The Anatomy of Industrial Order* △ TB/1082

FRANK H. KNIGHT: The Economic Organization TB/1214

FRANK H. KNIGHT: Risk, Uncertainty and Profit TB/1215

ABBA P. LERNER: Everybody's Business TB/3051

PAUL MANTOUX: The Industrial Revolution in the Eighteenth Century ° △ TB/1079

HERBERT SIMON: The Shape of Automation: *For Men and Management* TB/1245

PERRIN STRYKER: The Character of the Executive: *Eleven Studies in Managerial Qualities* TB/1041

PIERRE URI: Partnership for Progress: *A Program for Transatlantic Action* TB/3036

Contemporary Culture

JACQUES BARZUN: The House of Intellect △ TB/1051

CLARK KERR: The Uses of the University TB/1264

JOHN U. NEF: Cultural Foundations of Industrial Civilization △ TB/1024

PAUL VALÉRY: The Outlook for Intelligence △ TB/2016

Historiography & Philosophy of History

JACOB BURCKHARDT: On History and Historians. △ *Intro. by H. R. Trevor-Roper* TB/1216

J. H. HEXTER: Reappraisals in History: *New Views on History & Society in Early Modern Europe* TB/1100

H. STUART HUGHES: History as Art and as Science: *Twin Vistas on the Past* TB/1207

GEORGE H. NADEL, Ed.: Studies in the Philosophy of History: *Essays from History and Theory* TB/1208

KARL R. POPPER: The Open Society and Its Enemies △
Vol. I: The Spell of Plato TB/1101
Vol. II: The High Tide of Prophecy: Hegel, Marx and the Aftermath TB/1102

KARL R. POPPER: The Poverty of Historicism °△ TB/1126

G. J. RENIER: History: Its Purpose and Method △ TB/1209

W. H. WALSH: Philosophy of History △ TB/1020

History: General

L. CARRINGTON GOODRICH: A Short History of the Chinese People. △ *Illus.* TB/3015

DAN N. JACOBS & HANS H. BAERWALD: Chinese Communism: *Selected Documents* TB/3031

BERNARD LEWIS: The Arabs in History △ TB/1029

History: Ancient and Medieval

A. ANDREWES: The Greek Tyrants △ TB/1103

P. BOISSONNADE: Life and Work in Medieval Europe ° △ TB/1141

HELEN CAM: England before Elizabeth △ TB/1026

NORMAN COHN: The Pursuit of the Millennium △ TB/1037

CHRISTOPHER DAWSON, Ed.: Mission to Asia △ TB/315

ADOLF ERMAN, Ed.: The Ancient Egyptians TB/1233

HEINRICH FICHTENAU: The Carolingian Empire: *The Age of Charlemagne* △ TB/1142

F. L. GANSHOF: Feudalism △ TB/1058

DENO GEANAKOPLOS: Byzantine East and Latin West △ TB/1265

MICHAEL GRANT: Ancient History ° △ TB/1190

W. O. HASSALL, Ed.: Medieval England: *As Viewed by Contemporaries* △ TB/1205

DENYS HAY: The Medieval Centuries ° △ TB/1192

J. M. HUSSEY: The Byzantine World △ TB/1057

SAMUEL NOAH KRAMER: Sumerian Mythology TB/1055

NAPHTALI LEWIS & MEYER REINHOLD, Eds.: Roman Civilization. *Sourcebook I: The Republic* TB/1231

NAPHTALI LEWIS & MEYER REINHOLD, Eds.: Roman Civilization. *Sourcebook II: The Empire* TB/1232

FERDINAND LOT: The End of the Ancient World and the Beginnings of the Middle Ages TB/1044

G. MOLLAT: The Popes at Avignon: 1305-1378 △ TB/308

CHARLES PETIT-DUTAILLIS: The Feudal Monarchy in France and England ° △ TB/1165

HENRI PIRENNE: Early Democracies in the Low Countries TB/1110

STEVEN RUNCIMAN: A History of the Crusades △
Volume I: *The First Crusade and the Foundation of the Kingdom of Jerusalem. Illus.* TB/1143
Volume II: *The Kingdom of Jerusalem and the Frankish East, 1100-1187. Illus.* TB/1243

F. VAN DER MEER: Augustine the Bishop △ TB/304

J. M. WALLACE-HADRILL: The Barbarian West △ TB/1061

History: Renaissance & Reformation

JACOB BURCKHARDT: The Civilization of the Renaissance in Italy △ Vol. I TB/40; Vol. II TB/41

JOHN CALVIN & JACOPO SADOLETO: A Reformation Debate. *Edited by John C. Olin* TB/1239

G. CONSTANT: The Reformation in England △ TB/314

WALLACE K. FERGUSON et al.: The Renaissance: *Six Essays. Illus.* TB/1084

JOHN NEVILLE FIGGIS: Divine Right of Kings TB/1191

JOHN NEVILLE FIGGIS: Political Thought from Gerson to Grotius: 1414-1625 TB/1032

FRANCESCO GUICCIARDINI: Maxims and Reflections of a Renaissance Statesman *(Ricordi)* TB/1160

J. H. HEXTER: More's Utopia: *The Biography of an Idea. New Epilogue by the Author* TB/1195

HAJO HOLBORN: Ulrich von Hutten and the German Reformation TB/1238

JOHAN HUIZINGA: Erasmus and the Age of Reformation.△ *Illus.* TB/19

JOEL HURSTFIELD, Ed.; The Reformation Crisis △ TB/1267

ULRICH VON HUTTEN et al.: On the Eve of the Reformation: *"Letters of Obscure Men"* TB/1124

PAUL O. KRISTELLER: Renaissance Thought: *The Classic, Scholastic, and Humanist Strains* TB/1048

NICCOLÒ MACHIAVELLI: History of Florence and of the Affairs of Italy TB/1027

GARRETT MATTINGLY et al.: Renaissance Profiles. △ *Edited by J. H. Plumb* TB/1162

J E. NEALE: The Age of Catherine de Medici ° △ TB/1085

ERWIN PANOFSKY: Studies in Iconology △ TB/1077

J. H. PARRY: The Establishment of the European Hegemony: 1415-1715 △ TB/1045

J. H. PLUMB: The Italian Renasisance △ TB/1161

A. F. POLLARD: Henry VIII °△ TB/1249

A. F. POLLARD: Wolsey: *Church and State in 16th Century England* ° △ TB/1248

CECIL ROTH: The Jews in the Renaissance. *Illus.* TB/834

A. L. ROWSE: The Expansion of Elizabethan England. °△ *Illus.* TB/1220

GORDON RUPP: Luther's Progress to the Diet of Worms °△ TB/120

FERDINAND SCHEVILL: Medieval and Renaissance Florence. *Illus.* Volume I: *Medieval Florence* TB/1090
Volume II: *The Coming of Humanism and the Age of the Medici* TB/1091

G. M. TREVELYAN: England in the Age of Wycliffe, 1368-1520 °△ TB/1112

VESPASIANO: Renaissance Princes, Popes, and Prelates: *The Vespasiano Memoirs* TB/1111

History: Modern European

MAX BELOFF: The Age of Absolutism, 1660-1815 △ TB/1062

ASA BRIGGS: The Making of Modern England, 1784-1867: *The Age of Improvement* °△ TB/1203

CRANE BRINTON: A Decade of Revolution, 1789-1799. * *Illus.* TB/3018

D. W. BROGAN: The Development of Modern France. °△
Volume I. *From the Fall of the Empire to the Dreyfus Affair* TB/1184
Volume II: *The Shadow of War, World War I, Between the Two Wars. New Introduction by the Author* TB/1185

J. BRONOWSKI & BRUCE MAZLISH: The Western Intellectual Tradition: *From Leonardo to Hegel* △ TB/3001

ALAN BULLOCK: Hitler, A Study in Tyranny ° △ TB/1123

E. H. CARR: The Twenty Years' Crisis, 1919-1939 °△ TB/1122

GORDON A. CRAIG: From Bismarck to Adenauer: *Aspects of German Statecraft. Revised Edition* TB/1171

FRANKLIN L. FORD: Robe and Sword: *The Regrouping of the French Aristocracy after Louis XIV* TB/1217

RENÉ FUELOEP-MILLER: The Mind and Face of Bolshevism TB/1188

C. C. GILLISPIE: Genesis and Geology: *The Decades before Darwin* § TB/51

ALBERT GUÉRARD: France in the Classical Age △ TB/1183

CARLTON J. H. HAYES: A Generation of Materialism, 1871-1900. * *Illus.* TB/3039

J. H. HEXTER: Reappraisals in History: *New Views on History & Society in Early Modern Europe* △ TB/1100

STANLEY HOFFMANN et al.: In Search of France TB/1219

DAN N. JACOBS, Ed.: The New Communist Manifesto & Related Documents. *Third edition, Revised* TB/1078

HANS KOHN: The Mind of Germany △ TB/1204

HANS KOHN, Ed.: The Mind of Modern Russia TB/1065

FRANK E. MANUEL: The Prophets of Paris: *Turgot, Condorcet, Saint-Simon, Fourier, and Comte* TB/1218

KINGSLEY MARTIN: French Liberal Thought in the Eighteenth Century TB/1114

L. B. NAMIER: Personalities and Powers △ TB/1186

L. B. NAMIER: Vanished Supremacies ° △ TB/1088

JOHN U. NEF: Western Civilization Since the Renaissance: *Peace, War, Industry, and the Arts* TB/1113

JOHN PLAMENATZ: German Marxism and Russian Communism. °△ *New Preface by the Author* TB/1189

PENFIELD ROBERTS: The Quest for Security, 1715-1740. * *Illus.* TB/3016

PRISCILLA ROBERTSON: Revolutions of 1848 TB/1025

LOUIS, DUC DE SAINT-SIMON: Versailles, The Court, and Louis XIV △ TB/1250

A. J. P. TAYLOR: From Napoleon to Lenin: *Historical Essays* ° △ TB/1268

A. J. P. TAYLOR: The Habsburg Monarchy, 1809-1918 °△ TB/1187

G. M. TREVELYAN: British History in the Nineteenth Century and After: *1782-1919* △ TB/1251

H. R. TREVOR-ROPER: Historical Essays °△ TB/1269

JOHN B. WOLF: The Emergence of the Great Powers, 1685-1715. **Illus.* TB/3010

JOHN B. WOLF: France: 1814-1919 TB/3019

Intellectual History & History of Ideas

HERSCHEL BAKER: The Image of Man TB/1047

R. R. BOLGAR: The Classical Heritage and Its Beneficiaries △ TB/1125

J. BRONOWSKI & BRUCE MAZLISH: The Western Intellectual Tradition: *From Leonardo to Hegel* TB/3001

ERNST CASSIRER: The Individual and the Cosmos in Renaissance Philosophy. △ *Translated with an Introduction by Mario Domandi* TB/1097

NORMAN COHN: Pursuit of the Millennium △ TB/1037

C. C. GILLISPIE: Genesis and Geology: *The Decades before Darwin* § TB/51

ARTHUR O. LOVEJOY: The Great Chain of Being: *A Study of the History of an Idea* TB/1009

FRANK E. MANUEL: The Prophets of Paris: *Turgot, Condorcet, Saint-Simon, Fourier, and Comte* TB/1218

RALPH BARTON PERRY: The Thought and Character of William James: *Briefer Version* TB/1156

BRUNO SNELL: The Discovery of the Mind: *The Greek Origins of European Thought* △ TB/1018

PAUL VALÉRY: The Outlook for Intelligence △ TB/2016

PHILIP P. WIENER: Evolution and the Founders of Pragmatism. △ *Foreword by John Dewey* TB/1212

Literature, Poetry, The Novel & Criticism

JACQUES BARZUN: The House of Intellect △ TB/1051

JAMES BOSWELL: The Life of Dr. Johnson & The Journal of a Tour to the Hebrides with Samuel Johnson LL.D. ° △ TB/1254

ABRAHAM CAHAN: The Rise of David Levinsky TB/1028

ERNST R. CURTIUS: European Literature and the Latin Middle Ages △ TB/2015

A. R. HUMPHREYS: The Augustan World: *Society in 18th Century England* °△ TB/1105

ALDOUS HUXLEY: Brave New World & Brave New World Revisited. °△ *Introduction by Martin Green* TB/3501

ARNOLD KETTLE: An Introduction to the English Novel. △
Volume I: *Defoe to George Eliot* TB/1011
Volume II: *Henry James to the Present* TB/1012

RICHMOND LATTIMORE: The Poetry of Greek Tragedy △ TB/1257

J. B. LEISHMAN: The Monarch of Wit: *An Analytical and Comparative Study of the Poetry of John Donne* ° △ TB/1258

J. B. LEISHMAN: Themes and Variations in Shakespeare's Sonnets °△ TB/1259

SAMUEL PEPYS: The Diary of Samuel Pepys. ° *Edited by O. F. Morshead. Illus. by Ernest Shepard* TB/1007

V. DE S. PINTO: Crisis in English Poetry, 1880-1940 °△ TB/1260

C. K. STEAD: The New Poetic: *Yeats to Eliot* ° △ TB/1263
HEINRICH STRAUMANN: American Literature in the Twentieth Century. △ *Third Edition, Revised* TB/1168
PAGET TOYNBEE: Dante Alighieri: *His Life and Works. Edited with Intro. by Charles S. Singleton* TB/1206
DOROTHY VAN GHENT: The English Novel TB/1050
E. B. WHITE: One Man's Meat TB/3505
BASIL WILLEY: Nineteenth Century Studies: *Coleridge to Matthew Arnold* °△ TB/1261
BASIL WILLEY: More Nineteenth Century Studies: *A Group of Honest Doubters* ° △ TB/1262
RAYMOND WILLIAMS: Culture and Society, 1780-1950 ° △ TB/1252
RAYMOND WILLIAMS: The Long Revolution °△ TB/1253

Myth, Symbol & Folklore

JOSEPH CAMPBELL, Editor: Pagan and Christian Mysteries. *Illus.* TB/2013
MIRCEA ELIADE: Cosmos and History § △ TB/2050
MIRCEA ELIADE: Rites and Symbols of Initiation: *The Mysteries of Birth and Rebirth* § △ TB/1236
DORA & ERWIN PANOFSKY: Pandora's Box: *The Changing Aspects of a Mythical Symbol.* △ *Revised Edition. Illus.* TB/2021
HELLMUT WILHELM: Change: *Eight Lectures on the I Ching* △ TB/2019

Philosophy

G. E. M. ANSCOMBE: An Introduction to Wittgenstein's Tractatus. ° △ *Second edition, Revised* TB/1210
HENRI BERGSON: Time and Free Will °△ TB/1021
H. J. BLACKHAM: Six Existentialist Thinkers ° △ TB/1002
CRANE BRINTON: Nietzsche TB/1197
ERNST CASSIRER: The Individual and the Cosmos in Renaissance Philosophy△ TB/1097
FREDERICK COPLESTON: Medieval Philosophy ° △ TB/376
F. M. CORNFORD: Principium Sapientiae: *A Study of the Origins of Greek Philosophical Thought* TB/1213
F. M. CORNFORD: From Religion to Philosophy § TB/20
WILFRID DESAN: The Tragic Finale: *An Essay on the Philosophy of Jean-Paul Sartre* TB/1030
A. P. D'ENTRÈVES: Natural Law △ TB/1223
PAUL FRIEDLÄNDER: Plato: *An Introduction* △ TB/2017
W. K. C. GUTHRIE: The Greek Philosophers: *From Thales to Aristotle* ° △ TB/1008
F. H. HEINEMANN: Existentialism and the Modern Predicament △ TB/28
EDMUND HUSSERL: Phenomenology and the Crisis of Philosophy TB/1170
IMMANUEL KANT: The Doctrine of Virtue, *being Part II of the* Metaphysic of Morals TB/110
IMMANUEL KANT: Groundwork of the Metaphysic of Morals. *Trans. & analyzed by H. J. Paton* TB/1159
IMMANUEL KANT: Lectures on Ethics §△ TB/105
IMMANUEL KANT: Religion Within the Limits of Reason Alone. § *Intro. by T. M. Greene & J. Silber* TB/67
QUENTIN LAUER: Phenomenology TB/1169
GABRIEL MARCEL: Being and Having △ TB/310
GEORGE A. MORGAN: What Nietzsche Means TB/1198
MICHAEL POLANYI: Personal Knowledge △ TB/1158
WILLARD VAN ORMAN QUINE: Elementary Logic. *Revised Edition* TB/577
WILLARD VAN ORMAN QUINE: from a Logical Point of View: *Logico-Philosophical Essays* TB/566
BERTRAND RUSSELL et al.: The Philosophy of Bertrand Russell Vol. I TB/1095; Vol. II TB/1096
L. S. STEBBING: A Modern Introduction to Logic △ TB/538
ALFRED NORTH WHITEHEAD: Process and Reality: *An Essay in Cosmology* △ TB/1033
PHILIP P. WIENER: Evolution and the Founders of Pragmatism. *Foreword by John Dewey* TB/1212
WILHELM WINDELBAND: A History of Philosophy
Vol. I: *Greek, Roman, Medieval* TB/38
Vol. II: *Renaissance, Enlightenment, Modern* TB/39
LUDWIG WITTGENSTEIN: The Blue and Brown Books ° TB/1211

Political Science & Government

JEREMY BENTHAM: The Handbook of Political Fallacies. *Introduction by Crane Brinton* TB/1069
KENNETH E. BOULDING: Conflict and Defense TB/3024
CRANE BRINTON: English Political Thought in the Nineteenth Century TB/1071
ROBERT DAHL & CHARLES E. LINDBLOM: Politics, Economics, and Welfare TB/3037
F. L. GANSHOF: Feudalism △ TB/1058
G. P. GOOCH: English Democratic Ideas in Seventeenth Century TB/1006
SIDNEY HOOK: Reason, Social Myths and Democracy △ TB/1237
DAN N. JACOBS, Ed.: The New Communist Manifesto & *Related Documents. Third edition, Revised* TB/1078
DAN N. JACOBS & HANS BAERWALD, Eds.: Chinese Communism: *Selected Documents* TB/3031
KINGSLEY MARTIN: French Liberal Thought in the Eighteenth Century △ TB/1114
ROBERTO MICHELS: First Lectures in Political Sociology. *Edited by Alfred De Grazia* ¶ ° TB/1224
BARRINGTON MOORE, Jr.: Political Power and Social Theory: *Seven Studies* ¶ TB/1221
BARRINGTON MOORE, JR.: Soviet Politics—The Dilemma of Power ¶ TB/1222
JOHN B. MORRALL: Political Thought in Medieval Times △ TB/1076
KARL R. POPPER: The Open Society and Its Enemies △
Vol. I: *The Spell of Plato* TB/1101
Vol. II: *The High Tide of Prophecy: Hegel, Marx, and the Aftermath* TB/1102
JOSEPH A. SCHUMPETER: Capitalism, Socialism and Democracy △ TB/3008

Psychology

ALFRED ADLER: The Individual Psychology of Alfred Adler △ TB/1154
HERBERT FINGARETTE: The Self in Transformation ¶ TB/1177
SIGMUND FREUD: On Creativity and the Unconscious § △ TB/45
WILLIAM JAMES: Psychology: *Briefer Course* TB/1034
C. G. JUNG: Psychological Reflections △ TB/2001
C. G. JUNG: Symbols of Transformation △ Vol. I TB/2009; Vol. II TB/2010
JOHN T. MC NEILL: A History of the Cure of Souls TB/126
KARL MENNINGER: Theory of Psychoanalytic Technique TB/1144
ERICH NEUMANN: Amor and Psyche △ TB/2012
ERICH NEUMANN: The Origins and History of Consciousness △ Vol. I *Illus.* TB/2007; Vol. II TB/2008
JOHN H. SCHAAR: Escape from Authority: *The Perspectives of Erich Fromm* TB/1155

Sociology

JACQUES BARZUN: Race: *A Study in Superstition. Revised Edition* TB/1172
BERNARD BERELSON, Ed.: The Behavioral Sciences Today TB/1127
ALLISON DAVIS & JOHN DOLLARD: Children of Bondage ¶ TB/3049
ST. CLAIR DRAKE & HORACE R. CAYTON: Black Metropolis △ Vol. I TB/1086; Vol. II TB/1087
ALVIN W. GOULDNER: Wildcat Strike ¶ TB/1176
R. M. MACIVER: Social Causation TB/1153
ROBERT K. MERTON, LEONARD BROOM, LEONARD S. COTTRELL, JR., Editors: Sociology Today: *Problems and Prospects* ¶ Vol. I TB/1173; Vol. II TB/1174
TALCOTT PARSONS & EDWARD A. SHILS, Editors: Toward a General Theory of Action TB/1083
ARNOLD ROSE: The Negro in America TB/3048
PHILIP SELZNICK: TVA and the Grass Roots TB/1230
GEORG SIMMEL et al.: Essays on Sociology, Philosophy, and Aesthetics. ¶ *Edited by Kurt H. Wolff* TB/1234

HERBERT SIMON: The Shape of Automation △ TB/1245
PITIRIM A. SOROKIN: Contemporary Sociological Theories: *Through the first quarter of the 20th Century* TB/3046
MAURICE R. STEIN: The Eclipse of Community: *An Interpretation of American Studies* TB/1128
W. LLOYD WARNER & Associates: Democracy in Jonesville: *A Study in Quality and Inequality* TB/1129
W. LLOYD WARNER: Social Class in America TB/1013

RELIGION

Ancient & Classical

J. H. BREASTED: Development of Religion and Thought in Ancient Egypt TB/57
HENRI FRANKFORT: Ancient Egyptian Religion TB/77
C. RACHEL LEVY: Religious Conceptions of the Stone Age *and their Influence on European Thought* △ TB/106
MARTIN P. NILSSON: Greek Folk Religion △ TB/78
H. J. ROSE: Religion in Greece and Rome △ TB/55

Biblical Thought & Literature

W. F. ALBRIGHT: The Biblical Period from Abraham to Ezra TB/102
C. K. BARRETT, Ed.: The New Testament Background: *Selected Documents* △ TB/86
C. H. DODD: The Authority of the Bible △ TB/43
M. S. ENSLIN: Christian Beginnings △ TB/5
JOHN GRAY: Archaeology and the Old Testament World. △ Illus. TB/127
JAMES MUILENBURG: The Way of Israel △ TB/133
H. H. ROWLEY: Growth of the Old Testament △ TB/107
D. WINTON THOMAS, Ed.: Documents from Old Testament Times △ TB/85

The Judaic Tradition

MARTIN BUBER: Eclipse of God △ TB/12
MARTIN BUBER: For the Sake of Heaven TB/801
MARTIN BUBER: The Knowledge of Man △ TB/135
MARTIN BUBER: Moses △ TB/827
MARTIN BUBER: The Origin and Meaning of Hasidism△ TB/835
MARTIN BUBER: Pointing the Way △ TB/103
MARTIN BUBER: The Prophetic Faith TB/73
GENESIS: *The NJV Translation* TB/836
SOLOMON GRAYZEL: A History of the Contemporary Jews TB/816
FLAVIUS JOSEPHUS: The Great Roman-Jewish War, *with* The Life of Josephus TB/74

Christianity: General

ROLAND H. BAINTON: Christendom: *A Short History of Christianity and its Impact on Western Civilization.* △ *Illus.* Vol. I TB/131; Vol. II TB/132

Christianity: Origins & Early Development

AUGUSTINE: An Augustine Synthesis. △ *Edited by Erich Przywara* TB/335
ADOLF DEISSMANN: Paul: *A Study in Social and Religious History* TB/15
EDWARD GIBBON: The Triumph of Christendom in the Roman Empire. § △ *Illus.* TB/46
MAURICE GOGUEL: Jesus and the Origins of Christianity ° △ Vol. I TB/65; Vol. II TB/66
EDGAR J. GOODSPEED: A Life of Jesus TB/1
ROBERT M. GRANT: Gnosticism and Early Christianity △ TB/136
ADOLF HARNACK: The Mission and Expansion of Christianity *in the First Three Centuries* TB/92
R. K. HARRISON: The Dead Sea Scrolls ° △ TB/84
EDWIN HATCH: The Influence of Greek Ideas on Christianity § △ TB/18
ARTHUR DARBY NOCK: St. Paul ° △ TB/104
ORIGEN: On First Principles △ TB/310
SULPICIUS SEVERUS et al.: The Western Fathers: *Being the Lives of Martin of Tours, Ambrose, Augustine of Hippo, Honoratus of Arles and Germanus of Auxerre.*△ *Edited and translated by F. R. Hoare* TB/309
JOHANNES WEISS: Earliest Christianity Vol. I TB/53; Vol. II TB/54

Christianity: The Middle Ages and The Reformation

JOHN CALVIN & JACOPO SADOLETO: A Reformation Debate. *Edited by John C. Olin* TB/1239
G. CONSTANT: The Reformation in England △ TB/314
JOHANNES ECKHART: Meister Eckhart: *A Modern Translation by R. B. Blakney* TB/8
DESIDERIUS ERASMUS: Christian Humanism and the Reformation TB/1166

Christianity: The Protestant Tradition

KARL BARTH: Church Dogmatics: *A Selection* △ TB/95
KARL BARTH: Dogmatics in Outline △ TB/56
KARL BARTH: The Word of God and the Word of Man TB/13
RUDOLF BULTMANN et al.: Translating Theology into the Modern Age: *Volume 2 of* Journal for Theology and the Church, *edited by Robert W. Funk in association with Gerhard Ebeling* TB/252
WINTHROP HUDSON: The Great Tradition of the American Churches TB/98
SOREN KIERKEGAARD: Edifying Discourses △ TB/32
SOREN KIERKEGAARD: The Journals of Kierkegaard ° TB/52
SOREN KIERKEGAARD: The Point of View for My Work as an Author § TB/88
SOREN KIERKEGAARD: The Present Age § △ TB/94
SOREN KIERKEGAARD: Purity of Heart △ TB/4
SOREN KIERKEGAARD: Repetition △ TB/117
SOREN KIERKEGAARD: Works of Love △ TB/122
WALTER LOWRIE: Kierkegaard: *A Life* Vol. I TB/89 Vol. II TB/90
JOHN MACQUARRIE: The Scope of Demythologizing: *Bultmann and his Critics* △ TB/134
JAMES M. ROBINSON et al.: The Bultmann School of Biblical Interpretation: New Directions? *Volume 1 of* Journal for Theology and the Church, *edited by Robert W. Funk in association with Gerhard Ebeling* TB/251
F. SCHLEIERMACHER: The Christian Faith. △ *Introduction by Richard R. Niebuhr* Vol. I TB/108; Vol. II TB/109
F. SCHLEIERMACHER: On Religion: *Speeches to Its Cultured Despisers. Intro. by Rudolf Otto* TB/36
PAUL TILLICH: Dynamics of Faith △ TB/42
EVELYN UNDERHILL: Worship △ TB/10
C. VAN DER LEEUW: Religion in Essence and Manifestation: *A Study in Phenomenology.* △ *Appendices by Hans H. Penner* Vol. I TB/100; Vol. II TB/101

Christianity: The Roman and Eastern Traditions

DOM CUTHBERT BUTLER: Western Mysticism § ° △ TB/312
A. ROBERT CAPONIGRI, Ed.: Modern Catholic Thinkers I: *God and Man* △ TB/306
A. ROBERT CAPONIGRI, Ed.: Modern Catholic Thinkers II: *The Church and the Political Order* △ TB/307
THOMAS CORBISHLEY, S. J.: Roman Catholicism TB/112
G. P. FEDOTOV: The Russian Religious Mind: *Kievan Christianity, the 10th to the 13th Centuries* TB/70
G. P. FEDOTOV, Ed.: A Treasury of Russian Spirituality TB/303
ÉTIENNE GILSON: The Spirit of Thomism TB/313
DAVID KNOWLES: The English Mystical Tradition TB/302
GABRIEL MARCEL: Being and Having TB/310
GABRIEL MARCEL: Homo Viator TB/397
GUSTAVE WEIGEL, S. J.: Catholic Theology in Dialogue TB/301

Oriental Religions: Far Eastern, Near Eastern

TOR ANDRAE: Mohammed § △ TB/62
EDWARD CONZE: Buddhism ° △ TB/58
ANANDA COOMARASWAMY: Buddha and the Gospel of Buddhism. △ *Illus.* TB/119
H. G. CREEL: Confucius and the Chinese Way TB/63
FRANKLIN EDGERTON, Trans. & Ed.: The Bhagavad Gita TB/115
SWAMI NIKHILANANDA, Trans. & Ed.: The Upanishads: *A One-Volume Abridgment* △ TB/114

Philosophy of Religion

NICOLAS BERDYAEV: The Beginning and the End § △ TB/14
NICOLAS BERDYAEV: Christian Existentialism △ TB/130
NICOLAS BERDYAEV: The Destiny of Man △ TB/61
RUDOLF BULTMANN: History and Eschatology ° TB/91
RUDOLF BULTMANN AND FIVE CRITICS: Kerygma and Myth: *A Theological Debate* △ TB/80
RUDOLF BULTMANN and KARL KUNDSIN: Form Criticism: *Two Essays on New Testament Research* △ TB/96
MIRCEA ELIADE: The Sacred and the Profane TB/81
LUDWIG FEUERBACH: The Essence of Christianity. § TB/11
ÉTIENNE GILSON: The Spirit of Thomism TB/313
ADOLF HARNACK: What is Christianity? § △ TB/17
FRIEDRICH HEGEL: On Christianity TB/79
KARL HEIM: Christian Faith and Natural Science △ TB/16
IMMANUEL KANT: Religion Within the Limits of Reason Alone. § *Intro. by T. M. Greene & J. Silber* TB/67
K. E. KIRK: The Vision of God TB/137
JOHN MACQUARRIE: An Existentialist Theology: *A Comparison of Heidegger and Bultmann.* ° △ *Preface by Rudolf Bultmann* TB/125
PIERRE TEILHARD DE CHARDIN: The Divine Milieu ° △ TB/384
PIERRE TEILHARD DE CHARDIN: The Phenomenon of Man ° △ TB/383

Religion, Culture & Society

C. C. GILLISPIE: Genesis and Geology: *The Decades before Darwin* § TB/51
KYLE HASELDEN: The Racial Problem in Christian Perspective TB/116
WALTER KAUFMANN, Ed.: Religion from Tolstoy to Camus. *Enlarged Edition* TB/123
JOHN T. MCNEILL: A History of the Cure of Souls TB/126
H. RICHARD NIEBUHR: Christ and Culture △ TB/3
H. RICHARD NIEBUHR: The Kingdom of God in America TB/49
TIMOTHY L. SMITH: Revivalism and Social Reform: *American Protestantism on the Eve of the Civil War* △ TB/1229
ERNST TROELTSCH: The Social Teaching of the Christian Churches ° △ Vol. I TB/71; Vol. II TB/72

NATURAL SCIENCES AND MATHEMATICS

Biological Sciences

CHARLOTTE AUERBACH: The Science of Genetics Σ △ TB/568
LUDWIG VON BERTALANFFY: Problems of Life △ TB/521
HAROLD F. BLUM: Time's Arrow and Evolution TB/555
JOHN TYLER BONNER: The Ideas of Biology Σ △ TB/570
WALTER B. CANNON: Bodily Changes in Pain, Hunger, Fear and Rage. *Illus.* TB/562
W. E. LE GROS CLARK: The Antecedents of Man ° △ TB/559
W. H. DOWDESWELL: Animal Ecology. △ *Illus.* TB/543
R. W. GERARD: Unresting Cells. *Illus.* TB/541
ADOLF PORTMANN: Animals as Social Beings ° △ TB/572
O. W. RICHARDS: The Social Insects. △ *Illus.* TB/542
P. M. SHEPPARD: Natural Selection and Heredity △ TB/528
EDMUND W. SINNOTT: Cell and Psyche: *The Biology of Purpose* TB/546
C. H. WADDINGTON: How Animals Develop. △ *Illus.* TB/553
C. H. WADDINGTON: The Nature of Life △ TB/580

Chemistry

J. R. PARTINGTON: A Short History of Chemistry △ TB/522

History of Science

MARIE BOAS: The Scientific Renaissance, 1450-1630 ° △ TB/583
W. DAMPIER, Ed.: Readings in the Literature of Science. *Illus.* TB/512
A. HUNTER DUPREE: Science in the Federal Government: *A History of Policies and Activities to 1940* △ TB/573
ALEXANDRE KOYRÉ: From the Closed World to the Infinite Universe: *Copernicus, Kepler, Galileo, Newton, etc.* △ TB/31
A. G. VAN MELSEN: From Atomos to Atom: *A History of the Concept* Atom TB/517
O. NEUGEBAUER: The Exact Sciences in Antiquity TB/552
HANS THIRRING: Energy for Man △ TB/556
LANCELOT LAW WHYTE: Essay on Atomism △ TB/565

Mathematics

E. W. BETH: The Foundations of Mathematics △ TB/581
H. DAVENPORT: The Higher Arithmetic △ TB/526
H. G. FORDER: Geometry: *An Introduction* △ TB/548
S. KÖRNER: The Philosophy of Mathematics △ TB/547
D. E. LITTLEWOOD: Skeleton Key of Mathematics: *A Simple Account of Complex Algebraic Problems* △ TB/525
GEORGE E. OWEN: Fundamentals of Scientific Mathematics TB/569
WILLARD VAN ORMAN QUINE: Mathematical Logic TB/558
O. G. SUTTON: Mathematics in Action. ° △ *Illus.* TB/518
FREDERICK WAISMANN: Introduction to Mathematical Thinking. *Foreword by Karl Menger* TB/511

Philosophy of Science

R. B. BRAITHWAITE: Scientific Explanation TB/515
J. BRONOWSKI: Science and Human Values △ TB/505
ALBERT EINSTEIN et al.: Albert Einstein: Philosopher-Scientist Vol. I TB/502; Vol. II TB/503
WERNER HEISENBERG: Physics and Philosophy: *The Revolution in Modern Science* △ TB/549
JOHN MAYNARD KEYNES: A Treatise on Probability. ° △ *Introduction by N. R. Hanson* TB/557
KARL R. POPPER: The Logic of Scientific Discovery △ TB/576
STEPHEN TOULMIN: Foresight and Understanding △ TB/564
STEPHEN TOULMIN: The Philosophy of Science △ TB/513
G. J. WHITROW: The Natural Philosophy of Time ° △ TB/563

Physics and Cosmology

JOHN E. ALLEN: Aerodynamics: *A Space Age Survey* △ TB/582
STEPHEN TOULMIN & JUNE GOODFIELD: The Fabric of the Heavens: *The Development of Astronomy and Dynamics.* △ *Illus.* TB/579
DAVID BOHM: Causality and Chance in Modern Physics. △ *Foreword by Louis de Broglie* TB/536
P. W. BRIDGMAN: Nature of Thermodynamics TB/537
P. W. BRIDGMAN: A Sophisticate's Primer of Relativity △ TB/575
A. C. CROMBIE, Ed.: Turning Point in Physics TB/535
C. V. DURELL: Readable Relativity △ TB/530
ARTHUR EDDINGTON: Space, Time and Gravitation: *An Outline of the General Relativity Theory* TB/510
GEORGE GAMOW: Biography of Physics Σ △ TB/567
MAX JAMMER: Concepts of Force TB/550
MAX JAMMER: Concepts of Mass TB/571
MAX JAMMER: Concepts of Space TB/533
G. J. WHITROW: The Structure and Evolution of the Universe: *An Introduction to Cosmology.* △ *Illus.* TB/504